FOLLOW ME, AKHI

HUSSEIN KESVANI

Follow Me, Akhi

The Online World of British Muslims

HURST & COMPANY, LONDON

First published in the United Kingdom in 2019 by
C. Hurst & Co. (Publishers) Ltd.,
41 Great Russell Street, London, WC1B 3PL
© Hussein Kesvani, 2019
All rights reserved.
Printed in the United Kingdom by Bell & Bain Ltd, Glasgow

The right of Hussein Kesvani to be identified as the author
of this publication is asserted by him in accordance with the
Copyright, Designs and Patents Act, 1988.

Distributed in the United States, Canada and Latin America by
Oxford University Press, 198 Madison Avenue, New York, NY 10016,
United States of America.

A Cataloguing-in-Publication data record for this book
is available from the British Library.

ISBN: 9781787381254

This book is printed using paper from registered sustainable
and managed sources.

www.hurstpublishers.com

CONTENTS

CONTENTS

CONTENTS

CONTENTS

ACKNOWLEDGEMENTS

Thank you first and foremost to my parents, my mother Nushret Manji and my father Muhammad Rafik Kesvani. For your love, wisdom and willingness to let me determine my own faith while keeping me on the right path. Thank you for your patience, which I have no doubt tested, throughout the years as I tried to figure out who I was, and the type of person I wanted to become. This book would not have seen light without your patience, your hard work, your dedication to education and, most of all, your prayers.

To my sister, Shaheen. I am in constant awe of your intelligence and unwavering loyalty, even in the worst of times. Out of us, you have always been the most put together, and there are so many insights from our conversations about our faith and culture that informed this book. I promise you'll get credit for that whenever I talk about it.

I am extremely grateful to the team at Hurst. Michael Dwyer took a chance on me, then a twenty-five-year-old journalist who had just been made redundant, to pursue this ambitious project, in our shared belief that the British Muslim experience deserved better writing. I will be in debt to my editor, Farhaana Arefin, for the rest of my life. Thank you for your patience with me, for affording umpteen deadline extensions when I absolutely did not deserve it, and for showing me what good writing looks like.

Additionally, I would like to thank my agent Matthew Turner, and the team at Rogers, Coleridge & White, for all their support and guidance as the book was near completion. I promise I'll show up on time in future.

I could not have written this book without the guidance, support and care shown by Elizabeth Oldfield, Nick Spencer and everyone at Theos think tank. Thank you for taking me in, letting me be part of your world, and showing me the possibilities faith offered when I was so close to losing it. And thank you so much for always keeping me in your prayers.

Alan White, my former editor, provided invaluable advice and support with writing this book, and helped me to find my voice after I left BuzzFeed News. Thank you for your unconditional care, guidance and continued support for my bad tweets. In the same vein, I am grateful to all my friends and former colleagues at BuzzFeed, who are the most innovative and intelligent people working in media today. They believed even more than I did that covering Muslim issues was just as important as Westminster politics, and supported my work right until the end. In particular, I am extremely grateful to Aisha Gani, who took over the 'Muslim beat' after I left, and who showed how coverage of Muslims in Britain could be done fairly and with care—and without being fixated on extremism.

I am grateful to all my colleagues at *MEL* Magazine for giving me the time and space to work on the book, while letting me experiment with half-baked ideas every week. *MEL* ran some of the early sections of this book and I am so grateful to my editors Alana Hope Levinson and Josh Schollmeyer for believing in the value of these stories, even when I didn't myself.

In addition, I would like to thank the editors who let me write for them as a freelancer, and provided space for some of the early ideas that developed later in this book. In particular, I would like to thank Jamie Clifton and Simon Childs from *Vice*, and Samir Raheem and Stephanie Boland at *Prospect* magazine.

My thanks go to the Carey Institute for Global Good and John Logan, who provided me with a Logan Non-Fiction fellowship at a time when I needed it the most. More than just providing a serene environment to write the final pages, it provided exposure and friendships among a community of the most intelligent, talented and empathetic writers working today.

For their friendship, I want to thank everyone on the *Trashfuture Podcast*: Riley Quinn, Milo Edwards, Nate Bethea and Olga Koch and Alex Kealy. This was the only place I could unwind from the stresses of writing a book, by going into hour-long conversations about whether coffee is a kind of soup, or whether the pyramids were built by the Irish. I am looking forward to causing more international drama in the coming years.

For tolerating me at the worst of times, I owe a debt of gratitude to my friends: Rachael Krishna, Alicia Melville-Smith, Rohan Banerjee, Pav Dhande and Amna Saleem. Undoubtedly I have missed some people from the list; please know I owe you the same gratitude as well.

Most importantly, this book would not have been possible without the unconditional love of one person. Jasmin, you are the most incredible person I know, and I love you so much. I am so thankful for your intelligence and wit, your empathy and understanding. You are such a smart and brilliant writer, and you are the best partner one could ask for. I am so thankful that you believed in this book at a time when I was full of doubts about whether I was the right person to tell these stories. Thank you for being there always.

Finally, I wish to thank my extended family across the UK, Canada and the USA for their thoughts and prayers as I have written this, and to the community at Hyderi Islamic Centre,

ACKNOWLEDGEMENTS

which has always informed the foundations of my Muslim identity.

And to my late grandmother, Gulshanbanu, my *maa*. The first person to teach me how to read the Holy Qur'an, and to tell me the stories of the Prophet and his companions, *Ahl-ul-Bayt*. This book is dedicated to you, in memory of your strength, resilience, intelligence and willingness to see the best in people. I am so sorry for everything that happened. I love you and miss you so much.

NOTE ON THE TEXT

Some names have been changed at the request of interviewees to protect their identities.

INTRODUCTION

My call to war came at 3 a.m. via WhatsApp. A simple list of instructions, telephone numbers, and a list of what to bring on my journey—warm jacket, extra pairs of socks, hot water bottle. 'In the Name of Allah, the Most Gracious, the Most Merciful,' the message began. 'You won't regret this ... I'm so much happier than I ever was in *Dar al-Kufr*,'—the land of disbelief—'so much more at peace.'

'Follow me, *akhi*,' the message ended, addressing me as 'brother' in Arabic. 'I will help you make *hijrah* here.'

I had known Abu Antaar for a little over a year when he asked me to join his holy war in Syria. It was November 2015, and I was an ambitious, young reporter, keen to make my mark in the cut-throat world of London media. As one of the only Muslim reporters working in a national newsroom, I had been assigned to cover stories about the British Muslim community, and, in particular, their propensity for radicalisation. For months, I had been trying to secure an exclusive interview with a British Muslim who had opted to leave their privileged, Western lifestyle in the pursuit of jihad. I saw this as the key interview that would prove my abilities as a reporter and take me one step closer to my dream job as a political correspondent with a desk in Parliament.

At the time—in a media cycle that had yet to be touched by Brexit, Donald Trump and the rise of 'anti-globalism'—the objects of national fear were Muslims, found in the estates of East London and the suburbs of former industrial cities in the North. According to one British politician, thousands of Britons had fled to fight among 'Islamist militants' in Iraq and Syria.[1] Though official estimates at the time were much lower—at about 500 people—the migration still provoked anxiety that Muslims in Britain weren't loyal to their country of birth, that they were unable to 'integrate' into society, and that Islam was not compatible with 'British values'.[2]

* * *

I knew two Abu Antaars, and both were defined by the internet. The first was the religious zealot. He was a tall, lanky and shadowy figure, dressed in camouflage overalls, his face obscured by a black balaclava. His online profile pictures showed eyes so dark they were close to black, and while little of his face was visible, you could make out small, ashy bags beneath his eyelids. He changed his social media pictures frequently. Sometimes, they would just be screenshots of passages from the Qur'an, or stock images of lions—a popular symbol among young jihadis in the so-called Islamic State (ISIS) who styled themselves as noble warriors for Islam. Other times, he uploaded pictures of himself. In some, he held combat knives, or guns. In others, he sat in front of ISIS's black-and-white flag, holding up his index finger—symbolising *tawhid*, or the oneness of God.

This Abu Antaar was exactly what you'd expect of an ISIS fighter. His social media posts fixated on the importance of jihad, or on how Muslims living in the West were 'lazy', 'materialistic' and living in *jahiliyyah*, a 'state of ignorance'. This Abu Antaar would use his online platform to argue against other Muslims and to refute 'liberal scholars' who he believed were 'deceiving Muslims from fulfilling their duties'. When questioned about ISIS, he would post quotes from *hadiths* that supposedly justified their actions, declaring that he was 'following the path of *Ahl-ul-Sunnah*'—those who adhere to the way of the Prophet Muhammad—a 'pure' Islam that he believed wasn't tainted by cultural traditions or 'Western adaptations'. It was a path that he claimed he'd been searching for all his life, and one that he was willing to die for.

The other Abu Antaar I knew was the twenty-four-year-old Londoner who told me he had worked as a trader in the City's financial district and who passionately supported Arsenal football club. As we got to know each other, he would tell me about his old life riding glass elevators and donning Armani, Gucci and Prada suits. He spoke about his client meetings on the rooftops of exclusive bars in Mayfair and Kensington, and how multimillion-pound cash transfers were part of the average work day. 'I had it all, but I didn't feel good,' he wrote to me on Telegram, a direct messaging app. 'I always knew there was something missing.' There were times when he would feel 'empty' and 'isolated' at his work desk. When he went to glitzy corporate events, he would sit at the bar, slightly tipsy, and feel 'a great amount of sadness.' Abu Antaar had pondered this deep-seated feeling of emptiness, and concluded that 'there was more to life than just money and nightclubs'.

It seemed clear to me that Abu Antaar had constructed this narrative, of unhappiness followed by conviction and purpose, to justify to himself his decision to go to Raqqa and fight. He claimed that he had 'left a life of luxury to fight for the sake of Allah'. When I asked him about the specifics of travelling to Syria, he either refused to disclose details or circled around the questions: Who were his connections? How did he cross the border from Turkey? Did he travel on his own? He only responded by saying that he had travelled by 'Allah's guidance'.

Despite missing parts of his old life (more than once, he asked me to update him on football scores, or complained about how he missed Wispa chocolate bars), he needed to believe he was fighting for a bigger cause: to establish a true, Islamic caliphate.

He had spoken about the caliphate since he was a teenager—but not at the mosque or the madrassa, or to his family and friends. Instead, these conversations took place in the dead of night, on internet forums like The Student Room, a popular message board for British university students. Other times, he would take to darker, more obscure communities like Totse, 4chan and Ebaums World—sites where users could openly be rude and degrading and even post illegal material like computer hacking guides and PDFs of *The Anarchist Cookbook*. On these forums, under the username 'Al Siraat', he would post long messages criticising British military involvement in Iraq, or 'George Bush's war for oil', praising Al-Qaeda fighters as those simply resisting 'Western warmongers'. To Abu Antaar, a caliphate was the only way for the Muslim *ummah*—the supposed 'global community' of Muslims—to be united in fighting against Western imperialism. Other users on these forums laughed at him. Some down-voted his posts so his comments would be buried at the bottom of threads. Others reported him to community moderators, some of whom banned him from forums for 'advocating harm and/or violence'. None of this deterred him, or made him want to reconsider his beliefs.

'By the grace of Allah, I knew I was right,' he told me.

* * *

Abu Antaar's story intrigued me and prompted me to write this book, not because he had joined ISIS or because he was another case study in 'online radicalisation'. Rather, it was because his story was so familiar to me. Growing up, he attended school, went to the mosque and spent his weekends at family functions trying to avoid questions from prying aunties about when he planned to get married. But online, he lived a separate life. In the dead of night, he would assume aliases inspired by characters from science fiction films like *The Matrix* and *Andromeda*.

Like me, Abu Antaar came from a strict Muslim family that looked unfavourably on free-mixing between men and women. In some of our earliest conversations together we spoke about the romantic relationships we had developed with girls we met online and had only known through the internet. Through peer-to-peer networks like Kazaa and Limewire we both illegally downloaded extensive collections of music from bands like Rage Against the Machine, Nirvana and System of a Down, as well as American hip-hop artists like Lupe Fiasco, Wu-Tang Clan and NWA. Their messages of revolution and rejection of authority were infinitely appealing to us, angry teenagers who couldn't relate to the white indie-rock groups that dominated the charts in the mid-2000s.

Like me, Abu Antaar had used the internet to navigate his religious doubts and confusion. He went through a 'hard line atheist phase', devouring books by Christopher Hitchens and Richard Dawkins that he downloaded from chat groups in which people were often hostile to religion in general, though they mainly focused on refuting Christianity and the power of the Church of England. After the bombings in London on 7 July 2005 (7/7), Abu Antaar told me, he'd taken a more religious turn, developing a much keener interest in downloadable Islamic lectures and spending hours on the internet reading about Islamic history and philosophy. The turn, he told me, came from feeling isolated from the online communities he'd once been part of. Because of his Muslim name he was being taunted at school, while on the forums he'd spent years reading and posting in, people had suddenly become obsessed with insulting Muslims and Islam. 'They were making fun of Muslims,' he told me on

WhatsApp. 'They called Muslims "turban bombers" ... they made disgusting remarks about Muslim women looking like animals ... it was pure hatred. It wasn't my world.'

Abu Antaar's feelings of alienation resonated with me, as did his inclination to express those vulnerabilities on the internet. In many ways, he and I had lived the same life, one in which 'code switching'—variously adopting multiple identities to appease different groups of people—was a habitual part of everyday experience. For both of us, the internet had allowed us to be our true selves. Through anonymous profiles on message boards and pseudonyms in chatrooms, we could talk about anything, however we liked, without fear of reprisal. Moreover, we could do so without the burden of preconceptions about who we were based on our race or religion. We did not have to worry about being labelled and judged by our families or members of our religious communities—or by our predominantly white colleagues at work. In short, online, we could be whoever we wanted to be.

I haven't spoken to Abu Antaar since the night he tried to convince me to come to Syria. I still think of his journey—or at least, what I imagine it to have been—frequently. I often wonder whether a younger version of myself—angry, mired in self-doubt and in the throes of an identity crisis that every British Muslim faced in the wake of the 7/7 bombings—would have made the same decision he made if the online social networks that exist today had been around in 2005. Abu Antaar and I sought answers about our faith and identity not in the mosques that our parents frequented or from the elders in our community, but in online communities of people we didn't know and whose motives we could never be sure of. Despite that, seeking comfort on the internet felt like a normal thing to me.

The looming question that preoccupied me as I wrote this book is why Abu Antaar and I ended up making different choices. Why, in spite of occupying the same online environments and having near-identical online experiences, did I decide to stay in the United Kingdom and to use journalism as a way to explore my religious identity, while he gave up his life, his friends and his family to fight in a brutal foreign war in pursuit of the same goal? I wondered how our journeys online had contributed to those choices. Were there other young Muslims who were also struggling to come to terms with their religious identities? How have the expansion of mobile technology and the dominance of social media platforms in nearly every aspect of our lives shaped their paths?

* * *

Over years working as a journalist on British Muslim culture, I realised that for thousands of Muslims across the UK, the internet represents a place where they can contend with difficult and often multifaceted questions about religious identity, and in turn shape their religious identities on their own terms. I have reported on stories ranging from how Muslims in Britain were using WhatsApp to organise fundraising initiatives or making private Facebook groups for women seeking to leave abusive relationships, to how people across the globe had adopted their own shared language and hashtags on Twitter to assert their identities as minorities within Muslim communities. I have witnessed how online spaces can become safe havens for those who have left Islam, as well as for those who face hostility from their family and friends for joining the religion. And I have also seen how the internet has been used to raise awareness of Islamophobic attacks and anti-Muslim abuse, and how distrust toward mainstream media outlets led some British Muslims to develop their own platforms and outlets in order to represent the needs and concerns of their communities.

According to census figures in 2011, there were 2.7 million Muslims living in the UK that year,[3] about half of whom are under the age of twenty-five.[4] In the years since the 11 September 2001 (9/11) attacks in the United States and the 7/7 bombings in London in 2005, there have been countless studies, TV programmes, polls and articles about the UK's Muslim population. Their focus has ranged from what Muslims in the UK believe in, how 'tolerant' they are of non-Muslims, whether their religion is compatible with 'British values', and indeed even whether one can truly be both British and a Muslim. In recent years, more nuanced books about British Muslim communities have emerged too, from Shelina Janmohamed's *Generation M: Young Muslims Changing the World*, which explores how young Muslims are crafting their identity through pop culture and fashion, to Baroness Sayeeda Warsi's *The Enemy Within: A Tale of Muslim Britain*, which charts the author's years as the British government's most senior Muslim advisor, criticising its counter-terrorism policy for alienating the country's Muslims.

The vast majority of these studies and volumes, while useful, have tended to focus on what 'British Muslim communities' are imagined to be in physical or geographical terms. In my career as a reporter, there have been countless times when senior editors and producers assigned me to report on a 'Muslim story', for which I would be asked to scope the 'opinions of British Muslims'. This would almost always mean a day-return trip to Bradford, a city that is home to one of the UK's largest Muslim populations, or spending a few hours in Tower Hamlets, an area of London where many Muslim Bengalis have settled since the 1970s, to ask Muslims for 'their view' on terrorism and extremism.

Other studies of British Muslims, such as Phillip Lewis and Sadek Hamid's *British Muslims: New Directions in Islamic Thought, Creativity and Activism*, have expanded the scope of analysis by examining the lived experiences of British Muslims as both Muslims and British citizens. Even in these cases, however, the framework is constructed around physical Islamic spaces, meaning that mosques, imams and community centres have been the reference points for trying to understand what a 'British Muslim' is.

* * *

I wrote this book at a time when disillusionment and pessimism toward social media platforms were at an all-time high, to such an extent that many people in 'Generation Z'—those born from the mid-'90s to the '00s and who have grown up in the 'internet age'—are leaving social media for good.[5] In the time that I spent researching and writing, platforms like Facebook and Twitter have gone from being seen as revolutionary technologies that would empower ordinary citizens to stand up to tyrannical regimes and strongman dictators,[6] to being blamed for accelerating seismic shifts toward nationalistic and xenophobic forms of political populism, notably in the election of Donald Trump in the United States and the UK's decision to leave the European Union, as well as the election of European populists like Italy's foreign minister, Matteo Salvini, and Viktor Orbán in Hungary—both of whom were able to use their social media followings on Facebook to reach millions of impressionable voters.[7] Twitter, the social network where users must post their thoughts in 280 characters or less, once considered the primary vehicle for driving the Arab Spring, has been accused by both its users and the UK Parliament of turning a blind eye to abuse and harassment, particularly toward marginalised groups like women of colour, Jews, Muslims and the LGBTQ community, to name just a few.[8]

As social media increasingly becomes an integral part of everyday experience, particularly for consuming and sharing news, questions about its hand in acts of civil unrest and violence have also become prominent. In 2018, human rights groups accused the Burmese military of encouraging violence toward the Rohingya Muslim minority by 'exploiting Facebook's wide reach in Myanmar, where it is so broadly used that many of the country's 18 million internet users confuse the Silicon Valley social media platform with the internet', leading to the displacement of over 700,000 Rohingya who were forced to flee to neighbouring Bangladesh.[9] In India, WhatsApp has been accused of struggling to limit the distribution of fake news across its private channels—a problem that is said to be driving the growth of violent Islamophobia and that, in 2018, even led to the deaths of nine people who were falsely accused of being 'child kidnappers'.[10]

Social media has also been shown to dramatically alter the way individuals perceive their political identities, and how they see themselves as participants in the political process and as citizens. Following the 2016 US presidential election, there was an upsurge in research papers, journal articles and op-eds in newspapers and magazines arguing that social media platforms had created a polarised political landscape. By using users' demographic and behavioural data to customise their online experiences, social media reinforced individuals' biases by creating 'echo chambers', in which users would only see content that algorithms predicted they would click on.[11] Others argued that the structure of social media platforms, which act as a hybrid of social networks, news websites and shopping forums, meant that any candidate running for political office would have to create a 'social media identity' in order to show they were listening to the concerns of voters, as a means of 'leveraging their voting power'.[12] These scholars, journalists and political analysts all argued that achieving political currency was no longer dependent on how someone appeared in newspapers and on television to a mass audience, but rather, it mattered how they presented themselves online, and whether or not they could tailor their messages to individualised experiences and address the grievances of potential voters.

INTRODUCTION

While there has been much analysis of the influence of social media on political identity, there is remarkably little work in the public domain that explores the relationship between social media and the formation of religious identity. Furthermore, while some studies, like Gary Bunt's *Hashtag Islam*, have looked at how 'cyber-Islamic environments' have been formed internationally, especially across the Middle East and South Asia, they are limited in scope when exploring how Britain's Muslim communities interact with social media.[13]

* * *

This volume will explore how social media and internet culture have affected how British Muslims see themselves, both online and offline, in terms of their faith and their relationships with each other.

The stories in this book largely stem from my time as a reporter working on the religion beat, trying to explain, to both Muslim and non-Muslim readers, how social media networks and the decentralised nature of the internet were challenging traditional structures and authorities that have characterised the 'British Muslim experience'. In some cases, this would be in the form of charismatic individuals who were able to use platforms like YouTube and Instagram to deliver Islamic sermons to tens of thousands of people, a much greater reach than traditionally trained imams were likely to achieve. In other cases, these stories would involve groups of Muslims forming their own online spaces and networks outside of the traditional mosque structure—spaces that they could use to talk more openly, and in ways that physical spaces would be unable to facilitate. This book aims to show how British Muslims, particularly younger generations who were born in the UK and grew up in the age of the internet, have been able to use social media to explore their own religious identities, in many cases finding places where they could express themselves on their own terms and in environments that they built and curated themselves.

This book does not seek to undermine traditional Islamic structures, nor does it aim to reduce their importance to British Muslim communities. Mosques, madrassas and Islamic centres are still vital components of British Muslim identity, and I do not contend that the internet or social media operate as replacements for them. Instead, I try to show that analysis of British Muslim communities has for too long relied on self-styled 'gatekeepers' and 'community leaders' to define what being a British Muslim is, a simplistic framing that has shaped both government policy and societal perceptions of Muslims. This is a reductive lens, and one that I believe has alienated many young British Muslims, both from their national identities and their cultural ones.

It is against this backdrop that a younger generation of Muslims, mostly born in the West, are forming online communities. On the internet, young Muslims are free to express themselves in ways they cannot offline, whether this means being more open in expressing their sexual orientations, political affiliations, or even their doubts and fears about their faith. Young people who have found it difficult to express themselves or their views in mosques or Islamic schools can find communities who will listen to them online, where the barrier to entry when it comes to getting a platform is considerably lower. Such changes will naturally have a significant impact on Muslim communities across the country. At a time when Muslims are under scrutiny, traditional structures like mosques have often been at the centre of debates around the role of Islam in the UK and have been pressured to 'integrate' with British society, ranging from providing lectures in English (rather than in Arabic or other community language) to hosting interfaith initiatives and doing charity work to prove themselves as part of their local societies. Conversely, on the internet, such pressure is largely absent. As one young Muslim told me, 'Online, I can be whatever Muslim I choose to be ... I am not labelled, I don't define my faith by what mosque I go to, or what sheikh I listen to. I am just a Muslim—the way that Allah intended me to be.'

Ultimately, this book aims to show that the internet is a crucial component to understanding what contemporary British Muslim identity looks like. It is in the online world that young British Muslims are making the choices that define the nuances of their religious identity, and discover how that relates to other parts of their identity. At a time when, as a society, we are coming to terms with the effects of social media, and how it has impacted our politics and democracy, such an interrogation seems more important than ever.

1

PREACHERS AND MOSQUES

The New Khutbahs

On a Friday afternoon, in Muhammad Khan's two-bedroom, newly built flat in Poplar, East London, he and his roommate Asif Khan had just finished their *wudhu*—ritual washing—and were preparing for the weekly *jumu'ah* prayer. Asif took a seat on the floor, on the crimson-and-green embroidered faux-Persian rug that he'd ordered on Amazon. He rolled up the sleeves of his pink, Oxford collar shirt and dried off the remaining droplets of water. Muhammad was trying to adjust an old cable that linked his MacBook to the 50-inch, high-definition plasma TV. 'I should have really got a Bluetooth one—it would have been so much easier!' he laughed. The two men didn't have much time to finish praying, and maybe grab a sandwich, before they would have to jump on the bus back to work.

For the past year and a half, Muhammad and Asif, twenty-seven and twenty-four respectively, have been praying together every Friday. In an ideal world, they said, they wouldn't have to do this. After all, they used to pray at a space near their office, in

15

two small deteriorating portacabins on a central London side street that would always be filled to maximum capacity by the time they arrived for prayers. 'If you got there early then you'd be crammed into a corner by the time everyone showed up, and if you showed up late, you'd either have to wait for the second *jumu'ah* prayer, or pray outside, where there's people walking right behind you,' Muhammad explained.

The shortage of space wasn't the only thing that bothered them. The quality of the lectures was also an issue. 'The imam gave the *khutbahs* [sermons] in Bengali, so neither of us knew what was going on,' Asif recalled with a smile. 'I don't speak or understand Bengali, and Muhammad doesn't know it well enough to know what was being said. ... We'd just find ourselves staring into space, or playing on our phones, until the *adhaan* was recited.'

They had tried other *jumu'ah* places near their office, but encountered similar problems. Either they would find themselves having to pray outside because the spaces were too small, or they were uninspired by the quality of the lectures. Even when these were in English, 'they were just boring and I didn't learn anything,' Muhammad said. 'It was always something to do with manners, or the importance of giving to charity or helping your parents. Things that we all do anyway.' Both men wanted more from their *jumu'ah* prayers, and said that if they were going to take time off work to attend, they wanted to use the time well. 'One *jumu'ah* prayer I went to, I zoned out,' Muhammad remembered. 'I wasn't paying attention at all ... it just didn't seem like the best way to spend our time, or enrich our understanding of the *deen* [religion].'

Muhammad and Asif instead decided to hold their own *jumu'ah* prayers, an idea they hatched during a late-night Facebook Messenger discussion. They felt that it would be more intellectually enriching. From the comfort of their home, they would have the power to decide what imam to listen to, or what subject they wanted to hear about. 'If something in the news interests us, for example,' Muhammad told me, 'like the situation in Palestine, or what the religious rulings are when it comes to interest rates and *riba'a* [usury], we'll talk about it during the week on Facebook, and then on Friday, we'll find a video—sometimes a *khutbah* or an Islamic video, sometimes just part of a documentary—and then use that to reflect on what Islam teaches. Other times, we'll watch speakers who give out Islamic reminders about ways to keep on the *deen*.'

Asif told me that the week before my visit, they had watched a twenty-minute video on *Surat al-Waqi'ah*, the fifty-sixth chapter of the Holy Qur'an, delivered by the Pakistani American Islamic preacher Nouman Ali Khan—the founder of the Bayyinah Institute and, according to the Royal Islamic Strategic Studies Centre of Jordan, one of the 500 most influential Muslims in the world.[1] A month ago, they listened to a lecture by Sheikh Hamza Yusuf, an American Muslim scholar and convert to Sufism, about the virtues of patience based on Islamic history.[2] Occasionally, the lectures they choose aren't 'Islamic' at all—instead they might opt for 'motivational talks' by YouTube personalities like Gary Vaynerchuk and Jay Shetty, both of whom make YouTube videos about topics ranging from tips for entrepreneurs when starting a business to 'breaking out of lazy habits in life'.[3]

'The subjects vary,' Muhammad said. 'But, everything we listen to is in English.' This week, they were listening to a lecture on *taqwa*—piety, or fear of God—by Ustadh Wahaj Tarin, the dean of students at the Australian Islamic College and one of the most well-known Islamic motivational speakers in the world, whose videos frequently garner tens and hundreds of thousands of views.

* * *

What Muhammad and Asif are doing might seem insignificant. After all, people choose whom and what they want to watch or listen to every day. But for them, their Friday prayer sessions mark a radical departure from traditional worship. *Jumu'ah* prayer, after all, takes place every Friday, the holiest day of the week in Islam, and is a time to congregate and pray alongside other Muslims, regardless of their social, economic or political background. To give an idea of how large a Friday prayer gathering is: the East London Mosque, one of the UK's most prominent Islamic centres, frequently reaches its full capacity of 3,000 people on Fridays, and often hold more than one *jumu'ah* prayer in order to avoid worshippers needing to pray outside the mosque.[4] For many Muslims, the community aspect of *jumu'ah* is the main priority. But for some people, like Muhammad and Asif, *jumu'ah* meant more than just the physical act of praying together—it should be about 'intellectual nourishment' too.

For Muslims who use the internet as a means to explore and understand their faith, YouTube now plays a central role, not only because it hosts thousands of hours' worth of Islamic videos and lectures, but also because of how it facilitates theological, social and political conversations, both in the comments on the site, and on other social media channels where YouTube videos can be shared. Users themselves can upload Islamic lectures directly to the platform for millions of people to access. On top of this, speakers can record themselves giving sermons to a live audience, and people across the world can play their lectures back on YouTube. In the course of researching this book, I attended countless *khutbahs* across the country and often heard imams reference YouTube during their speeches, telling their congregations to 'watch my lecture on YouTube if you are confused', or directly speaking to audiences outside of the physical space of the mosque, addressing them as 'our brothers and sisters who are not with us today, but who are tuning in on YouTube'.

Only beaten by music videos, 'religion'-related videos comprise the second-largest category on YouTube, and within the religion category itself, the majority of content relates to Islam.[5] In 2012, more than 5,000 Islamic videos were published on the platform each week, according to YouTube's own figures.[6] While there is no exact, publicly available figure for Islam-related videos uploaded to YouTube today, it's likely that the number has not significantly declined since then. If anything, the amount of Islam-related content has probably increased as a result of the 'Arab spring' in 2011, the Syrian civil war, and the subsequent refugee crisis across Europe. Videos range from explainers about Islam and its role in shaping Middle East politics, to calls by preachers and Islamic centres for donations and volunteering. Of course, a number of videos have also been anti-Islam, produced by far-right figures and populist parties across Europe with anti-refugee and anti-Muslim agendas.

For the most part, conversations around the influence of YouTube on Muslim identity in the UK have tended to take place as part of wider discussions around Islamic extremism and the influence of YouTube on radicalisation. In 2016, the House of Commons Home Affairs Committee accused YouTube and other large social media companies of being 'the vehicle of choice in spreading propaganda', saying they had 'become the recruiting platforms for terrorism'.[7] In 2017, the committee doubled down on these claims in a report suggesting that young British people who had travelled to fight with ISIS had been influenced by videos the group had uploaded to YouTube.[8]

As Mosemghvdlishvili and Jansz argue, while traditional media outlets in Britain, like newspapers and television, have scrutinised mosques and Muslim community centres, the experiences of British Muslims on the internet have hardly garnered attention, despite the huge number of conversations, debates and communities being formed on comment threads, social media pages and online forums. At the same time, they argue, the pro-liferation of user-generated online media provides a platform for Muslims to define their own narratives and how to represent themselves to the rest of the world.[9]

* * *

This freedom was also what drove Salmaan Saleem, a forty-eight-year-old optician from Birmingham, to join YouTube in 2006, only a year after the site was founded. Salmaan is a man of average build, with a shaved head and thin, well-combed beard. We met in his flat in Birmingham, a few miles from the city centre, where he lives with his wife and his six-year-old daughter. Salmaan describes himself as a devout, practising Sunni Muslim, and, like many Muslims who grew up in the late '80s and early '90s, as a young man he was active in giving *da'wah*—teaching people about Islam—and helped to produce and distribute Islamic pamphlets, which he would give out on high streets and outside shopping centres. Though he 'wasn't ever really inter-ested in the internet, or computers', he said that he had a 'drive to call people to Islam' from his youth, wanting to 'share this beautiful religion with as many people as possible'. Saleem believed that giving *da'wah* was his duty as a Muslim, and that as someone devoted to his faith, it was his responsibility to spread the message of Islam.

It was because of this that he was drawn to YouTube when it launched in 2005. He had been sent a link to a five-minute reci-tation of *Surat al-Fatihah*, the first chapter of the Qur'an. 'It was just amazing hearing it come out of the computer for the first time, knowing that I could access it whenever I wanted,' he said. Eventually, he began to upload his own collection of recordings of the Qur'an and *du'ahs*—prayers, supplications—to YouTube, mostly taken from old CDs and cassette tapes. 'Lots of people I knew were doing the same,' he remembered. 'For some people it was to use in their communities, or help teach their children

Qur'an, but for others, it was just the excitement of being able to do it, and seeing your video being listened to by hundreds of people. Now it's nothing, but at the time it was incredible.'

Today, Salmaan contributes videos and recordings to the YouTube channel Epic Islamic Lectures.[10] Founded in 2016, the channel has more than 19,000 followers at the time of writing, and uploads weekly lectures that are similar to those Muhammad and Asif listen to on Fridays. Salmaan has run a number of different channels in the past, with content ranging from recordings of Qur'an recitations he hosted, to videos of speakers giving lectures, which he sometimes filmed at the mosque, or republished from other YouTube channels. In some cases, he uploaded clips of lectures broadcast on Islamic TV channels based outside of the UK, for Urdu- or Hindi-speaking audiences. When I asked Salmaan how he would define Epic Islamic Lectures, he laughed. 'Epic! It's a channel that is designed to make the believer feel good.'

To Salmaan, the mission of his YouTube channel is exactly the same as his reason for giving *da'wah* two decades ago. 'One of the key tenets of being a Muslim is to spread the word of Allah,' he said. 'We spread the word of Allah, and the message of the finality of Prophet Muhammad, that's my duty. With the YouTube channel, I want to provide the tools and knowledge for any Muslim to improve their understanding of the *deen*, through recitations, translations, and so on. At the same time, I also upload inspirational speeches from imams and other people of knowledge, because this is important as well. There might be Muslims who go on YouTube whose belief is not strong, who are struggling with Islam, and they won't want to click on a video that is just a recitation of the Qur'an. They are looking for something that will help them out of their struggle, that will motivate them to pray.'

Those kinds of videos, Salmaan told me, were the ones that tended to resonate most with young Muslims living in Britain, who he said are 'more likely to struggle when they're surrounded by temptations: barely dressed women, drugs, violence ... all things that are *haram*'—forbidden. In fact, Salmaan said he frequently receives 'thank you' messages and emails for his uploads, and that his channel has helped more than ten young men either to return to Islam, or not to leave. 'My videos are always there whenever people need them. It doesn't matter what time it is, what day it is, and it doesn't matter what kind of a person you are. The videos are always there.'

That's not to say that YouTube lectures are necessarily a replacement for traditional Friday *khutbahs*; *jumu'ah* prayers in mosques are still well attended across the United Kingdom. But for young people like Muhammad and Asif, as well as for people like Salmaan who use the internet to spread Islamic content, what YouTube really offers is a wider choice of listening material. Before the age of social media, Muslims could only listen to the imam at their local mosque, or to whatever lectures they had recorded on video tapes or CDs. Social media has expanded the scope of available material for Muslims to engage with in order to think about and negotiate their faith. Those wanting to learn about specific subjects—about *fiqh* (jurisprudence) or *nafs* (the ego or self)—can easily find videos and audio recordings online, and can decide what speakers they want to listen to on the topic. Those who want to listen to more contemporary Islamic lectures, about politics or social issues, can use the internet to find lectures that interest them too. Videos from internationally renowned speakers, like UAE-based Mufti Menk or US-based Khalid Yasin, who talk about gender and race in Islam, regularly amass tens of thousands of views on YouTube, while they achieve a comparable number of cross-platform shares across Facebook, WhatsApp and Instagram.

* * *

Choosing what and whom to listen to was 'really something that's only been normal for our generation,' Muhammad said when he had finished praying. 'Our parents had an attachment to their *masjid*, because they were immigrants to the UK, they had family all in the same area, and also because they didn't have a choice but to listen to the local imam, who for us was just a local family friend that my granddad had grown up with in Karachi.'

To Muhammad and Asif, who both grew up in areas of London where there were various Muslim communities of different cultures and ethnicities, their identities would inevitably differ from their parents. 'All my friends were Muslim,' Asif said, 'but very few were Pakistani. Most were Nigerian, Ghanaian, or Iraqi. So even though we all prayed together, we all saw ourselves as Muslim before anything else.'

Both men feel this spirit of openness resonates with younger generations of British Muslims, particularly those who have grown up in multicultural environments and, more importantly, with the internet. 'We're a generation that isn't just aligned to one speaker or imam; we listen to so many people so we can get a better knowledge of Islam and of how to be better Muslims,' Asif said. '[In Islam] we're told to constantly study and acquire knowledge [of Islam] so we can please Allah. You can't do that by just listening to one person—you have to be open to other people's interpretations and views so you can strengthen your own faith ... we might be doing it by watching lectures on YouTube rather than at the *masjid*, but the intention of gaining the knowledge and becoming a better Muslim is still the same.'

The Online Imams

Nahiem Ajmal, known online as Mufti Abu Layth, laughed into his phone camera. A well-built man with broad shoulders, a neatly trimmed, thin moustache and goatee, and a full head of jet-black hair, combed back, he was attempting to answer a question received on his Facebook live stream, about the age at which it's appropriate for a Muslim man to take a second wife. 'First, you've got to ask yourself, are you ready for it? Hahaha! Let me tell you something ... let me tell you something. Lots of young men, they have, what do you call it ... libido! They think they can marry another person because they have energy. But they don't! And it's always likely to end badly, hahaha!' Nahiem, sitting cross-legged on the floor, shifted and took a sip of Coca Cola from a pint glass branded with a Strongbow logo.

Mufti Abu Layth's weekly live streams take place from 10 p.m. to 12 a.m. on Monday nights.[11] He films them in his study in Birmingham, against the backdrop of his collection of gold-embossed Islamic books—volumes of *hadith* narrations, *tafsir* (Qur'an commentary), and guides to *fiqh*—a collection which, for the most part, one would associate with older Islamic scholars who sport white beards, wear traditional Islamic dress and wouldn't dream of drinking from glasses that had been designed for alcoholic beverages.

When I interviewed Nahiem in June 2018, he had just finished one of his Monday sessions. Over 500 people tuned in to the live stream on Facebook, and within a week, it had been watched by more than 2,000 people on YouTube. That might be a modest number compared to some of YouTube's biggest stars and personalities, but for Muslim preachers—especially those who, like Nahiem, are classically trained in traditional *madhhabs*, or Islamic schools of thought (Nahiem studied in the Maliki tradition, but doesn't subscribe to any particular Islamic school of thought)—a viewership of that scale is rare, and highly desired.

Tonight, Nahiem wore a tight black T-shirt with a large white skull, reminiscent of Marvel's 'The Punisher'. It hugged his biceps and showed the contours of his pecs, which, during his live streams, he sometimes tightens and flexes unknowingly. He uses his Monday nights to field questions from his followers, which he estimates to be around 10,000 people from all over the world. The questions he receives range from the strictly theological ('Was Mary a prophetess of God?' 'Do we accept *mutawatir hadith* if they contradict the Qur'an?' 'Is there even such a thing as *mutawatir hadith*?') to more practical elements of everyday life for practising Muslims ('Can Muslim women go out without their husband's permission?' 'Is smoking *haram*?' 'Can Muslims keep dogs as pets?').

Nahiem is thirty-nine and has been on the Islamic preaching circuit for over a decade. He has spoken at mosques across the UK, as well as in the US and in Pakistan. He has participated in debates with some of America's most well-known preachers, such as Bayyinah Institute founder Nouman Ali Khan, and has taught at the prestigious Jami'ah Muhammadiyyah Institute in Islamabad. It might be easy to dismiss Mufti Abu Layth as a self-styled preacher, who, like others in the online world, has made a name for himself by engaging in Islamic apologetics. But Nahiem has credentials, and is respected by trained Islamic scholars, not least because he studied Islamic theology in Damascus and later in Karachi, where he became a *hafiz*—someone who has memorised the Qur'an and *tafsir*—a feat that can be challenging even among the most pious of Muslims. At the same time, Nahiem does not embody the aesthetic expected of a 'person of knowledge', a term used by Muslims online to describe a person who has dedicated part of their life to studying Islam. Some of his fans—and his critics—describe his look as one of a 'jacked-up bodybuilder'. Others liken him to 'those Asian men who hang out outside of shisha bars before going clubbing'.

Nahiem's appearance has attracted criticism from some Muslims online, some of whom accuse him of 'mocking the *deen*' with his unconventional clothes that show off the shape of his body and his arms. 'He has no sense of *gheerah* [honour]!' one person posted on the Islamic forum Ummah.com in 2018.[12] Others criticise the choice of topics Nahiem chooses to talk about on his live streams, especially when it comes to topics like sexuality.

In 2017, Mufti Abu Layth received a lot of attention after a clip of his Monday-night live stream about the permissibility of masturbation went viral.[13] In his video, Nahiem said that masturbating was 'not clear-cut *haram*' and that there was evidence that early Muslims, the *Salaf*, encouraged masturbation as a way of avoiding committing major sins. 'He should not be talking about these subjects, especially when there are young people watching,' read one YouTube comment under the video. 'This is not the example we want to be setting for the next generation.'

In all the time I'd spent covering Muslim news, as a reporter and later researching this book, I hadn't ever come across someone like Mufti Abu Layth, a man who seamlessly navigated traditional conservative Islamic values and translated them onto the internet, so successfully that even the simplest live stream set up—an iPhone attached to a tripod—could result in hundreds of views every week.

'I don't believe what I'm doing is special in any way,' Nahiem told me. 'At the core of it I'm just talking about Islam, in a way that I would do in a *masjid* or a school. Maybe that's the appeal of my videos: that I don't appear like I'm an authority, or that I'm better than anyone. I'm not denominational, not attached to a particular mosque or community. I just act like myself, and I make comments based on what I know and what I've learnt. And if there's anything I don't know, I will be very open in saying I don't know.'

Nahiem attributes his success to what he believes is his 'authenticity'. For his audience, that means that while he has the authority of a trained scholar, he is able to exert his influence outside of traditional Islamic institutions. He can stream his lectures live to much larger audiences than can be expected to gather at the mosque. Rather than being limited by their location or their relationship to the local community, his audience can tune in anywhere, and at any time. Most of his audience, Nahiem said, seek him out directly on social media. The majority are long-time listeners, who 'connect with what I am saying, and the values that I hold'.

Mufti Abu Layth is considered by many to be one of the UK's most notable 'online imams'. He isn't connected to a specific mosque or a specific *madhhab*. His accessibility comes from his theological ambiguities.

As one of his viewers told me when I contacted them on YouTube, 'I find Mufti much more engaging than imams I have seen at *masjids*. The imams in the *masjid* tend to be quite dull, or they're very preachy. They will have one topic that they have been preparing for a long time, and they don't deviate from that ... Mufti is much more fast-paced. He has more energy and he also has views on what's happening in the real world—I feel that I learn much more from watching his videos than I have learned from other imams.'

* * *

While social media is saturated with Islamic lectures, the vast majority of them tend to be recordings of imams giving *khutbahs* in mosques or at Islamic events to live audiences. But although very few established scholars make content specifically for online platforms, Mufti Abu Layth is not the only one to do so. More and more young imams are using social media to share content, like London-based Abu Abdul Aziz Ahmed, a student at the King Saud University in Saudi Arabia, who uses Instagram's 'stories' feature and Snapchat to make short videos about Islamic history, etiquette and *tafsir* for his audience of 7,000 followers.[14] Abu Safiyyah Mohammed Osman, a London-based preacher and former student of *hadith* at Madinah University, also uploads videos to his Instagram and Facebook pages, in which he talks about Islamic issues ranging from the 'scholastic history of the *Sahabah* [companions of the Prophet]' to 'Islamic lessons about hardship, success and seeking knowledge'.[15]

Most of these preachers are relatively young, in their mid-twenties to their late forties. They make most of their online content in English, and the issues they focus on almost always relate to youth culture. 'There's a reason why Allah wants you to stay off the streets,' says Abdul Mohammed, an Islamic speaker from New York, in an Instagram story to over 53,000 followers in January 2018. '*Shaitan* [Satan] wants to see you go back to the gang life. To the music, to the drugs, to the girls. He's telling you that it'll make you happy. Fight it, fight it! Allah has so many more rewards for you in *Jannah* [Paradise], *inshallah*, if you fight it!'[16]

This style of preaching has become hugely popular amongst Muslims online. For most people who watch them, the appeal of these videos is that they are short and digestible, and that the preachers are direct and personable. Twenty-two-year-old Sara Salih, a young Muslim who lives in Kent and who regularly watches Islamic videos on Instagram, explained: 'I like that I can get important messages, and reminders within a few seconds. I can watch these videos on my way to work, or to college, or just when I have a spare moment in my day. It's nice to be able to hear an Islamic reminder, or positive Islamic messages, without having to watch videos that are hours and hours long, or ones that require you to have a deep historical knowledge to get any benefit.' Sara told me that her Muslim friends feel the same way. Though they regularly attend their mosque for prayers, they don't feel they have an affinity or a relationship with the mosque imam. Even though the online imams might live in different cities, or entirely different countries, their messages were more relatable. To Sara, this might be a generational issue.

'Our parents, grandparents, are the ones who set up these mosques, and for them the mosque is a part of their community. I think with younger Muslims like us, we're less inclined to attach ourselves to one place—we grew up online, so we know Muslims all over the UK who have had the same experiences as us, the same interests as us. I think that's why imams who aren't attached to one place—who can deliver messages that are universal—are more appealing to the younger generation.'

This is the central reasoning behind groups like Imams Online, a British organisation that aims to provide a voice for aspiring Muslim religious leaders across the UK by helping them to use social media to deliver their messages.[17] Based in an industrial park just outside of London, the project began in 2014 as a cross-denominational project, in the wake of news that young British Muslims were attempting to join ISIS in Syria. In July that year, Imams Online launched its first online campaign, a professionally shot video featuring British imams from across the country who refuted the theological claims ISIS was using to assert its legitimacy. 'ISIS are cowboys. They don't represent the religion and are not qualified to represent the religion,' says Sayed Ali Rizvi, one of the imams featured in the video. 'We are Muslims united against ISIS, against terrorism, against atrocity, against pain and suffering.'[18]

'That was really just the start,' Shaukat Warraich, the organisation's founder and chief editor, explained to me. 'Imams Online isn't just there to combat ISIS or extremism; it also exists because we recognised that there was a disconnect between the youth and the traditional places of worship. As Muslims, we've heard about all these preachers who know how to use social media, but they didn't necessarily have the knowledge to know what they were preaching, or how harmful it could be. And because there's no one regulating it, all you need to have religious influence is a camera and a laptop—obviously that can be a problem, not just when it comes to extremism, but also people who end up hearing twisted interpretations of the religion and believe that to be the truth.'

For that reason, Shaukat added, Imams Online exists to help traditionally trained imams learn how to use social media well enough that they can distribute more accurate and nuanced religious lessons. The organisation helps to set up social media pages, provides consulting work regarding social media strategies, and works together with tech companies like Google and Twitter.

And while Imams Online isn't quite a lobbying group or an activist campaign, Shaukat and others involved in the project say that its purpose is to 'reclaim internet spaces' from extremists, both within Muslim communities and amongst far-right, anti-Islam groups who 'want to define what Islam is and who Muslims are'. Speaking to BBC News, Qari Asim, one of the organisation's imams, urged that 'someone has to reclaim that territory from ISIS, and that can only be imams: religious leaders who guide and nourish their community'. Asim noted that 'in a digital mobile world', fewer young people were attending the mosque, and advised imams to 'reach out to them'.

* * *

Mufti Abu Layth agrees. 'My goal is to subvert the dogmas that exist in the Muslim community, and to challenge people who set themselves up as authorities or believe that they automatically have authority to dictate what Muslims should do,' he told me. 'The internet has made it easy to do that—you can claim that you're an authority, an expert, as long as you dress right and have the right books in the background. So when I do my [live streams] my job isn't just to disseminate knowledge ... it's also to recognise that we live in a digital age, where people can get more confused and can be misled, and to call out those people who are deceiving others.'

This, Nahiem added, wasn't a new innovation. In fact, he argued, what he is attempting to do in his videos is part of a much longer, historical tradition in Islamic preaching. 'Islam was never supposed to be institutionalised, and I feel that the online world has forced so many imams to recognise that now,' he said. 'I was just ahead of the game.'

The Da'wah *Showdown*

One night in January 2016, as I was sleeping, my phone came to life with the chimes of continuous WhatsApp messages. At the time, I was a reporter at BuzzFeed News working on the extremism beat, so an onslaught of messages suggested to me that some sort of attack had occurred, and that I would need to start making phone calls to police departments. Bleary-eyed, I pulled myself up and turned to my phone, to find that the messages were more erratic and excitable than I was anticipating. 'It's proper beef you know!' one message read. 'I can't believe it's still going on, it's like a boxing match!' read another. 'Is it going to be streamed?' someone else wrote, followed with a string of laugh-cry emojis.

The succession of messages had come in response to a video uploaded to YouTube and Facebook by Imran Ibn Mansur, a twenty-nine-year-old online Muslim personality who goes by the moniker 'Dawah Man'. With a tall, slim figure and a scruffy black beard—shaped in accordance with the teachings of the *Sunnah*—Ibn Mansur's aesthetic is a blend of traditional Islamic clothing and contemporary streetwear, popular among young people living in London. In most of his videos, he wears a black skullcap and designer sports jackets, under which he wears a traditional *thawb*.

Most Muslims who are active online will have heard of Ibn Mansur. He is one of the leading figures of *da'wah*, or Islamic

proselytising. As a young Muslim, Ibn Mansur was a pioneer—
one of the first Muslims to put videos of himself performing
da'wah on the internet, and developing a style that was highly
relatable to young Muslims growing up in cities and towns
around the UK. Sprinkling his speech with Arabic words and
citations from the Qur'an and *hadith*, with the tonal inflections
of South London 'road' talk more commonly associated with
grime musicians, Ibn Mansur initially put out videos that were
zany in their content and gonzo in style. In one video uploaded
in 2013, he asked drunken club-goers on the streets of Kingston-
upon-Thames whether their intentions that night were to find
someone to have sex with. In another video from 2015, Ibn
Mansur stands outside the Arabic hookah bars on Edgware Road
in West London, berating Muslims for smoking shisha in celebration of the end of Ramadan. Addressing a crowd of observers,
Ibn Mansur shouts through tears:

> Imagine if the Prophet stood right here! ... After Ramadan! Thirty
> days we stood [praying] in the last third of the night, crying to
> Allah, saying, 'Allah, forgive me for my sins!' Then literally the next
> day, the Prophet saw us out here, free mixing, boys and girls, dressed
> inappropriately, smoking shisha! *Wallahi* I am not judging anyone.
> I'm here just to give you the reminder that Allah told me to give you.
> But how embarrassed and sad would you feel that the Prophet *sallal-
> lahu alaihi wasallam* would see you in such a state. ... My brothers
> and sisters, take yourself to the Day of Judgement ... *wallahi* your
> mum will smile at you burning in the hellfire.[19]

Ibn Mansur has long been a controversial figure, and while his
supporters and sympathisers say that his work has been beneficial
in helping young Muslims to stay on the path of Islam, others
believe his fiery approach to *da'wah* has been unhelpful, even
detrimental to spreading the message of the faith. As someone
who used to promote Ibn Mansur's videos on social media told
me: 'I still believe that Imran is a sincere brother; he has a lot of

faith in Allah. But his approach was always very aggressive, and very black and white. If you didn't agree with him, his first instinct was always to attack ... maybe that's because of his background in the hip hop scene, but when you're giving *da'wah*, especially when you're giving *da'wah* to people who don't know about Islam but who nonetheless have strong opinions about it, it's not the best way to approach it.'

Other people point out that Ibn Mansur's choice to make content about deliberately controversial topics, such as sexual morals, homosexuality and sectarianism, has done little to benefit Muslims struggling in their faith and religious identity, and has instead driven some Muslims further from Islam. Writing for The Muslim Vibe, Amir Webb says that Dawah Man's videos are 'spreading hatred as nonchalantly as I spread jelly on my toast in the morning.' Webb writes that Ibn Mansur's confrontational attitude to those with different opinions and his ignorance about issues such as the history of Shi'ism or of Islam and black Muslims in Africa make him 'genuinely dangerous', as his dogmatic views and myth-peddling will inevitably make an impact on his scores of young, impressionable followers. Moreover, Webb argues that Ibn Mansur's videos have promoted toxic messages when it comes to sexual decency. He cites a video on 'dressing modestly', in which Ibn Mansur approaches three teenaged girls and interrogates them about why they 'enjoy dressing "sexy"', eventually asking the group 'if they would consider themselves possible rape victims'. 'This is how our young Muslim community is radicalized,' Webb warns. 'This is how they are taught to devalue women, hate anyone that disagrees and internalize racism and ignorance.'[20]

* * *

Up until the end of 2015, Ibn Mansur's reputation didn't go much further than his videos. In conversations I had with both imams and London-based Muslim community leaders at the time, they told me they saw 'Dawah Man' as an online persona, and as an example demonstrating that when 'young men get too excited about *da'wah*, they perform it incorrectly'. Still, they would give Ibn Mansur the benefit of the doubt. 'His methods are unconventional but he is not giving out Islamic rulings,' one imam told me in October 2015. 'If he is bringing youth to the *masjid* then *alhamdulillah* [praise be to Allah], may Allah reward him *inshallah*.'

But in late 2015, some believed that Ibn Mansur had overstepped his boundaries, when he got into a highly publicised feud with Imam Asim Hussain. Hussain is one of Bradford's most well-known Islamic preachers, and the founder of the Al-Hikam Institute, one of the UK's leading Islamic seminaries for aspiring imams and 'students of knowledge'. The dispute was over the legitimacy of celebrating Mawlid—the Prophet Muhammad's birthday. Mawlid has always been a contentious issue among Muslim communities. In Sunni Islam, Muslims who follow the Shafi'i *madhhab* or school of thought see the Mawlid as a legitimate celebration, and Muslims around the world, including in Egypt, Morocco, the Caribbean, India and Pakistan, celebrate by holding gatherings, marching in parades, and singing *nasheeds*. In the UK, many Muslim communities across different sects recognise the Mawlid too, by fasting throughout the day, gathering together for prayers and communal meals, and hanging lights outside their mosques. Other Muslims—often those who are affiliated with Salafism or Wahhabism—reject the idea of celebrating Mawlid, arguing that there is no evidence in the Qur'an, the *Sunnah* or the *hadith* to imply that the Prophet's birthday was ever marked or held in high veneration.

On 26 December 2015, Ibn Mansur posted a one-and-a-half-hour video called 'The TRUTH about the MAWLID!!!' He argued that the Mawlid is '*bid'ah*', an Islamic term for a man-made innovation that did not exist during the time of the Prophet Muhammad or the *Sahabah*, the righteous followers of the Prophet, who were trusted with continuing the religion upon his death. Throughout the video, Ibn Mansur backed up his argument with quotations from Islamic scholars. He ended with an exhortation:

> *Wallahi* we need to study our religion ... the longer you guys carry on being ignorant from the religion of Allah, you are just gonna be spoon-fed and misguided from people that they themselves don't know any better. So I urge you, go out there, study from a person who teaches you the *Sunnah* [way of the Prophet] according to the *Salaf* [early Muslims] ... because if not, you're gonna learn from people that are just trying to brainwash you, confuse you, pull the wool over your eyes.[21]

The video received only a few hundred views, until it was picked up by Imam Asim Hussain. Himself an advocator for recognising the Mawlid, Hussain made a response video that he and hundreds of his supporters shared on social media, refuting Ibn Mansur and inviting him to a conference to debate the issues around the Mawlid and the concept of *bid'ah*.[22]

What happened afterwards is less clear, and the story largely depends on whose side you're on. Those supporting Dawah Man say that Hussain didn't disclose the location or time for the debate, and subsequently failed to attend debating venues that were offered. On YouTube, Instagram and Snapchat, Ibn Mansur and those who manage his social media accounts repeatedly 'called Hussain out' for his 'misrepresentations' of Ibn Mansur and for his evasion of opportunities to debate. Those on Hussain's side, on the other hand, argue that Ibn Mansur failed to respond to invitations to debate, and that he had even disrespected Hussain by posting a derogatory cartoon of him online. Writing on Facebook in January 2016, Hussain wrote: 'It's sad to see that brother Imran has resorted to depicting me in this cartoon. I must say the turban is on point and I look whiter than usual. Very sad to see him depicting the *Na'l Mubarak* [Prophet Muhammad's sandals].'

* * *

It wasn't really the content of the debate that made the conflict such a spectacle—it was the optics. Dawah Man's videos were recorded in the empty spaces of his house, or sometimes in a car. Meanwhile, nearly all of Hussain's were recorded in his study, with a camera set up to show his lavish collections of gold-lettered Islamic literature, *hadith* commentary and other texts that would only be available to those pursuing the study of Islam as a way of life. To observers, this was more than a matchup between two Muslim men. It was a conflict between traditionally trained imams and a younger generation of YouTube-savvy religious Muslims. It was a showdown between those who led congregations inside the mosque, and those who could command bigger followings from bedrooms all over the world.

'It just felt like entertainment, like it was some kind of rap battle,' said Suffian Mannan, the administrator of the WhatsApp group 'Muslim News and Events UK'. Suffian watched things escalate on the group as the conflict between Ibn Mansur and Hussain heated up. 'It was weird', he recalled. 'I wouldn't really update the group unless there was some kind of event, or a *janazah* [funeral], or requests for *du'ah* [prayers] to be made. But all of a sudden, people were posting in the group every day—sometimes every hour. They would say things like "Look what Dawah Man's just put up, he's challenging the imam again". Or they would comment on the type of language they were using. Like they would get really excited if either of them was visibly angry.'

To Suffian, who lives in Birmingham, the incident was telling of how social media is increasingly influencing British Muslim culture, and how even the most mundane theological debates, when they take place online, can blur the boundaries of who can call themselves an authority. 'I was genuinely surprised by how many people took Ibn Mansur to be a legitimate scholar—even he doesn't say he is!' he said. 'But it was the way he dressed, and that he was able to imitate the way that scholars speak in the mosque. He was able to broadcast that to a huge audience and many of those people took that seriously.'

'The whole fight might have been funny to us initially,' he added. 'Of course, the problem is that many of our imams, our scholars who have studied [Islamic] knowledge for years and years, don't have the advantage of knowing how to use social media in the same way that these young guys do.'

For Suffian, that might cause serious problems for British Muslims in the future, especially if social media becomes the main place where young Muslims gain religious knowledge. He believes that extremists—including people who advocate physical violence—might be able to harness more influence than traditionally trained imams who are less internet-savvy. 'Eventually, you might have someone who is more extreme than Dawah Man, someone who is actually dangerous, who can end up being the main influence for young Muslims who are confused about practising the *deen*.' And if that happens, he believes, even an imam with more charisma than Ibn Mansur won't be able to bring them back to the right path.

Speakers' Corner

On a cold Sunday morning in April 2018, in Speakers' Corner, an area of London's Hyde Park, I was standing in a large circle watching two men loudly argue about whether or not the Prophet Muhammad was a paedophile. Dozens of phone cameras were out as more people moved in to watch the argument between the men—one, a Muslim man of South Asian origin, medium height, with a short, well-groomed beard and gelled black hair; and the other, a tall, slightly plump and clean-shaven white man wearing a tight T-shirt that bore a picture of Donald Trump.

'He married his wife when she was seven and consummated that marriage when she was nine. That's paedophilia, admit it!' the white man shouted, gesturing towards the audience. The statement was met with a mix of applause, boos and head-shaking. 'There is no passage in the *hadith* that verifies this,' the Muslim man retorted. 'Besides, if you are so concerned about paedophilia and child abuse, why don't you look back at your own history?'

This debate went on for over an hour. The circle around the men kept growing, and even more people brought out their phones to record or live stream. After a while, the men started to refer to their audience—offline and online—in every other sentence. 'Are you going to lie to everybody on camera, mate? Everyone's watching you ... you've exposed yourself!' the white man shouted. 'Everyone who is watching this will just see how stupid your arguments are,' the Muslim man responded. 'You're just showing you're a typical racist Islamophobe.'

I witnessed conversations like this quite regularly when I visited Speakers' Corner, an open-air arena for public speeches and debate, close to the site of the old Tyburn Gallows, where public executions used to take place until 1783. The tradition of open-air speech started because those due for execution were allowed to make one final statement before being hanged, during which many would chastise, ridicule and mock the monarch and the state authorities.[23]

When the site of the executions moved, Speakers' Corner hosted a number of English and international movements—for example, the Reform League, which in 1865 campaigned for universal male suffrage. It was also frequented by Karl Marx, and by George Orwell, who described it as 'one of the minor wonders of the world,' where he listened 'to Indian nationalists, temperance reformers, Communists ... freethinkers, vegetarians, Mormons, the Salvation Army ... and a large variety of plain lunatics.'[24]

In 1872, the British Parliament officially made Speakers' Corner a protected area for public speaking. Since then, the park has hosted some of the world's best orators, including C.L.R. James and Marcus Garvey. But it also has a reputation for being a place where conspiracy theorists—whose platform is usually confined to internet forums, where they rant behind pseudonyms—can openly speak about 'chemtrails', the New World Order or how the government is trying to control our minds by putting fluoride in water.

Yet, if you go to Speakers' Corner today, you'll find that these 'traditional' conspiracy theorists have largely been pushed to the sidelines. Instead, as some veterans and former veterans of Speakers' Corner told me, 'Every conversation is now about Islam. Everyone is obsessed with Islam and Muslims, and every conversation is either about whether Islam is bad, or it's Muslims who come to the park to preach about the virtues of Islam.' One man who has been going to Speakers' Corner for over two decades told me he had become so concerned by this that he set up an online petition called 'Make Speakers Corner Great Again'. The petition complained that: 'In recent years the range of speakers has reduced significantly and religion, increasingly just Islam, has become the main subject. This has more recently been accompanied by an increase in violence and intimidation and attempts to control who comes to the Corner and what they are permitted to say.'

* * *

To an extent, the man was right. While researching for this book, I was privy to countless conversations and debates at Speakers' Corner about whether Islam 'originated from Satanism', whether 'all true Muslims believe in Sharia law', and whether 'Islam and British values are compatible', and on every visit I made there since 2016, I found it only took a few minutes to find someone debating Islam.

Part of this surge in Islam-related debates at Speakers' Corner has come from the anti-Muslim rhetoric on social media, which, for some speakers, has helped them amass a huge public following. Stephen Yaxley-Lennon, known as Tommy Robinson, the former leader of the right-wing English Defence League (EDL) and now a prominent anti-Islam public figure, chose Speakers' Corner as a venue to hold a rally in May 2018, after Martin Sellner, the leader of the racist far-right movement Generation Identity, was barred from entering the UK. Robinson's speech brought thousands of his supporters to the park—most of whom are just as hostile to Islam and Muslims as he is, if not even more so. At the rally, some of Robinson's supporters told me that 'Muslims have taken over Speakers' Corner' and were 'threatening free speech'.

At the same time, the boost in Islam-related content has been driven by the demand of online audiences, particularly on YouTube, where videos streamed from Speakers' Corner can reach tens of thousands of people across the world, and where creators of Speakers' Corner videos know that speeches about Islam will get views. A rudimentary search on YouTube of Speakers' Corner videos shows that videos with titles like 'MUSLIM VS JEW', 'ISLAMOPHOBE vs MUSLIM MAN' and 'ATHEIST EVOLUTIONIST DEBATES MUSLIM' amass over half a million views each, while YouTube channels like 'Content Over Everything', 'O.S.S.C Dawah' and 'BlackDunya', which put out professionally filmed and edited videos from Speakers' Corner, have tens of thousands of subscribers. No one running one of these huge YouTube channels was willing to talk to me for this book, but the popularity of Islam-related content hasn't gone unnoticed by those running smaller channels, or streaming debates on social media.

'I usually get a few thousand views a week,' says thirty-four-year-old Ahmed, who runs 'Living Dawah', a YouTube channel with around 2,000 subscribers. Like others, Ahmed live streams debates from Speakers' Corner on YouTube and Facebook, using an iPhone 6 and a selfie stick. For Ahmed, his channel is a form of *da'wah*, and an effective one to boot. 'I was like all the other *da'wah* people a few years ago—the guys you see outside of Earl's Court tube station with their stalls, trying to give out literature about Islam ... I remember thinking to myself that it was just ineffective, you know? You would spend hours on the stall, trying to convince people to talk to you, and then you'd just end up talking to tourists. ... It is important, but it wasn't an effective way to convince people to come to the *deen*.'

As a devout Muslim who believes it is his a duty to bring as many non-Muslims to Islam as possible, Ahmed struggled to figure out what he should do. It was one night in 2017, while he was on YouTube looking for clips from a football match, that he came across Speakers' Corner videos.

'I was watching a debate between Hamza Myatt'—a notable Sunni speaker—'and an atheist who was trying to debunk Islam. It was this hour-long video, and I just remember how Hamza carried himself so confidently and managed to win the debate—it was amazing, you know? And then when I was reading the comments, I was seeing atheists actually [concede]. Like, they were saying, "I'm not a Muslim but Hamza made some good points".'

Ahmed suddenly grasped the potential of the internet to spread his message. 'I realised that it was way more effective to put those kinds of debate on YouTube, so you can at least reach people who are curious about Islam to give them *da'wah*, rather than random people who really couldn't care less.'

Since then, Ahmed has been travelling from his home in Essex to Hyde Park on Sundays, often staying until the evening, in order to film debates. It's a sacrifice for Ahmed, who spends the rest of the week working as an Uber driver in order to support his wife and two children. But for him, it's also an extension of his duties as a Muslim. 'I do spend less time with my family,' he tells me. 'But they understand why. They understand that it's important work, that it's my Islamic duty.' He quotes a verse from *Surat an-Nahl* to justify his point: 'Invite (all) to the way of thy Lord with wisdom and beautiful preaching; and argue with them in ways that are best and most gracious' (Qur'an, 16:25).

'I have received messages from people who have seen my videos telling me that they were driven to learn more because of them, or that they had come back to Islam because of them,' Ahmed adds. 'So to me, it's a sign that it's working.'

* * *

Of course, not all Muslims are as optimistic about the effectiveness of *da'wah* at Speakers' Corner compared to older or more traditional methods. The main criticism, according to the Muslims I interviewed, was that Speakers' Corner inspired 'aggression'. 'It encourages you to have to be loud, to be rude and to be arrogant in order to make your point, which isn't what the Prophet taught us,' said one former attendee. Most of the Muslim women I spoke to said they wouldn't go to Speakers' Corner, because it was 'dominated by macho *akhs* [bros] who are looking for fights'. 'It feels like it's just a playground for men to let out their aggression, rather than to have a genuine conversation.'

But there was one criticism that emerged again and again— that 'Speakers' Corner is just a platform for people who want to be famous online, while thinking they're speaking up for Islam'. Another of my interviewees said: 'I don't want to doubt anyone's sincerity ... I just don't think Speakers' Corner is the right place to carry out acts in the name of Allah. In an environment like that, it's easy to play to the camera, or think your online audience is more important than the person you're talking to or even staying true to the path of Islam, which warns us about celebrity.'

And indeed, Speakers' Corner videos have turned some Muslim speakers into online celebrities, with thousands of social media followers. Such speakers include Shamsi, a notorious Salafi speaker, originally from Egypt. On YouTube, most of Shamsi's videos accrue thousands of views, while his debates with Christians and atheists can easily be watched more than 10,000 times in a matter of weeks.[25] Other well-known Muslim speakers who have made a name for themselves online include Mohammed Hijab, a tall, well-built man known for his calm, refined manner during debates as well as his penchant for mixed martial arts. A video of Hijab debating feminism at Speakers' Corner has been viewed more than 160,000 times.[26]

Another of these YouTube stars is Ali Dawah, a convert to Islam and one of the UK's first Muslim influencers. Dawah has been on YouTube for over five years, and was one of the first speakers to employ techniques used by traditional YouTube influencers to advocate a more literalist, Salafi interpretation of Islam. For example, some of his early videos included the now unavailable 'Haram Relationship Prank', in which he tried to convince his Muslim friends that he had been in an impermissible relationship, or 'MUSLIM MURDER EXPERIMENT!!!' in which he attempted to expose the double standards of the media in its reporting about Muslims and non-Muslims.[27]

Over the years, Dawah has received praise among Muslims for his attempts to give *da'wah* to younger, tech-savvy generations. But he has also received criticism. Some Muslims have accused him of sexism during videos in which he encourages women to wear hijab. Others say he is too aggressive when he presents his opinions about Islam online, or find him egotistic. 'I stopped following him when his beef with Tommy Robinson happened,' one of his former followers told me via Instagram, referring to when Dawah challenged the former EDL leader to a debate in mid-2018. 'I am sure he had good intentions, but that just showed that he was more interested in showing up Tommy on camera, which is fine when you are a sheikh, or a person of knowledge studying Islam. But you shouldn't be doing that if you're a YouTuber.'

When I spoke to him, Ali Dawah told me that he understood some of these concerns and admitted that 'my approach on certain subjects could have been worded better'. He attributed those mistakes in part to his age. Now twenty-nine, he said that both he and his content have matured. Most of his videos are now educational, 'involve talking to a scholar, or having a conversation with people who are learned', and are part of a professionalised media network called Salaam Studios, which Dawah runs alongside Mohammed Hijab. An online TV channel based in East London, Salaam Studios puts out a range of Islamic content, from debates and discussions to restaurant reviews, with the aim of 'tackling misconceptions by both Muslims and non-Muslims'.

While his online output had changed in some ways, Dawah emphasised that his 'overall objective' had stayed the same. 'My aim is to "enjoin the good and forbid the evil", as Allah has commanded us to do,' he said. 'We want to help Muslims find and stay on the correct path, and also to let them know there's nothing wrong with being creative, so long as it is halal.' When I asked him to expand on this, he referenced some of his earlier work that he now distances himself from. 'For example, we won't do any YouTube stunts, or lie to people for a joke,' he told me, adding that this remained a problem for many young Muslims making content for YouTube. 'The problem is that it can be tempting for so many people to do things that are impermissible—things like music, or [these kinds of] bad jokes, just to get clicks and views. You find that when Muslims start out on YouTube, they talk a lot about religion, but as their views go up, and their clicks go up, they talk about religion less and less, and sometimes they even compromise on Islam to maintain their following.'

When I asked whether it would be easier for more practising Muslims to stay off social media, he replied by saying that there was 'nothing *haram* about any of the social media platforms'. In fact, he said, 'Social media is a good way to connect with other Muslims, to give *da'wah* and also to get knowledge. It's about how you use those platforms, and what we want to show is how you can use them responsibly—in a way that is fun, that is [informative], and that also exposes things that are intellectually misleading in the faith, that can make people turn away from it.'

Though Dawah is still a regular at Speakers' Corner, he now attends less, so he can focus on building Salaam Studios into the 'best place for young Muslims and people interested in Islam to gain knowledge'. While he still thinks Speakers' Corner is an important place for spreading the message of Islam, he believes that YouTube culture has helped to turn the Hyde Park site into a place that is 'being used for all kinds of madness', which people use 'for their own ends, for fame or to attack people'.

'Sometimes at Speakers' Corner your points get lost, because of all the fighting and shouting,' he said. With his new venture, he hopes that he can use the following he has gained over years as an online influencer to teach people about Islamic ideas productively, in discussion with trained imams and scholars. 'With Salaam, we will teach people about their religion respectfully and calmly, and in a way that everyone can benefit from.'

Places to Pray

For the past few years, each Friday, Samira Khan, a thirty-five-year-old paralegal from North London, has hosted *jumu'ah* prayers from her living room. They are strictly women-only gatherings, and are usually attended by some of Samira's co-workers, her friends, and a couple of women living outside London who attend via video-link. Each week, the women sit together and read verses from the Qur'an, or listen to Islamic lectures on YouTube, usually relating to the *surah* they are reading. They also talk about events in the news that relate to their experiences as Muslims—this week, about the safety of wearing a hijab in public, and whether it is permissible to remove it if one is in danger—and consider the lessons offered by scripture and Islamic teachings. The session ends with one of the women leading the others in prayer.

Samira said the idea of hosting her own *jumu'ah* was born of frustration. She comes from a devout religious family, and Islam was always a central part of her life. 'Right from the beginning,' she said, 'I was always taught by my family—my father in particular—that Islam was about empowering women. I grew up with all the stories about the great women of Islam, like Khadija [the wife of the Prophet] and Fatima [the Prophet's daughter], how they were powerful because of their faith. They were always my role models, even when every one of my friends was looking up to actresses and pop singers.' Samira's devotion to her faith translated into her actions. She used her time to serve her community, holding charity events on behalf of the local mosque, travelling abroad to volunteer, and spending her weekends teaching in the madrassa. But one thing had irritated her since her teens. 'I wasn't allowed to pray in the mosque during *jumu'ah* ... all because I'm a woman.'

What started as a mild irritation intensified as time went on. At university, Samira was denied access to the campus prayer room by a group of Muslim men, who told her she could only use it when all the men had left. The incident prompted her to start 'thinking about how women were actually treated in all the mosques I'd attended'. After graduation, she went back to her local mosque more regularly, but became more aware not only of how small the women's section was, but also of how poorly their space was run. 'On our side you had paint peeling off the walls, no air conditioning, not even a proper space to perform *wudhu*— you'd have this one sink and bathroom, and everyone would have to take turns to quickly use it,' she remembered. 'On the men's side, there were more washing facilities, fans, windows ... it was just very unfair.'

Samira's repeated complaints were all ignored. 'I told my mum and my aunties about my frustrations and they just sort of shrugged it off,' she recalled. 'My mum basically told me that even though it was annoying, that's just the way things are.' Over a cup of tea and home-made biscuits after the *jumu'ah* prayer, Samira described how little has changed in traditional mosques when it comes to how women are treated and catered to in comparison to men. 'I'm sure there are plenty of mosques that are doing a good job, and they have women on their committees and are having these important conversations,' she said. 'But from my experience, this isn't the case for most Muslim women, living in the UK anyway.'

The turning point, when she decided she needed to take action on her own, came from Facebook.

'I'm a member of a lot of Islamic groups on there, just so I can get Islamic reminders, or keep up to date with Muslim events,' she said. 'Some of those groups are specifically there for Muslim women. I remember when I first found some, there was one group—I think it was just called "Muslim Women Chat Forum". It had about 200 members a few years ago. ... When I joined that group, it was the first space where there were female administrators. The conversation threads were about issues—not even just the standard issues you'd expect from a Muslim woman, like hijab or marriage—real political issues. There are always threads on there about the atrocities happening in Palestine, or the war in Syria. It was the first time I felt I could actually participate in that conversation and let people know how I felt about it. At least, people other than my husband at the dinner table!'

Samira used to spend hours in these Facebook groups. She would keep up with threads on her daily commute and during her lunch breaks. She'd talk about some of the conversations with her husband before bed. 'Even he was fascinated by them—it added a different perspective to the debates he would be having with his friends at the *masjid*, or the things he'd hear when he went to pray. He realised there was a lot he didn't know. He grew up hearing stories about Aisha and Khadija [wives of the Prophet], but he knew nothing about Sumayyah bint Khayyat, who's considered to be the first martyr of Islam. He didn't know about Arwa al-Sulayhi, one of the first women rulers in all of human civilisation, and who contributed so much to modern Islamic thinking. I hadn't heard of either of them until I joined the groups.'

* * *

It wasn't just on Facebook that Samira found a way to feed her religious curiosity. One of her favourite blogs, hosted by Tumblr, frequently came up in conversations on the Facebook group. Samira finds that it emphasises the 'real problems that Muslim women face when it comes to fighting for their own religious spaces'.

'Side Entrance' is one of the most popular Muslim blogs, and has opened a much-needed discussion about Muslim women's experiences in their places of worship. The blog's description says it is for 'Photos from mosques around the world, showcasing women's sacred spaces, in relation to men's spaces. We show the beautiful, the adequate and the pathetic.' The photos, contributed by the blog's loyal readership and curated by the American interfaith activist and educator Hind Makki, are often laid out so that pictures of large, lavish prayer spaces designed for men are juxtaposed with the considerably smaller, dreary settings for women. Makki has received pictures of women's prayer spaces not just from the West, but also from Muslim-majority countries across the Middle East, North Africa and South Asia. In an interview with the religion and culture website Patheos.com, Makki explained that her motive for creating the blog was to 'catalyze a discussion on Muslim male privilege,' adding:

> I realized that many Muslim men are ready to be allies; however, they typically don't know how bad some of these spaces are. When they find out about them, they are often surprised and dismayed about women's spaces and want to do something to fix these issues. The thing about privilege is that the ones who are privileged rarely know they are. So Side Entrance is a way to open that discussion among men, too.[28]

Makki has been criticised for her blog, often by men, she says, who accuse her of airing 'dirty laundry' in public. To her, however, the blog isn't about portraying Islam or Muslim communities negatively. Rather, she says, she is trying to alert Muslim communities to real problems that can have material consequences, namely in 'stopping Muslim women from wanting to attend the mosque or feeling welcome in it.' Responding to criticism, she adds:

> The mosque plays a certain role in Western Muslim communities— it's the glue that holds us together, teaching Muslims about Islam, providing a space for Muslims to be in community with one another. If mosques neglect the needs of women to prioritize men's needs, or are hostile toward women altogether to the point where women are leaving, that's a greater disservice to our beautiful faith than my publishing a few negative photos and catalyzing an online discussion about the spaces women occupy in our mosques.

* * *

For some Muslims, it's not just in prayer and worship where social media can facilitate conversations that are harder to initiate in the mosque. In 2016, Shareefa Iqbal, twenty, from Birmingham, ran a small Facebook group called 'Muslimahs UK', which she set up to discuss issues for and about Muslim women.[29] The group grew from five members, initially Shareefa and her friends, to around 500 members from across the country. Shareefa started the group because she found that too many discussions around Islam and Muslim identity were being led and controlled by men, both in real life and on the web.

'The majority of Muslim Facebook groups are run by men,' Shareefa says. 'That can make it difficult for women's issues to be made a priority in those groups, and often they would end up being pushed right to the bottom as soon as they were posted, because men in the group would just post things like YouTube videos, or reminders for events. That's not a problem, of course ... it's just that the groups weren't useful when it came to discussing really important issues around things like gender, family and marriage.'

There were persistent difficulties for women who tried to raise specific women's issues in these groups. Shareefa faced this challenge herself when, in a Facebook group for young British Muslims, she posted a link showing various hijab styles for women. She didn't give much thought to the article before sharing it, other than that other women might find it helpful. 'I just thought it might have been useful for some of the sisters in the group—ones who have just started to wear hijab, or find particular styles uncomfortable, especially because it was summer and very hot—there were styles which showed how to wear it a bit looser.'

When she returned to the group a few hours later, she found a thread of over eighty comments. 'I thought it would be a positive response.' Instead, she sighs, it had turned into a debate about 'what constituted the best way to wear the hijab'—a conversation dominated by male members of the group.

'It ended up in a situation where guys—or at least accounts with male names—were telling women that there was only one correct way to wear the hijab, posting lectures by male speakers, some that referred to women who wore it in any way that showed skin or hair as being "sluts" and "whores" who were "just as bad as underwear models". ... There were other guys who accused me of going against the rules of the group because I was supposedly spreading information that was *bid'ah* [innovation in religious matters]—this is despite the fact that some of these hijab styles have existed for hundreds of years outside of the Western world.'

Shareefa also received more than ten messages, all from men in the group, telling her to take down the post, warning her that she was spreading information that was 'un-Islamic' and that could cause young Muslim women to 'deviate from the commands of Allah'. 'These were guys who thought they were doing something [good], meaning well—like they started their messages by saying that they "wanted to give advice privately" ... but what actually made them qualified in the first place?'

Like many Muslim women-only groups online, Muslimahs UK was a private group with membership restrictions and set rules of conduct, from being respectful, refraining from swearing and applying a zero-tolerance policy towards public shaming. For Shareefa, it was imperative that the group operated as a 'safe space' for Muslim women to talk about the issues they faced without the threat of what she calls the 'male gaze'. For this, she has received more criticism from Muslim men.

'I think there are a fair number of Muslim men out there who don't really know what it's like to be a Muslim woman, apart from surface-level things,' she says, referring to the well-known challenges of being a Muslim who wears a hijab, niqab or jilbab in public. 'They understand the Islamophobia part, but not necessarily the battles we have to face within our communities. That's not just how we wear Islamic dress, or how we pray. It's also the difficulties we have if we want to run for leadership positions in our communities because they're considered "jobs for men", or even the challenges and prejudice we face pursuing careers as Muslim women.'

Shareefa blames some of these preconceptions on mosques and madrassas for not teaching young boys about the challenges Muslim girls will face. As a result, 'guys end up getting most of their knowledge about women from TV, or, these days, Instagram, Snapchat, just social media in general ... it's no wonder that they have all these ideas of what women are supposed to think and how they're supposed to behave.'

For Shareefa, her Facebook group was one of the only spaces where Muslim women could 'truly be themselves'. It was somewhere they could discuss anything, not just about religion—passages of the Qur'an, *hadiths* and Islamic reminders—but also things that were more mundane or funny. 'One of the most popular posts in that group was a video from the "Epic Meal Time" YouTube channel, where they just made this massive lasagne filled with bacon and Jack Daniel's whisky. You'd have women joking about how they would definitely take a sneaky bite of it, or commenting on the cooking style—just silly things. But it was great, because there wasn't as much of a fear of having your opinions shut down, or being told you weren't behaving properly by men who've almost certainly liked Emily Ratajkowski's Facebook page.'

More importantly, Shareefa notes, the group acted as a support network for women who had faced challenges in their lives and who felt unsupported by their communities. 'We had one member, Maryam, who had faced years of domestic abuse from her ex-husband,' Shareefa recalls. 'People in her community knew—she had told them—and all they said to her was to try not making him as angry—as if it were her fault.'

Maryam didn't know much about the legal system, and wasn't sure what she could do if she intended to terminate the marriage. Even more worrying to her was how her community would respond. After all, she was a stay-at-home wife, at the insistence of her husband. Out of the blue, Shareefa received a private message from Maryam—'help me', it said, followed by a telephone number. 'I put her in touch with a solicitor who spoke her home language, Bengali. We used code words to talk to each other so that she could communicate that she was in danger, and to protect her from being detected. Within a month I was able to organise a place she could stay via another member of the group, and the solicitor worked pro bono to ensure that she could get a divorce as quickly as possible.'

Although Shareefa doesn't want to be negative about mosques and their ability to handle situations like Maryam's, she recognises the power of online groups like hers to support people and achieve results in ways that mosques cannot. 'In a mosque, it's difficult to make friends, let alone divulge things that are very private and secret—you don't know who might accidentally tell your mum, or an auntie, and then how that might affect your reputation and future.'

At the mosque, she expands, 'it's difficult to know if you can trust someone with sensitive parts of your life'. The setting made it hard to be open. 'Online, it's different—you're speaking directly to people and you can build instant relationships. If it weren't for the group, and Maryam being able to speak to me directly, there's a big chance that she would still be in her marriage today, and probably in even more danger.'

But while Muslimahs UK gave Shareefa a chance to create a community focused on Muslim women's issues, she doesn't feel that the group was necessarily a replacement for the mosque, nor that it was always the ideal place to have sensitive discussions. 'Social media is the only tool available to us at the moment to have these conversations respectfully and honestly,' she says. But operating in a secular space, of course, poses challenges.

'For starters, it's easy for people to be targeted. Even if they don't use their real names or upload photos of themselves, being online means being in a space where you aren't governed by the same rules you would be if you were in the house of Allah [the mosque].' One of Shareefa's greatest worries was that members of the community would be 'doxxed', meaning that their personal information—names, addresses, contact info—had been accessed without their consent and made public. 'It would have put Muslim women in danger, and I wouldn't have been able to live with myself if that happened,' she says. 'Ultimately the *masjid* has to be the place that they can go to. [They need to] know that there's always someone there to speak to, that they can seek guidance on issues without having a man present, that they can even access a decent space. So many women in the group say they just don't like going to the *masjid* because it's physically uncomfortable.' Shareefa hopes that mosques will look into ways to make themselves more open to those who feel marginalised, particularly women. 'The big fear is having a generation of women younger than me—who've truly grown up on the internet, who have had all the big conversations about Islam on the internet—just find the *masjid* irrelevant. And that could really put their future at risk.'

* * *

It's a fear that Samira Khan shares. 'It's a shame that the types of discussions we have aren't had in the *masjid*, in the men's side and even in the women's side. I'm lucky to be able to have spaces, on the internet and in real life, where I can talk to other women about issues that affect us. But I know plenty of women who aren't as lucky.'

Like Shareefa, Samira doesn't believe that the internet is a replacement for the mosque, but rather that the former has become the main arena of debate and discussion for young Muslims. Although that can be positive, it also risks leading impressionable young Muslims down the wrong path, in terms of both understanding their religion, and being vulnerable to dangerous people. 'To a lot of young people, the mosque is just somewhere you go and pray, and that's it,' Samira said. 'If you want to learn something about Islam, countless people I've come across will immediately just search online, or ask someone directly on Twitter or YouTube.

'One reason I set up a *jumu'ah* in my house was because I know the importance of human interaction when you want to learn or discuss something as important as religion,' she added. 'But when you don't have those human interactions, and all your learning just comes from Google and YouTube videos, that can have real problems later down the line. That's where *masjids* really have to step in, before it's too late.'

Sheikh Google

Sara Sahir, a twenty-nine-year-old business management consultant in East London, had been staring at her computer screen for an hour, tapping her fingers on her desk. It was an hour until lunch, and her colleagues had been talking about a new fried chicken stall that had opened around the corner from her office near Spitalfields Market. The stall had only been around for a few weeks, but it had rave reviews, both on London's foodie websites and in *Time Out* magazine, which described the organic, Asian-style chicken as 'succulent', 'mouth-watering' and like a 'taste of heaven'. Her colleagues wanted to check the stall out, and had asked if she wanted to come. It should have been a no-brainer; after all, Sara describes herself as a 'fried chicken addict' and is always up for spicy wings, regardless of the time or place. The problem was that she wasn't sure if this premier fried chicken was halal.

With the clock counting down to 12.30, Sara did the only thing she could do: she turned to Google and typed, 'can praying on chicken make it halal?'

'It was a ridiculous question,' she laughs, when we speak on the phone. Sara went through over ten pages on her initial Google search, reading everything from Wikipedia pages on the rules of halal slaughter, to threads on Ummah.com, one of the biggest Islamic online forums, and Islamqa.com, a popular website where users can ask scholars based in Egypt and Saudi Arabia questions about the *Sunnah* and *fiqh* directly.

Reading the forums made her even more confused than she had been when she started. 'There were just conflicting opinions—some people said that eating meat that wasn't slaughtered in a halal way was prohibited at all costs. But at the same time, some said that you can only eat meat if you can *guarantee* the animal was slaughtered in a halal way, which maybe works if you're living in Pakistan, but in the UK, even in restaurants you can't see the animal being killed.'

With fifteen minutes left to go, Sara eventually stumbled across a website called Al-Mawrid.org, the official website of a Pakistani madrassa, which had a forum for people to ask questions to students studying to become imams. 'If Halal butchers/suppliers are not easily available to you and it is not easy to buy enough Halal meat for the period that you are not accessing the butcher/supplier then I think the advice of eating non-Halal chicken can be adopted,' the website said.[30] Sara had her justification. 'I knew my situation wasn't quite the same,' she says. 'But if there are rules that can be that flexible, I thought my situation would be fine. And just in case, I'd probably say *bismillah*'—in the name of Allah—'before eating.'

* * *

Sara's struggle to reconcile her religious beliefs with the pursuit of tasty chicken might seem minor. But it also captures one of the most common experiences of Muslims living in Britain when it comes to navigating and negotiating their beliefs. As Gary Bunt has argued, where Muslims lack access to imams or scholars who can adequately issue rulings, the internet has provided a repository of judgements and *fatwas*—guidance on everyday issues from an Islamic perspective—that can be accessed quickly and easily in English.[31] While *fatwas* are not absolute rulings but rather serve as learned opinions, their attachment to established Islamic scholars means that they are still deemed to have the authority to guide decisions.

At the same time, the new online *fatwa* culture frequently causes controversies. That wasn't the only time Sara had consulted Google to get Islamic advice. 'I use the internet a lot to learn about Islam,' she says. 'I've probably learnt more about Islam from reading forums, Facebook groups and watching videos than from any direct advice from an imam in real life.'

And Sara isn't alone. Across the world, more and more Muslims are turning to the internet to find answers about Islam, particularly on large public platforms like YouTube, where thousands of videos detail rulings on the minutiae of everyday life, from the permissibility of particular hairstyles, to halal and *haram* positions to sleep. More often than not, there is little consensus on these subjects, meaning that for Muslims whose primary resource for Islamic knowledge is the internet, they can choose from a plethora of opinions from both scholars and laymen. The phenomenon has become known as 'asking Sheikh Google'.

Concerns about Sheikh Google have long been voiced, both by scholars themselves and by Muslim community leaders and activists. One of the most stark warnings was from the Emirati imam Mufti Menk, who, in a 2013 lecture said:

> Nowadays that the globe is a small little village, people wait for loopholes. You know when someone says 'interest is *haram*,' we'll start Googling—they call it Sheikh Google, *mashallah*. Start

Googling: 'who says it's not?' When we find the *fatwa*, we quickly stick to it: 'I've found something else.' That's the attitude nowadays. We quickly go and use Sheikh Google in order to justify what we want to do, rather than surrendering to [Allah].[32]

In 2016, the Saudi Arabia-based sheikh Abdur Razzaq al-Badr also warned of the dangers of consulting Google over the *fatwas* of 'legitimate scholars' and 'people of knowledge', referring to those who had spent years, if not decades, studying Islam under a sheikh or in an established madrassa. 'Many of the Muslims nowadays do not know Ibn Qawqal [a companion of the Prophet Muhammad], may Allah be pleased with him, nor do they know many of the companions,' al-Badr says in the video, addressing his congregation of mostly older men wearing long beards, kurtas and white skullcaps. 'They don't know "Qawqal" but they know "Google". They know Google very well. Every day they're distracted by Google, and it brings them into a state of confusion and deviation.'[33]

* * *

Search engines—and indeed, the advanced internet—pose a challenge for many mosques, community leaders and local imams, not just in Britain but around the world. Some find themselves unable to compete with both the speed at which Google can deliver answers and the scope of its search results. For some imams, especially those who serve small communities, this can be worrying.

'As an imam, you have a lot of responsibilities, but with the internet being such a prominent part of our lives, especially if you're a young person, we have to learn how to combat bad ideas before our youth find them in the first place,' said Imam Mohammed Abidina. I met Mohammed, a tall, slim man of Somali background, with a small, trimmed beard lining his clearly defined cheekbones, in a café in Haworth, a small town near Bradford, where he teaches and gives lectures to a community of just over 1,000 people in a mosque converted from two suburban semi-detached houses.

Mohammed is a young imam, only thirty-five years old; he studied at Al-Azhar University in Cairo before coming to the UK with the aim of becoming a full-time imam. For him, being an imam is about giving back to the wider community, so beyond his normal duties of leading prayers, giving weekly sermons and providing counselling, he also helps organise charity events and interfaith workshops with local churches. He believes that one of the biggest challenges facing every Muslim community across the country is the internet, and its ability to 'capture the minds of young people quickly and more effectively than parents, community leaders or mosque leaders'.

'Extremism is only part of the story,' Mohammed said. 'The internet has other harms too, which, if you are young and impressionable, can be just as bad.' He described having to counsel young people who had got in physical fights with other Muslims because of religious disagreements. Another time, he had to rebuke a group of young men for sexist remarks they had made about Muslim women who didn't wear hijab after watching Islamic videos on YouTube featuring speakers who had also used derogatory language.

'It's difficult explaining to them that this kind of language is wrong, because they see a guy with a beard, a skullcap, who looks like any other Muslim speaker, say these things, and no one is there to question him or stop him. He's entertaining on screen, and that makes it enticing for teenage boys who are struggling with their identity.'

More important, Mohammed said, is that learning about Islam from the internet 'prevents young Muslims from developing both as people and in their *iman* [faith]'.

'When you are taught about Islam properly, you're taught how to be patient, compassionate and empathetic, because you're interacting with other Muslims you understand that everyone makes mistakes and no one is perfect. But online, perfection is demanded, and it can make you feel inadequate that you aren't a good Muslim, even though the person accusing you of that probably isn't any better.

'It's a big problem,' he sighed. 'We shouldn't be letting our youth go and essentially teach Islam to themselves.'

For Mohammed and other imams I spoke to, the conflict between traditional, pre-digital methods of teaching Islam and the vast array of information available on the internet needs to be addressed in Muslim communities around the country. Some imams say they run workshops for parents of young children to teach them how to use the internet safely to protect their children. Others have developed resources for parents and teachers to use when teaching Islam, including lists of refutations against inauthentic or inaccurate *fatwas*. Mohammed welcomes this, but worries that it might be 'too little and too late'. 'Besides,' he added, 'the types of things young people like are flashy, interactive and exciting. It's difficult to see where PowerPoint presentations and worksheets can be effective.'

* * *

Not everyone has a bleak outlook, however. Some feel that a holistic approach to Islamic learning can exist in conjunction with an ever-expanding internet. Writing in 2008, Yahya Birt diagnoses one of Sheikh Google's failings, noting that 'Electronic fatwas ... ignore any original context of time and place to speak for "Islam" globally, for Muslims everywhere, in soundbite format. This loss of context ... is injurious to intellectual expertise, proper deliberation and intra-religious pluralism.'

Birt paints a picture of what would be a 'nightmare scenario', in which:

Sheikh Google will lead the unified madhhab of the virtual umma in which a billion-plus, atomized Muslims project their subjective musings, screaming inanities into the ether in a dialogue of the deaf. Sheikh Google's umma would be protean, individualised, samizdat, postmodern, unregulated and without any agreed standards in interpretive technique. All differences would become mere subjectivity, reducing everything to the will for recognition manifested as the narcissism of small differences.

For Birt, a potential way for Muslim scholars and institutes to stave off this dismal future is to embrace what the internet offers to religious scholarship and to adopt the model of Wikipedia. 'Wiki-Islam', as he calls it, would allow individuals and groups to collaborate and reach consensus when interpreting Islam, creating an accurate, reliable resource for sharing Islamic rulings. Wiki-Islam, to Birt, would provide:

> a better possible future for Islam online, amenable to its unchurched nature. Creative collaboration between scholars, experts, intellectuals and Muslim publics would allow for the social and intellectual process of ijma [consensus] and ijtihad [independent reasoning] to become dynamic, relevant and infinitely refinable. ... [A] crucial first step ... to unlocking that potential is to recognize the collaborative creativity the digital age offers to a Muslim.[34]

Since Birt published his blog piece in 2008, some platforms have attempted to achieve this. The Saudi-based AMJA Online, for example, provides a 'Fatwabank' service, which allows scholars to set up accounts and submit edits, amendments and requests for corrections on *fatwas* published on the site.[35] The English-language version of IslamWeb offers a service allowing users to ask a sheikh, via an in-built messenger app, about the Islamic ruling on certain issues and to receive a direct response from schools associated with established scholars. For the most part, these websites are fairly basic, having been built in the early to mid-2000s, with no app versions and user interfaces that tend to be difficult to use on smartphone and tablet internet browsers.

In Britain today, mobile phones are the most popular devices used to access the internet.[36]

* * *

Yet, even though Sara and countless other Muslims use 'Sheikh Google' as a way of checking their actions are in accordance with Islam, it's unlikely that they see the internet as a replacement for mosques or imams themselves. Sara attends the mosque at least once a week, and she reads the Qur'an every day. She explains that to her, going to the mosque is an important part of being an active member of her local community in North London. She sees it as both a holy place and one of the few places in her quickly gentrifying neighbourhood that brings her 'back to her roots'. For Sara, Sheikh Google is no substitute for that, and is only a quick fix.

'It's not just about checking if something is halal or not, it's also just a useful Islamic reminder,' she adds. Using Google, she can find pockets of time each day to listen to part of a *surah*, or to be reminded to pray, be kind to people and give charity at the end of each month when she receives her pay cheque. It's a way of keeping Islam in her life as it becomes busier with work and day-to-day chores. 'I don't always get time to go to the mosque as much as I want, or to read Qur'an,' she says. 'Having all this material available to me means I don't have an excuse not to spend at least ten minutes a day reminding myself about my creator, or the religion that he's given me.' And while the internet has been a useful way for her to keep in touch with her faith, she still believes that learning about Islam offline is preferable.

'Sheikh Google only gets you so far,' she laughs. 'It might help you make a quick decision, but it's also a cop-out. The real Islam is spending years learning it with no motive other than devotion to Allah. You won't get that online.'

2

SEX AND DATING

The Halal Dating Revolution

It's 7.30 p.m. on a Thursday night and Saira Khan, a thirty-two-year-old advertising executive, is staring patiently at her watch, in a dimly lit corner of an Afghan restaurant in Swiss Cottage, London. She's been sitting at the table for a good fifteen minutes, and as the restaurant gets busier, she keeps anxiously glancing at the door, expecting her date to arrive. It's the first time she's been on a 'date' in over a year, after a long-term relationship and a planned marriage fell through unexpectedly. She is looking for a potential marital partner, and is worried that she's been stood up.

Saira, petite with fair skin and dark-brown curly hair that almost reaches her waist, has gone down 'traditional' routes of finding a partner in the past. Her grandmother in Lahore would often send her pictures of young men 'back home' who were lawyers, engineers and business owners. When she said she wasn't keen on marrying someone born and raised in Pakistan, her mother took over the search, using her contacts within their community to find eligible bachelors.

Her mother put together a 'CV'—a document detailing every aspect of her appearance, her educational history, and every job she had ever had—the idea being that elders in her community would be able to find the perfect match for her. But her first few dates were disappointing, mostly 'because the men were too eager and immediately started talking about marriage and kids'. In other cases, her dates were 'emotionally unready for marriage ... they liked the idea of getting married, but they didn't know how to talk to me, or to women! It ended up being lots of awkward conversation over dinners or mocktails, but with no emotional connection.'

In early 2017, Saira reluctantly joined the 'halal dating' app muzmatch after it was recommended by friends who had successfully used it to find stable relationships, and even engagements, that their parents had approved of. Muzmatch is one of the most popular Muslim dating apps, especially for young people who are looking to get married in an Islamically permissible way. 'It'll change your life,' one of Saira's friends claimed. Another friend, whose wedding Saira had attended only a few months ago, told her that muzmatch was 'better than any other system' when it came to finding a partner. Both of her friends felt that muzmatch's appeal came from being able to tailor your preferences on the app. 'It's like having a matchmaker, but without all the judgement you'd get from your mum or aunties,' Saira was told.

* * *

Saira is one of an estimated 600,000 members on muzmatch,[1] and one of millions of Muslims around the world who use marriage apps as their main way of finding prospective partners.[2] Muzmatch has the largest subscriber base of Muslim dating apps in the UK, but other apps, including Salaam Swipe, Minder, Muslima and Yelli also have thousands of members, with their user numbers growing dramatically year on year. Dating apps are particularly popular among young Muslims—a huge user base given that, according to data from the Muslim Council of Britain, around half of all Muslims in the UK are under twenty-five years old.[3] While no precise studies of halal dating app use are available, it's likely that demographic patterns are similar to those on non-religious dating apps, like Tinder and Bumble. According to the data collection service Statista, 60 per cent of people aged eighteen to twenty-five in the UK have used Tinder, and more than 20 per cent are current users.[4]

It's not difficult to see why dating apps would appeal to young people, who have different priorities from older generations when it comes to relationships, and who desire more choice and input into deciding who their partners should be. As Shahzad Younas, the twenty-nine-year-old creator of muzmatch, told me, 'The app gives people control of who they want to speak to and interact with, in a safe environment where there's no expectation from outside family members.'

A former investment banker, Shahzad started muzmatch because he felt that there were 'limits to how traditional match-making could work in the modern age'. The traditional ways to find partners—through relatives, community leaders and mosques—could still bear fruit for some Muslims, but Shahzad found that 'more and more people have different priorities' when it comes to marriage. 'Some want to get married young; others want to establish a career,' he said. 'Some want people who are less or more practising [religiously] than them. I wanted to create an app where people can find those kinds of people directly, without having to depend on other people.'

Since its creation, muzmatch has taken the UK's Muslim community by storm, with Shahzad and his co-founders making TV appearances and featuring in a multitude of international magazines and newspapers. The app is also a core part of British Muslim Bilal Zafar's Edinburgh comedy show 'Lovebots'.

Zafar talks about the trials and tribulations of finding love as a Muslim, where romance isn't just determined by mutual attraction, but also requires introspection about how important faith is to your identity.

Despite the fact that muzmatch's user interface emulates similar, non-Muslim dating apps, Shahzad stresses that his app isn't just catered to liberal-minded Muslims who are familiar with the rituals of Western-style dating. 'I always set out to be inclusive,' he told me. 'From the outset, we recognised that there is more than one kind of Muslim, so we've added functions in the app that cater to the needs of people who are more practising. For example, we have a function where you can indicate how religious you are, based on things like how often you pray or whether you fast.

'We also have functions that allow users to add a *mahram* [chaperone] to the experience,' he explained, an option for Muslims who believe that it is a religious requirement for a woman's male family member to be present whenever she meets a man who is not her relative. 'As the app grows,' Shahzad hopes, 'it will have features that cater to more specific needs of our users when it comes to expressing their faith. We want to help as many Muslims as we can to get married—our end goal is securing as many successful marriages as we can.'

* * *

Thirty minutes after Saira's arrival at the restaurant, and one bowl of chilli-and-lemon-flavoured peanuts later, she spots a man entering—he is well-built, average height, with medium-length, wavy black hair and a well-fitted blue suit. She notices that he is sweating slightly as he walks to her table. When he apologises for his lateness, telling her he had been stuck on the tube, Saira tells him not to worry about it, and that, from her experience on the Muslim dating scene, 'it happens all the time'.

Mohammed, Saira's date for the night, is thirty-five and works in hotel management. He was married once before, at eighteen— the match had been arranged by his mother. Two years ago, he got divorced, and, like Saira, has had little luck being set up by relatives. They immediately start talking about their experiences on muzmatch, about the times matches had freaked them out ('Within two minutes, he was talking about marriage, and whether I'd move to Bolton!' Saira exclaims), or how the experience often involves gauging how religious someone is ('She was afraid that I was too religious for her, because I said that I prayed every day,' Mohammed recalls). Both have spent weeks on muzmatch and talked to countless people. Over a shared platter of pomegranate pilau and lamb kebab, they share horror stories about past dates set up by their family members. 'He sounded fresh off the boat!' Saira laughs, remembering a time her mother had invited a distant relative's son over, supposedly spontaneously. 'I just thought, if I got married to him, I'd have no idea what he was saying.'

For Saira, the worst part of being on muzmatch is receiving occasional 'dirty messages'—the smutty comments that are almost inevitable on any dating service. But while on other dating apps, users tend to ignore these comments unless they threaten violence, the 'halal' environment of Muslim dating apps means that sexually explicit messages are prohibited in the terms of service, and so Saira reports her harassers immediately. She brushes these incidents off, saying that 'it's part and parcel of dating online' and something 'every woman on the internet has been through'.

For the most part, Saira's experiences on muzmatch and other dating apps have been positive. But, she recognises that as a fair-skinned woman who doesn't wear a hijab or niqab, who can appear both offline and online to be religiously ambiguous, dating can be easier. Men are likely to approach her 'because they don't see me as strict or religious'. Muzmatch's users don't uniformly see marriage as their immediate goal, and many consider it to be like most other 'dating' apps, using it for just that—dating. Because Saira doesn't wear hijab, men are likely to consider her more 'liberal', meaning her profile gets more engagement and right swipes.

* * *

Nafisa, twenty-eight, from Birmingham, has had a very different experience on halal dating apps. She describes herself as a 'strict, practising Muslim'. She wears hijab and meets prospective partners with her brother as a *mahram*. Like Saira, she had not had any luck with traditional matchmaking methods and was unable to find a potential partner through the mosque, something she suggests might have been because 'I was considered to be too old.' As a result, Nafisa created accounts on muzmatch and Minder. 'I was sceptical at first,' she laughs. 'It was fun ... I have work friends who talk about Tinder all the time, and it felt like a way of having the same kind of fun—swiping, but obviously in a way that was halal.'

Yet, despite over a year on the apps, and frequent meet-ups, Nafisa has not found anyone she could see herself marrying. It upset her initially, and she felt there was something wrong with her. 'I would speak to men, and initially it would be nice, very respectful,' she says. 'But I think having a *mahram* present in these online conversations was intimidating. Eventually they would stop replying to my messages, even simple ones like "how's your day". Some of them unmatched as soon as they remembered a *mahram* was present—it was all very weird because I didn't know what these men expected, especially when I said I was very religious from the outset, and I wanted to conduct any form of courtship and marriage in the most halal way possible.'

To Nafisa, Muslim dating apps work well if you're 'liberally minded and accustomed to the Western model of marriage'. She describes Muslim friends who went on dates un-chaperoned, were willing to meet in places where alcohol was served, and, in some cases, were even willing to hold hands and kiss—acts that are largely seen as taboo in halal marriage arrangements. But in her case, 'I didn't want to compromise my *deen*, or allow my *iman* to be weakened by a desire to get married. ... Even if it takes longer, and *inshallah* it will not, my religion will always come first. A lot of the guys I spoke to had said they were religious, and I assumed they had the same outlook on faith as I did. But it just became clear that in most cases, they weren't, and that they aren't always using these apps for the sole purpose of getting married Islamically.'

To Nafisa, her experiences on marriage apps illustrate the difficulties of navigating even the most Islamically designed online spaces as a visibly practising Muslim woman. She believes that there is a pressure on these apps for women to 'act religious on the outside, while being willing to compromise with men' in the same space. Sometimes men present her with blunt requests for compromise; she has been asked whether she 'would ever take off the hijab if I wanted you to', or, conversely, if she would be willing to start wearing a niqab in public as part of a marriage agreement. More often, however, her religious identity is challenged in more subtle ways.

'Men will see my hijab and make so many assumptions about me,' she says. 'For example, they will assume that I'm hard-line religious, so you can tell they are uncomfortable when speaking to me. In other cases, even supposedly religious, practising men will expect me to be meek—one time I made a joke while I was talking to a man, and he was just taken aback by it! Like he had never expected a woman wearing a hijab to be anything other than meek and soft-spoken.'

While these problems aren't unique to Muslim dating apps, and Nafisa recognises that such assumptions are made offline too, she believes that the apps 'make these problems much more obvious'.

'When you're online,' she says, 'I think there's a temptation to say whatever is on your mind without thinking it through. With these apps it's the same—and the kind of thinking about hijabi and niqabi women that I and others have received—lots of Muslim men probably think this way—but the app ... the distance it gives you from another person ... I think they feel it gives them permission to air their prejudices openly.'

* * *

It's not just Nafisa who's made the observation. On blogs, Facebook posts and YouTube videos, young Muslims, particularly women, have spoken out about their experiences of discrimination when using halal dating apps—even when there are systems in place that are designed to make the experience easier. In June 2018, YouTuber Diaspora Ukhti, an African American Muslim, published a video called 'Black, Muslim and Struggling to Get Married', drawing on her experiences talking to non-black Muslims on marriage apps.[5] She would often receive racist comments from men who claimed that 'my parents wouldn't approve of me marrying a black woman'. Diaspora Ukhti believes that marriage apps make it easy for black Muslims both to be filtered out and potentially subjected to abuse in what they imagine is a safe environment. These forms of discrimination, politely presented as 'preferences' on halal dating apps, are often reflective of problems that exist in the dating game more generally.

For example, a 2014 study carried out by OkCupid co-founder Christian Rudder found that most men on the website rated black women as less attractive than women of other ethnicities.[6] The same study also showed that Asian men were ranked the lowest in terms of attractiveness and desirability by the site's female users. Meanwhile on Tinder—still the world's most popular dating app—data released by the company in 2017 showed that 'sexual racism' was commonplace and that black and South Asian users received fewer matches and messages than their white counterparts.[7] Things aren't always better for people from ethnic-minority backgrounds when they do receive messages. The internet is crowded with anecdotes and screenshots of racial abuse and fetishism on online dating services. In some cases, Muslims on mainstream dating apps have reported receiving Islamophobic comments. An American Muslim woman interviewed by Mic described a man who harassed her on OkCupid with 'unprovoked and unsolicited ... messages about Islam'. The man described Prophet Muhammad as 'a child molester' and referred to Islam as 'a religion of VIOLENCE'.[8]

'Wherever there are Muslim women, there is always going to be abuse and harassment,' says Salima Haris, a twenty-seven-year-old optician who lives in North London. Salima describes herself as a 'secular Muslim'; while her religion means a great deal to her, she doesn't want to exclusively date Muslims and is open to marrying a non-Muslim. Salima has signed up to 'almost every dating app you can imagine'.

Salima uses each platform a little differently. 'For example,' she says, 'I might post bikini pictures on Tinder, but I won't on Salaamswipe'. Despite these differences, across the board, Salima has faced discrimination. 'It ranges from white, non-religious guys on Tinder asking obscene questions like whether I'm looking to avoid an arranged marriage, to religious Muslim guys telling me I would have to give up my career if we got married,' she says. 'On halal dating websites, I've spoken to guys who say that they would want to go out on a date, but that they'd never marry me because they want someone with "fair skin"—this is on a Muslim dating website, from guys who say they're religious and talk about the "beauty of the *ummah*" in their biographies, it's ridiculous!'

Like many women, Salima goes through cycles of deleting dating apps and later re-downloading them in the hopes that things have changed. 'I reinstalled Tinder a month ago, and pretty much all my matches either decided to send me dirty messages looking to hook up, or immediately started talking about Islam and Muslims. Not all of it is Islamophobic, of course, but my thinking is: if the first thing you notice in me is my Muslimness—like, if that's the only part of me that matters to you—I don't want to be with you.'

For Salima, dating apps 'amplify being a Muslim above every-thing else' and place 'unfair expectations on women from Muslim backgrounds'.

'No one is saying that the Muslim part of me should be ignored, but at the same time men need to recognise that it's only one part of my identity. All my dating bios talk about how I love music and dancing, how I support Chelsea Football Club with all my heart, how I like hiking and running—yet I've never ever been asked about these things by a man on a dating app in all the years I've been on them.'

Salima still uses a few apps, but she says that the situation has worried her, especially as she wants to get married soon. She feels reluctant to get an old-fashioned arranged marriage like her parents and grandparents had. But her bigger fear is that dating and marriage apps have so thoroughly taken over the general dating scene that finding her perfect match might end up an impossible task—and one she sees as uniquely arduous for women, rather than men.

'Regardless of which app you use, the preconceptions will always be there—I'll always be regarded as oppressed to non-Muslims, or as too liberal by Muslim men. Or I'll be seen as "exotic" by white guys who fetishise women of colour, and as too promiscuous by Muslim men who would rather I wore a hijab, and who think I would make a bad mother because my hair is uncovered.

'Honestly, dating as a Muslim woman really isn't fun,' she sighs.

* * *

Saira's date with Mohammed went well. After dinner, they went to an ice cream parlour for dessert, and made plans for a second date. When I checked in with Saira a few months later, however, she said that in the end it didn't work out. Mohammed had been going on dates with other women he had been talking to on Muzmatch—something he hadn't told her—and, a few weeks after their dinner, he messaged her to say he was engaged, and that the *nikah* or marriage ceremony was set to take place in six months' time.

Saira was disappointed, but tells me 'it wasn't surprising'. Hers was a familiar story that she had heard from friends, and read online—of guys using the app in order to get married as fast as they could, and 'playing the numbers game' when it came to online dating. Sometimes, promising prospective partners disappear without so much as a word, a practice known as 'ghosting'. In a video called 'We met on MuzMatch but He Won't Marry Me', YouTuber Bintou Waiga reads a letter from one of her viewers with a marriage app predicament. 'You say you haven't heard from him in four months? And this is someone that wants to marry you?'[9]

Saira plans to go on more dates and hopes that she'll be able to find a partner before she's thirty-five. 'If I don't get married by then, I'll just settle into bad-ass single-lady life,' she laughs.

'Or, I'll take my grandma's advice and marry the nice boy from our village.'

Masturbating While Muslim

Ibrahim 'Ibby' Mamood was frantically typing on his laptop, his body shaking, droplets of sweat dripping down his forehead.

Every so often, he peered over his shoulder, just in case someone was awake and had come into his room.

'I did it again,' he wrote to the members of a private Facebook group. 'I lost control of myself. May Allah, the Greatest, the Most Kind, the Most Merciful, forgive me.'

Ibrahim, twenty-seven, lives in Birmingham, one of Britain's largest cities and home to the country's largest Muslim population outside of London. He is a practising Muslim who prays five times a day and teaches at a madrassa. He lives in a neighbourhood predominated by Muslim families, all of whom know each other, attend the same social events and congregate at the same mosque. This makes what he calls an 'addiction' to masturbation even harder to talk about. Calling me from a café in central Birmingham, far away from his home, he says that he started masturbating in his late teens 'without really knowing what I was doing'.

'It started, like most boys, with wet dreams. I thought I was wetting the bed. And it really developed from there. Later, I looked at pornographic images. Not because of a sinful sexual attraction. I wanted to figure out what was happening to my body.'

Ibrahim tells me that as he grew older—and with Islamic marriage on his mind—he attempted to become a more devout Muslim. Despite these intentions, however, he continued to look at pornography. 'I knew what I was doing was wrong ... I've always known that. But we live in a society where pornography is widespread, so even when I wasn't looking for porn, it was just there.'

* * *

Like many Muslim men in his situation—who find themselves unable to talk about sex, masturbation or porn in their communities, where such things are considered taboo—Ibrahim turned to the internet for help. In addition to private groups on

Facebook (the group Ibrahim is part of has more than 200 members) and WhatsApp, the biggest support network is on Reddit, where the 'MuslimNoFap' subreddit has about 2,000 followers.[10] On the surface, it might seem like the normal Reddit 'NoFap' community, a group of men whose choice of abstinence is driven by a desire for self-improvement.

But according to members of MuslimNoFap, who all wished to remain anonymous, their community is very different. As one person told me, 'People in the main NoFap community aim to somehow assert their masculinity through self-control, with the hope of sleeping with women outside of marriage.' Conversely, the MuslimNoFap community believes in the sanctity of marriage, and that 'any form of sexual activity' before marriage is prohibited. 'All we're trying to do is serve Allah, and to do what he commanded us to do.'

While the men I spoke to had joined the group for different reasons—some wanted to stop watching porn; others used the group to manage depression and anxiety—nearly all of them wanted to get married in a halal way, and were worried that their partiality to porn and masturbation would nullify their marriages in the eyes of God. It was also clear that, despite long being preoccupied with marriage, none of these men had been prepared for what would happen on their wedding nights.

'There's no way we can talk about sex, or anything to do with sex, at the mosque. It's impossible,' writes a Canadian man under the username 'Abu Khadeer'.

'Most of the people in these groups had a strict Islamic upbringing. They didn't have sex education in the madrassa, where they were prohibited from having girlfriends. Some date and have sex outside of marriage, but [most] are truly devoted to their religion. They end up giving into temptation ... usually because they're afraid they won't be competent when they finally get married.

'Mentions of sex in the [mosque] are usually associated with sin,' he adds. 'The attitude that the imams take is that any sort of deliberate extramarital sex is a severe sin—one that results in punishment in the *akhirah* [afterlife].'

Islamic scholars differ on this topic. The mainstream view, espoused by many world-famous preachers like Zakir Naik and generally agreed upon, is that anyone who engages in extra-marital sexual activities without repentance (in the form of fasting and prayer) will be sent to hell. However, disagreement arises on the topic of masturbation, as the Qur'an doesn't spe-cifically label the practice a sin. Some argue that self-stimula-tion is permissible, especially if it prevents someone from hav-ing sex outside of marriage.

Regardless of the grey area amongst scholars around masturba-tion, most devout Muslim men grow up being told to stay away from all types of sexual activity until marriage. As Abu Khadeer says, 'A lot of us are told to be celibate up to the point of marriage. And then when we get married, we're just expected to know what to do. One of the guys on the forum had to divorce his wife because he couldn't consummate his marriage. He literally didn't know how to have sex with her on his wedding night.'

* * *

It's difficult to quantify the problem, but most of the imams I spoke to recognised that there is a taboo against talking about sex. Ghulam Rasool of the progressive Imams Online network believes that Islamic leaders haven't really dealt with situations involving men and sex education, beyond very extreme situa-tions—ones where men believed they have been possessed by evil spirits, in which case imams recommend long periods of praying and fasting, or sometimes *ruqyah*, an Islamic exorcism ritual.

Things like sexual etiquette aren't taught in Islamic schools. 'The teachers believe it's a parent's duty to teach their children about sex, but many parents don't feel confident talking to their sons about sex either,' says London-based imam Muhammad Jafer. 'As a result, there are young men who reach their twenties knowing next to nothing about intimacy, or worse, they've learned about it by looking at sinful websites or talking to people about sex in *haram* environments.' Plus, as Ibrahim points out, 'Most [imams] are older men, who grew up at a time when getting married young was something everyone did, so they don't understand the world we're in today. They don't understand how sexualised our society is now. To say that we should abstain from pornography is impossible.'

'The problem begins when you say abstinence is the only option,' agrees Imtiaz Ayub, a social worker based in Derby, a small city in the north of England. Imtiaz isn't an imam, but much of his work involves supporting Muslim teenagers, including getting them to open up about sex. 'There's a wider problem here—in Muslim communities the idea of a very macho masculinity is imposed,' he explains. 'More and more young Muslim men are obsessed with how they look, how muscular they are, as a way to prove they're manly. But at the same time, they're not encouraged to talk about their own sexuality. That can be very confusing for them.'

In Imtiaz's opinion, teaching young men to disregard their sexuality is harmful. 'You're basically waiting for a volcano to erupt,' he remarks. 'Muslim boys aren't different to any other type of male—they're going to be sexually curious when they reach a certain age, and if communities care about them, they need to provide spaces where they can openly talk about sex without the taboos. You can't expect young Muslim boys to grow up and become men unless they're able to manage the period of growing up.'

His attitude is shared by others trying to offer better resources for Muslim men to talk about sex. In the US, a website called 'Purify Your Gaze' provides interactive sessions via Skype—usually involving a mentor—as well as other specially designed programmes, consisting of physical activities and prayer, to aid men as they attempt to 'heal' and cease porn consumption and masturbation.[11]

Others, like British imam Alyas Karmani, take a more modern approach—deeming masturbation not to be a major sin. This viewpoint has earned Karmani the title of the 'Muslim Sex Doctor' in some online circles.[12] Mufti Abu Layth achieved a similar level of notoriety when, in his weekly advice session on Facebook Live, he declared that masturbation wasn't prohibited in Islam at all. Quite the contrary—Abu Layth claimed past Muslim scholars had suggested that masturbation could be used to manage one's sexual desires in a halal way. To Imtiaz, Abu Layth's statements were a positive first step. 'The Mufti has a big public platform, and it was important for him to say that. Even if there are Muslim men who want to be celibate, who want to abstain until marriage, it's still important for them to understand that masturbation is a natural human thing.'

* * *

When I next speak to Ibrahim, he is in better spirits. He has blocked the porn sites he used to visit, and, following the advice and encouragement of other members of his support group, is trying to combat his sexual urges through studying Islamic books and spending more time outside of the house, playing football and going shopping.

'I'm fine during the day, when I can control my temptations. It's moments at night, when I'm alone ...' He takes a long pause, and then mumbles a short prayer in Arabic, asking for God's forgiveness. 'Those are the times I'm worried about. It's at night-time, when the devil likes to tempt us, especially on the internet.'

Muslim #MeToo Movements

In late 2017, as allegations of rape, sexual assault and sexual abuse of women were emerging against the prolific American film producer Harvey Weinstein, Farrah, thirty-five, was scrolling through Twitter looking at posts tagged #MeToo.[13] The hashtag was trending worldwide and had international variations, like #YoTambien in Latin America, #BalanceTonPorc (#DenounceYourPig) in France and #QuellaVoltaChe (#That TimeThat) in Italy. Thousands of women across the world were going online to talk about their own experiences of sexual abuse, misconduct and harassment in the places they worked in, walked through and lived in—experiences that, until this moment, they had largely kept to themselves, or had talked about openly only to be dismissed.

The origins of #MeToo began in 2006 when the American civil rights activist Tarana Burke used the term on Myspace, as part of a 'campaign for empathy' prompted by the story of a thirteen-year-old survivor of sexual abuse. Speaking to BuzzFeed in 2017, Burke said that the term was originally about supporting young women of colour, those 'who did not know where to turn, did not have any vital support in the healing process ... to help them get an entry point to healing.'[14] In 2017, as allegations against Weinstein, as well as scores of other powerful men in media, popular culture and politics, kept stacking up, #MeToo started being referred to as a 'movement'.

The #MeToo movement spread on social media, as high-profile women, like Alyssa Milano, encouraged others to tell their stories. Milano was one of the women abused by Weinstein, and in October 2017 she tweeted a screenshot of the statement: 'If all the women who have been sexually harassed or assaulted wrote "Me too." as a status, we might give people a sense of the magnitude of the problem.'[15]

Farrah was hesitant to tweet about her own story. She wasn't particularly active online, and worried that her story wouldn't have an impact. She has just over 100 followers, most of whom are friends and a couple of which are spam accounts. She mainly follows celebrity actors and sportspeople, as well as the Twitter accounts of newspapers and TV news stations.

But what seemed more important than her limited audience was that Farrah's story was different from the other #MeToo posts she had scrolled through, liked and retweeted.

'Almost all those stories were about women—mainly white women—working in offices and being harassed by colleagues. Or about being harassed on public transport,' she says. 'Some of them were about sexual abuse and violence by boyfriends, ex-husbands ... I didn't feel that mine was as relatable.'

When Farrah was twelve, she was molested by a man—a friend of her father's and a senior figure in her mosque—who was teaching her how to read the Qur'an. Few people knew the story—Farrah had only confided in her close friends and her younger sister about the trauma.

'It petrified me at the time,' Farrah recalls, on the phone. 'I wasn't sure what to do. I had grown up knowing this man, he would come to our house ... My father still speaks to him and he is still highly respected in our community.'

It was this dynamic that made it difficult for Farrah to tweet her story. For over a decade, she had kept what happened to herself—for the sake of her family, and out of fear that if she spoke up, she wouldn't be believed. She worried that as a young woman, she would be dismissed and disbelieved. She feared that her mother and her aunts would 'tell me not to worry ... that I was just seeing things, that Uncle was a good man, a religious man, that he wouldn't ever do anything like that.'

Farrah didn't tweet her entire story. Instead, she simply tweeted '#MeToo.'

Her tweet was retweeted more than twenty times, and engaged with by more than forty people. 'To this day, it's probably the best tweet I've ever done!' she laughs.

* * *

Farrah hasn't publicly spoken about what happened to her since that day. We met while I was working on a story for *MEL* Magazine about #MeToo and how abuse survivors from religious communities were interacting with the movement, and especially the unique challenges survivors face when they want to hold their communities accountable while also holding on to the faith they cherish.

While abuse in religious contexts wasn't at the forefront of the #MeToo movement, some survivors have used hashtags like #ChurchToo to speak about the specific experiences and difficulties of being both a survivor and a person of faith, especially when abuse happens from within a religious community. In an Islamic context, the Egyptian American activist Mona Eltahawy started the hashtag #MosqueMeToo.[16] Eltahawy, the author of several books on Islam and feminism, used the hashtag in a Twitter thread about her experience of sexual assault at fifteen, while she was on Hajj.[17] She told her followers that she was inspired to tell her story after reading a Facebook post by a young Pakistani woman, Sabica Khan, who describes being sexually harassed while performing *tawaaf* around the Kabah. The post was shared more than 2,000 times.[18]

The #MosqueMeToo tweet spurred hundreds of tweets of solidarity, as other women took to Twitter about their experiences being sexually harassed and abused not just while performing Hajj, but also in their own communities and mosques. Eltahawy wrote in *The Washington Post* that she was 'overwhelmed' by the number of responses to her tweet, but that she wasn't surprised that sexual assault in Muslim places of worship was so widespread.

'All those years of silence were for the same reason: We thought it was impossible that anyone else had gone through such a violation at such a sacred place,' she affirmed. At the same time, Eltahawy said, it was difficult for Muslim women to engage with the mainstream #MeToo movement because of their political situation—they felt their testimonies would inevitably be diminished not only because of patriarchy within Muslim communities, but also as a result of growing anti-Muslim prejudice, which meant they would be seen not as individual women, but rather as symbolic of Islam itself.

Eltahawy pointed out that this pressure from two sides made talking about sexual harm and abuse even less likely for Muslim women. Survivors believed that by speaking out, they would further tarnish the image of their religious communities, which for so long have been the subject of scrutiny in the public eye.

> Muslim women are caught between a rock and a hard place. On one side are Islamophobes and racists who are all too willing to demonize Muslim men by weaponizing my testimony of sexual assault. On the other side is the 'community' of fellow Muslims who are all [too] willing to defend all Muslim men—they would rather I shut up about being sexually assaulted during the hajj than make Muslims look bad. Neither side cares about the well-being of Muslim women. Reading the stories that women have shared with me of their sexual assaults during the hajj has undone something broken in me I thought I had stitched together. I was 15, traumatized and ashamed after I was sexually assaulted during the hajj. I am now 50 and shameless.[19]

The sentiment resonates with Farrah. 'As a woman who is visibly Muslim, there's a lot of responsibility placed on you,' she says. 'You're supposed to represent the family, you are supposed to represent the religion in a good light. At the same time, we [women] are the biggest victims of Islamophobic attacks, and there is always a worry that when you talk openly about sexual violence and harassment, people will assume that [it happens] because of Islam, or because of the Pakistani community. When it's not. ... This is to do with toxic masculinity, and it happens in every culture and every community.'

She adds that this feeling is shared by every hijab-wearing Muslim woman that she knows. 'It feels like you are dehumanised in every community you are part of.' This is partly because of the media backlash against the #MeToo movement,[20] and the wider issues around sexual harassment by Muslim men. 'I don't remember harassment ever being talked about in madrassa, or any mosque that I went to,' she laments. 'Even now, it's rarely spoken about, if ever. And when you're a teenager, all you're told is to "lower your gaze", and avoid situations where there is free mixing of genders. But that doesn't prepare someone for Hajj, where genders aren't segregated. And it doesn't prepare people to live in countries where you can't avoid free mixing.'

* * *

In some cases, Muslim scholars and public figures have spoken out against sexual harassment in Muslim spaces, analysing the #MeToo movement in the context of Islamic history. In September 2018, Yasir Qadhi, a well-known Pakistani American scholar with a large global following, gave a lecture at the AlMaghrib Institute in Houston, Texas, strongly condemning sexual harassment and intimidation as grave sins in Islam. '[Harassment] is a lived reality that many of our sisters are painfully aware of, and many of our brothers are completely oblivious to. ... Sexual crimes are indeed a crime in the eyes of Allah.'[21]

Shabir Aly, a Canadian Muslim preacher and the president of the Islamic Information and Dawah Centre in Toronto, has also spoken about the importance for Muslim communities to engage with #MeToo. In an interview with the YouTube channel 'Let the Qur'an Speak', he stated that:

It seems that this is not something that people come to imams with, and that itself is a problem. We need to let the community know that imams can actually deal with situations like this, and imams of course need to be trained to deal with situations like this. ...

We should look at the general picture and realise that most of the cases have to be true. ... Why would a woman put herself into the spotlight and talk about such things of such a private nature unless they were true? ... This is a reality. It is happening, and it is happening more than we should tolerate, much more than we should tolerate, and we cannot tolerate this as a society, whether we are Muslims or not. And especially because we are Muslims, we cannot tolerate such things happening.[22]

While some Muslim women activists welcome these discussions, most I spoke to said this sudden awareness from male scholars had arrived too late, and that as men were slowly starting to become conscious of the levels of misogyny in their communities, women were creating their own safe spaces—often online—to talk about sexual abuse and violence and form support networks.

'Private social media groups is where you'll find the true scale of the issue,' said forty-year-old Nasreen Shah. Nasreen is an administrator of the Islamic Women's Group, a small Facebook and WhatsApp group that has a network of around 1,000 members from across the world, a sizeable percentage of whom come from the UK.

Over Skype, Nasreen told me that the advent of modern social media and the proliferation of smartphones with internet access have meant that 'stories that were always there' can be more widely shared. 'Back in the old days, in my parents' generation and grandparents' generation, abuse—not just sexual, but all kinds—was just accepted as part of family life. I grew up in a house where my mum was verbally abused, not just by my father but by relatives too. It was always there—the only difference now is that it's easier to connect with people who have had similar experiences, and also to understand the cultural nuances.'

Nasreen is one of three women who oversee the Facebook group, which was set up in 2012. She told me that sexual abuse had previously been a problem that Muslim women only spoke about privately. 'Very rarely was there a chance you could speak about it openly in a mosque, and as a woman it is even more difficult to talk directly to an imam about it. We eventually turned to the internet because it was the only place where we could provide a safe environment to talk about our traumas and our histories, and to provide support for each other.'

The network is particularly important, she added, because of the number of women who are still in abusive relationships and marriages, and who have 'cultural pressure to maintain it'. 'Imagine living in a place where all you have is your religious community,' she said. 'Many women leave home to live with their husband's family to then find that they can't get out of their abusive relationships, and that they have no-one who under-stands what they're going through.' In these situations, the group provides support by way of comforting messages, oppor-tunities to talk privately to other survivors, and, in some cases, material support, like shelter and assistance with legal represen-tation for women planning to leave their abusive relationships. While Nasreen told me that there are established organisations, such as the Muslim Women's Network in the UK, that do simi-lar work, the primary purpose of the IWG group is simply to provide a safe space for women to talk without fear.

'For many women it's the first time they will speak openly about the trauma they've been through,' she said. Solidarity groups like hers offer a unique form of support, which, she believes, wouldn't be possible without the internet. 'It's a big step for them—without social media it's likely they'd never have had the opportunity to share.'

FOLLOW ME, AKHI

Inside the Muslim Abortion Network on Tumblr

Aisha was panicking. Her fingers trembled as, in the dead of night, she let the world in on her secret. 'I don't know why or how it happened. I was careful. I don't know what to do. I can't do this, my parents will kick me out of their house. I can't raise a baby on my own,' she wrote on Tumblr. 'Writing here, in case anyone can give some advice.'

Aisha's choice to confess on Tumblr was deliberate. When it was first launched in 2007, as one of the internet's first social networks, Tumblr was a blogging platform—one which functioned more easily than sites like WordPress and Blogger. Pictures, videos and hyperlinks could be integrated seamlessly, and new trends in internet culture, like gifs and image-based memes, could be made and shared by thousands of users instantly.[23]

As platforms like Facebook and Twitter dominated the social media market, Tumblr developed a reputation for being host to the internet's most niche online communities. More often than not, these are 'fandoms' populated by teenagers dedicated to Korean pop stars or actors in cult Netflix shows, as well as communities who consider themselves to be 'outsiders' on other mainstream social media platforms. In 2016, journalist Elspeth Reeve wrote that:

> Tumblr is the social network that, based on my reporting, is seen by teens as the most uncool. A telling post from 2014: 'I picked joining Tumblr and staying active on here because: 1. I'm not attractive enough to be a YouTuber 2. Not popular enough for twitter 3. Facebook is dumb.' You don't tell people your Tumblr URL, you aren't logging the banalities of your day—you aren't even *you*. On Tumblr, you can revel in anonymity, say whatever you want without fear of it going on your permanent record.[24]

Aisha, who is slender with dark skin, chestnut-brown eyes and dark-brown hair lightly covered in a thin, floral hijab, has been using Tumblr since her early teens. She follows hundreds of Tumblr accounts. Most are dedicated to her interests in anime (her favourite show is the popular series *Naruto*), or accounts that spout thousands of images of her famous crushes (Andrew Garfield and Zac Efron). Others fall into the 'Tumblr culture' bracket—anonymous profiles with huge followings, best known for their irony-laced takes on sensitive topics, including mental health, bullying, coming out to your parents and racism, to name a few.

A typical example of the kind of post that tends to gain traction on Tumblr:

> Me: My friends love me. They totally don't think I'm annoying!
> My Brain: Why the fuck you lyin? Why you lyin? Hmmmm. Oh God. Stop Fuckin Lyin.[25]

It's this kind of irreverence—dark, 'relatable' humour—and, more importantly, the encouragement of emotional honesty that separate the online culture of Tumblr from other social media outlets and make it, as *The Washington Post* declared in 2015, 'the new ground zero of the viral internet'.[26]

While platforms like Instagram, Facebook and Twitter expect users to reveal as much information as they can, including their real names, as well as to post the highlights of their personal lives, Tumblr errs in the opposite direction. Most active users post anonymously, under pseudonyms, without any resistance from Tumblr's moderators. As a freeform blogging network, Tumblr isn't constricted by the same limitations of other social media platforms. Unlike on Facebook and Twitter, Tumblr's users have never complained about new user interfaces and the layouts of their profiles being changed without prior notification; nor have they felt that the platform has compromised their personal information and security. In an interview with *The New Republic*, Tumblr user Jason Wong said he considered the platform to be a 'safe haven' for teens. 'On Tumblr they tell their most personal stories. They share things that they normally wouldn't share with their local friends because of the fear of judgment.'[27]

* * *

Aisha made her confession to her 4,000 followers in April 2015. At the time, she was six weeks pregnant. The father, her then-boyfriend whom she had been secretly dating for just under a year, refused to return any of her calls, texts or messages. She stopped messaging him once and for all when she received a text from one of his friends, threatening her to stop trying to communicate with him if she didn't want to be exposed 'as a slut'.

Meanwhile, living in a devout Muslim household—one in which framed *surahs* adorned the walls, where both her mother and father spent the evenings teaching children how to pray and read Qur'an, and where she was expected to be home in time for *maghrib* prayer—Aisha was more than alert to what the consequences of having sex out of wedlock, and the resultant pregnancy, would be. She was viscerally aware of the shame she thought she would bring to her family if her community found out.

When Aisha and I met in 2017, in an ice cream bar near my office in East London, she recalled the constant sense of panic that filled her every waking moment at that time. 'Even searching for help online, on websites like the NHS, made me panic, in case one of my family ended up seeing. I would delete my entire browser history every night before I went to sleep.' she remembered. 'I even borrowed money from my friend to buy pregnancy tests, and I took them in the toilets of a McDonalds.'

Living in a tight-knit Muslim community in East London, Aisha knew it was a risk to talk about her pregnancy even to her closest friends, who were all only separated by a few degrees from a relative or family friend whom her mother or father would inevitably see at the mosque. This fear also meant ruling out going to a clinic in her local area, in case someone she knew saw her going to see the doctor on her own. 'I felt trapped,' she said. 'Writing about my problem on Tumblr seemed like the only way I could let my secret out ... in a place I felt would be safe.'

Aisha cried herself to sleep the night she posted her confession. But at the very least, she said, 'I didn't feel as alone as I had done before.'

Aisha received a message on Tumblr the next day, from a user who called herself 'Narcissistic Anarchist'. Her profile picture was of Jungkook, a member of the hit sensation South Korean boy band BTS, and her profile largely consisted of images, gifs and posts about the band. All in all, the account looked like any one of the hundreds of fan accounts on Tumblr. 'I know people who have gone through the same thing as you. Are you in the UK? I can help you,' the message read.

Aisha didn't disclose the identity of Narcissistic Anarchist to me, only telling me that she lived near Manchester, came from a Muslim family and was around the same age as her. Her Tumblr account had only a few hundred followers—mostly other BTS fan accounts, but also, because she had reposted some Islamic *surahs* and reminders on her page, a scattering of Islamic-themed accounts as well.

Narcissistic Anarchist ended up getting Aisha to an abortion clinic safely. In the few days after responding to Aisha's initial message, she had formed a plan to get Aisha out of London temporarily. She booked her a train ticket, and more crucially, gave her an alibi. Aisha would add her on Facebook. She would 'like' her photographs—especially the ones of Islamic reminders and sayings. She would create the impression of a long friendship. And she would convince her parents to let her go to Manchester for a week, to visit the medical school at the university and spend time with another Muslim sister and her family.

As far as her parents were concerned, Aisha and Narcissistic Anarchist had met at an Islamic event, and they had kept in touch since.

Narcissistic Anarchist's plan worked, and in the first week of June 2015—one week before Ramadan—Aisha was escorted to a clinic and received the medication she needed to abort under the supervision of two doctors. She spent the next few days recovering in her new friend's bedroom, spending the time watching movies on Netflix, sleeping and processing everything that had happened—a trauma that still sometimes creeps up on her today.

Aisha agreed to speak to me on the condition that I wouldn't ask her personal questions regarding her abortion. But thinking back to that moment in her life, she says that, 'if it wasn't for Tumblr, and social media, I don't know what would have happened'. 'I could have been homeless,' she tells me, 'or forced to marry someone so I wouldn't have a baby that would be shamed in the community.' Without Tumblr, Aisha, as a young Muslim woman, would have felt she had no choice but to have a child she knew she wasn't ready for.

'I grew up going to Muslim schools, so we never learnt about sex education, or sexual safety. We were basically taught that you go get married, and then you have babies, and you raise them in Islam. That's it.' When contraception was ever brought up at her school, she says that it was mostly dismissed or frowned upon. 'The most we learnt about was condoms,' she said in hushed tones. 'Even then, they were not recommended. The point of sex—one of my teachers said—was for children.'

Most of Aisha's sex education came from candid conversations with strangers on platforms like Tumblr. And while this isn't uncommon among teenagers living in the online age, Aisha says that her experience as a Muslim, especially as a British Muslim woman, made learning about sex complicated. 'A lot of young

Muslims end up getting a distorted perspective about sex, because on one side, we are being taught that sex is just about having children when you're married. And then online, sex is so much more—it's about status, attractiveness, and also how real your relationships are.'

This dichotomy is one that many young Muslims like her struggle to navigate. 'The majority of my Muslim friends have had sexual encounters that no one knows about, or very few people do. ... Some have had boyfriends and girlfriends. Others have had flings, one-night stands. Sometimes girls feel pressured into doing things by boys that they like. ... They get the impression that if they don't do these things, the boys will lose interest in them.'

Aisha didn't tell me much about her ex-boyfriend, but she implied that she had felt pressured into having sex with him. 'I did love him, and I wanted to marry him eventually,' she explained. The memories were painful for her to recall, and throughout the interview, she sometimes paused to cry. 'He told me he loved me too ... that we would get married. That it was our destiny, when the time was right.'

Since her return to London from Manchester, Aisha thought about him less. She had stayed in touch with Narcissistic Anarchist, and reached out to her if she felt the need to talk about what happened. She was most thankful for how their friendship had blossomed—something that she privately felt might be a blessing from God during the most difficult time of her life.

'There's a saying by Imam Ghazali that the best of friends is someone who, when you ask them to follow you, won't say 'where?' but will simply come with you,' Aisha said. 'I have thought about that saying every day since I met her.'

3

ISLAMOPHOBIA AND THE ALT-RIGHT

The Impact of Islamophobia

In 1997, the Runnymede Trust, a race equality think tank, published the report 'Islamophobia: A challenge for us all', the first nation-wide survey into attitudes toward Islam and Muslims living in Britain.[1]

Launched in the House of Commons by the then home secretary, Labour MP Jack Straw, the paper found that there was a 'small, but growing amount' of anti-Muslim prejudice in the UK, much of which was expressed in the form of negative opinions about Islam as a religion, following events such as the 1979 Iranian revolution and the First Gulf War. The paper warned that discrimination toward Muslims was on the up, and in the context of UK policy-making, is considered to be the first to use the distinct term 'Islamophobia', which the report defined as an 'unfounded hostility towards Islam' and the practical consequences of such hostility, including 'unfair discrimination against Muslim individuals and communities' and 'the exclusion of Muslims from mainstream political and social affairs'.

Since the landmark report's publication, levels of 'Islamophobia' in the UK have increased. The years 1997–2007 were considered to be the 'first decade of Islamophobia',[2] partly defined by the 11 September 2001 terrorist attacks, the subsequent 'War on Terror' in Iraq and Afghanistan, and the 7 July 2005 attacks in London. Instances of Islamophobia ranged from negative coverage about Muslims and Islam in mainstream newspapers and on television, to violent attacks and harassment toward people who outwardly 'looked like they were Muslim', such as women who wore headscarves and Sikh men who had beards and wore turbans.

According to Runnymede, hostility toward Muslims in Britain became even further entrenched as time went on. In 2017, the think tank published a report titled 'Islamophobia: Still a challenge for us all', noting a number of changes in the intervening twenty years since the 1997 report.[3] The report highlighted ways that Islamophobia had been institutionalised and internalised in society; beyond hate crime, it affected the everyday experiences of British Muslims. Speaking to Al Jazeera, Farah Elahi, a research and policy analyst at Runnymede, said:

> We have an understanding of how Islamophobia impacts hate crime, but when somebody applies for a job and they get an interview, those stereotypes can remain in an employee's mind, even when they go to the doctors, when they go to school. ... Policy focus and media representation which frame Muslims in a particular way [feed] particular stereotypes about Muslims. They all feed off each other and the effects manifest in larger labour market penalties, larger mental health impact, and penalties in the criminal justice system.[4]

Islamophobia manifested itself in new and manifold ways, not only in overt racism, or in individual hate crimes as a reaction to the rise of ISIS and ISIS-inspired 'lone-wolf' attacks, but also because increased access to social media meant that 'Islamophobic narratives are now reproduced and shared globally'.

Runnymede were not the only ones to warn of the dangers of social media when it came to proliferating anti-Muslim hatred. In his paper analysing online Islamophobia on Twitter and Facebook, Mattias Ekman argues that the internet has 'facilitated a space where xenophobic viewpoints and racist attitudes toward Muslims are easily disseminated into public debate.'[5] He explains that the relatively relaxed attitude by social media platforms towards monitoring and regulating anti-Muslim speech allowed 'Islamophobic actors to push the boundaries of publicly accepted speech on Muslims and immigration', especially in the moments after a terrorist attack has taken place, or in the context of 2015's refugee crisis.

Significantly, what changed between 2007 and 2017 was the way that Islamophobic material was transmitted on the internet. Though anti-Muslim material has long existed online, it had tended to only proliferate in obscure online communities and forums largely populated by gamers, hackers and technology enthusiasts, on websites like Totse.com, 4chan, and 4chan's relative 8chan during the pre–social media age. The transition of this content to mainstream social media platforms, partly because its former online hosts were shut down for explicit and violent content, and partly because of the increasing domination of Facebook, Twitter and Google, meant that it wasn't just individual users who were able to create, promote and share anti-Muslim material online.

As Ekman notes, online Islamophobia today also emanates from organisations, from far-right populist parties like the Dutch Party for Freedom and the Danish People's Party, to street protest groups like the English Defence League (EDL), to right-wing think tanks hostile to Islam, such as the Organization for Security and Co-operation in Europe, the International Civil Liberties Alliance, and the International Free Press Society.[6] Though all these groups in the online 'counter-jihad' movement have different political goals, they promote and bolster each other, pointing to the high levels of online engagement with their anti-Muslim sentiments to legitimise their aims. This strategy hasn't just impacted the nature of Islamophobia on the internet, but it has also facilitated a shift in political discourse around Islam.

Rather than focusing only on the threat of terrorism, the period between 2007 and 2017 saw Islamophobia morph into fears about migrant criminality. Anti-Muslim bloggers portray Islam and Muslims as being fundamentally and culturally opposed to Europe and its values—a resurrection of the old 'clash of civilisations' trope. Blogs including 'Gates of Vienna', 'The Geller Report', 'The Religion of Peace' and 'Jihad Watch' perpetuate this analysis. Tens of articles are posted on these sites every day on Muslim refugees entering Europe, reporting on their supposed criminal behaviour, sexual misconduct and alleged links to militant Islamist groups. The posts often draw their information from other right-wing websites, blogs and Twitter feeds, and it is an understatement to say the data isn't necessarily verified before publication. The blogs share their content via social media, which means that a single post can be shared over 1,000 times and appear on the news feeds of thousands more on Facebook alone.

Other organisations have reported a rise in Islamophobia in Britain in recent years. In July 2018, Tell MAMA, a national project to record anti-Muslim incidents in the UK, found that there had been a record number of Islamophobic attacks in 2017.[7] Though two-thirds of the 1,201 verified cases concerned incidents that had occurred offline, the 26 per cent surge in reports since 2016 also accounted for an increase in online incidents of anti-Muslim abuse.[8] Furthermore, previous Tell MAMA reports found a majority of Islamophobic incidents occurring online, and in 2014, 73 per cent of its reports of anti-Muslim abuse took place online.

'What we're seeing is a growing network of individuals and groups who are using their online profiles to spread Islamophobic messages, which are reinforced into expanding networks online,' says Steve Rose, a researcher at Tell MAMA. Rose has been tracking the rise of far-right groups across the world since 2013, and emphasises the key role played by these groups in creating an online climate that encourages Islamophobia. Far-right groups have been very successful in exploiting populist talking points to build up their following—one prime example being the fascist street movement Britain First. 'At their height, Britain First had around 2 million Facebook likes. Not all of [those likes] came from content that was anti-Muslim.'

In fact, one of the biggest drivers of traffic to Britain First's page was its memes—about animal cruelty. 'They would make memes that would have an image of say, a wounded English Greyhound, and they would encourage their followers to share the image across their networks, write to their MPs, and then follow the page afterward.' Rose says that other far-right groups employ similar tactics, creating shareable short videos, audio clips and images about anything from recipes for traditional food to videos of national celebrations. This non-Islamophobic material attracts large numbers of likes and shares, and builds a ready audience primed for more insidious anti-Muslim messaging.

'It ends up creating a cottage industry in which Islamophobic content is built and transmitted, and then amplified, by groups with large followings, often consisting of the same people,' Rose adds. 'In many ways it's not the dark web, but it is an alternative social network that exists in plain sight. It uses the same sorts of techniques that brands use to advertise products, and they reach a huge number of people who aren't aware of the motivations of these individuals and groups. By the time people do realise what these far-right groups are doing, it's too late, the damage is already done.'

* * *

And the damage has been done. For many British Muslims, the growth of online Islamophobia has made them uncomfortable having an online presence, especially if they want to use their platform to speak about current affairs, their faith, or their lived experiences.

One such person is twenty-seven-year-old Hala, a London-based masters student researching decolonial movements in North Africa. Prior to taking up further education, Hala was a volunteer and activist. When we met in a café near her university campus, she had just come back from a demonstration outside the Yarl's Wood detention centre, protesting the government's mistreatment of immigrant and refugee women being held there. What was immediately noticeable about Hala was her commitment to activism: in black Arial Bold her T-shirt proclaimed 'No One Is Illegal', and was covered with badges promoting causes including veganism and the 'Boycott, Divestment, Sanctions' campaign to end Israel's oppression of Palestinians. Her hijab was red, black and white, which she said was to express solidarity with women suffering in Syria.

Hala had been active on social media ever since she got a Myspace account in the mid-2000s, she told me. 'As someone from an Egyptian background, my parents were very strict—no parties, no boyfriends, all of that. So social media was initially what I used so I could be like my mostly white friends and secretly talk to boys.' Later in her teens, particularly following the events of 7/7 in 2005, she became more politically active. She went to rallies demonstrating against the wars in Iraq and Afghanistan, volunteered at Islamic charities helping to deliver aid, and became involved in women-led liberation movements like Southall Black Sisters and Sisters Uncut. When she joined Facebook in 2010, she used the platform to share articles about the mistreatment of women across the world, as well as about anti-Muslim attacks—particularly 'on women who wore niqab, jilbab and hijab', she said. 'Most of these attacks were carried out by men, and no one was saying anything about that. I wasn't able to use Facebook like my school friends did—in that I didn't have pictures of myself at parties, or in a relationship—so I used it to learn more about politics and activism, and to try to get people to join the causes.'

In 2017, however, Hala decided to delete all her social media accounts. Every post she had ever made; every photo from rallies, marches and activist events; all of her connections to the people she had met through her online activism, ever since the days of Myspace.

'I couldn't be a Muslim on the internet anymore,' she explained. Stirring her coffee in small, quiet circular motions, she recalled the months of online abuse she had received after posting photographs of herself protesting against a march led by Tommy Robinson and the Football Lads Alliance, a right-wing street group made up of football fans, current and former EDL members, and members of other identitarian groups.

In June 2017, the FLA had held its first march through London to protest against 'extremism and terrorism' in the UK.[9] The march attracted well over 10,000 people, one of the biggest demonstrations that the UK had seen for nearly five years. Though the FLA said that the group welcomed people from 'every race, colour and creed'—a statement that its founder John Meighan reaffirmed to the press—this hadn't stopped other right-wing groups and figures that had made racist and anti-Muslim comments from throwing their support behind the group.

The counter-demo wasn't the reason for Hala's decision to leave social media. 'The march was fine,' she said. 'As usual the anti-fascist groups were kept at a distance from the [FLA] and I didn't experience problems marching.' Rather, it was the aftermath of posting pictures of herself on Twitter, wearing a

Palestinian flag as a hijab, with a group of her female friends holding placards saying, 'Fascist scum off our streets!' and 'FLA, EDL not welcome here!' 'I had put the photos up for fun,' she remembered. 'We were out protesting, but also it was a sunny Saturday, and it was just a casual picture with my friends.'

Within a couple of hours, Hala had received over 600 notifications, and none of them were positive. She had become the target of 'visibly far-right accounts'.

'They were retweeting my photo with all the disgusting things you could imagine. Some of them called me a "filthy Muzzie bitch"; there were others that made disgusting jokes about how my husband would "stone me to death if I protested in Saudi Arabia".'

Few of the accounts that Hala saw had profile pictures of real people; they instead displayed pictures of the England flag, Tommy Robinson and Donald Trump. 'Some of the accounts used Pepe the Frog,' she said, referring to a web comic character popularly used by Trump supporters, especially by the white nationalist 'alt-right' wing, to conceal their identities online. 'I was receiving so many messages at once, all telling me to leave the UK, to kill myself, that because I was Muslim, I was a threat. I even had some accounts tag the Metropolitan Police saying that I had a bomb in my bag and encouraging them to arrest me.'

The abuse continued in the weeks, even months, after the FLA's march, Hala remembered. She received Islamophobic private messages on her Twitter and Facebook accounts, calling her a 'Muslim bitch', a 'filthy terrorist' and a 'mentally retarded product of first-cousin marriage'. Though she deleted the picture she had uploaded on the day of the protest, it was still being circulated across right-wing media. She was sent edited versions where she was photoshopped to wear a niqab or had been implanted into the scene of an ISIS beheading. 'It was just relentless,' she recalled. 'And they were attacking me for being a woman, for being an ethnic minority and, of course, for being Muslim. It had a really severe impact on my mental health, in a way that I hadn't experienced before.'

Hala had seen this happen to other Muslims before. She had Muslim friends from university whose pictures showing them with long beards had been turned into anti-Muslim memes. She remembered an image that had been circulating online only a few months earlier, of a Muslim woman walking across Westminster Bridge after the terror attack in March 2017. Right-wing commentators around the world had accused the woman—and by extension, British Muslims—of being indifferent to the attack.[10]

Though Hala reported hundreds of accounts to Twitter and Facebook, little was done to stop the onslaught of abuse. Twitter found that the majority of accounts she had reported 'didn't violate any specific terms and conditions', and held that the threats weren't specific enough to warrant punishment. And even when some accounts were banned, it made little difference, because 'five more would pop up after'.

Hala finally decided enough was enough when the harassment went beyond social media. In the middle of the night, she received a phone call to the landline of her family home, where she lived with her parents and two sisters. 'Fucking Muslim bitch!' the caller shouted. 'Fuck off out of the UK!' The line went dead, leaving her in shock.

For the next few days, the phone calls continued—all from blocked numbers—with the same kind of abuse. One night, her father picked up the phone instead of her. 'Muslims are traitors,' said the voice on the line. 'Britain doesn't want you.'

* * *

Hala's experiences, she told me, aren't unique. Her visibly Muslim friends posted on social media very rarely, cautious to protect themselves from abuse for taking part in social activism online. For the most part, Hala tended to talk about politics only in private WhatsApp groups with her friends and fellow activists. Even then, she didn't use pictures of her face—her profile picture was a flower garden she had found from a Google image search.

Looking back on the incident, Hala said that the abuse she received might not have been as intense if social media didn't make it so easy to harass people, enabled by easy search functions and the wide reach of some users who encourage harassment. 'They all followed these big right-wing accounts, and only one of them, with a couple of thousand followers, is needed for the rest to pile on. Twitter, Facebook—most social media platforms—don't offer any kind of protection against that. So if you're from a marginalised group, you are left to your own devices to fight against hundreds of accounts that are attacking every part of your identity.' Crucially, the internet also allows people to feel a certain distance from the people they abuse. 'People feel empowered when they can attack someone so directly and there isn't any consequence,' she explained. 'Most of the accounts that attacked me were anonymous.'

When I interviewed her in June 2018, Hala said she was in an 'emotionally better place' compared to where she'd been in 2017, but remarked that the experience was still traumatic. She told me that the incident demonstrated not only how prevalent anti-Islam rhetoric is on the internet, but also how dangerous it can be if unmoderated. 'If you look at all anti-Muslim right-wing attacks,' she pointed out, 'every person who has carried out an attack has been influenced and radicalised on the internet—usually by the same blogs read and retweeted by the accounts attacking me. I was lucky that I was only harassed online and with telephone calls—I got off lightly. But if they were able to get my home phone number, they probably could have got my home address too. And then what would have happened? It only takes one person to come to my house and carry out a physical attack, all because these social media platforms make it easy to cast powerless people as enemies.'

These days, Hala still goes to protests and marches, but she stays away from cameras out of fear that she might be recognised or again face abuse. 'It's sad,' she sighed. 'I wanted to be an activist to make change, you know? I grew up reading Malcolm X, Audre Lorde, Assata Shakur, all these powerful, brave activists that I wanted to emulate.' She paused. 'But if I can't face down a Twitter mob, well, maybe I'm not as brave as them.'

Muslims and the Media

In the years I have worked as a journalist reporting on 'Muslim issues', one of the most frequent complaints I hear from British Muslims is that media coverage about Islam and Muslims is so often inaccurate and unfair. For them, mainstream news outlets only focus on Muslims in the context of jihadi extremism, crime, and segregation, and stories about Islamophobia, anti-Muslim hate crimes and the plight of Muslims abroad are 'ignored' or 'whitewashed'.

It's not difficult to see where this animosity toward the mainstream media comes from, amidst sensationalist headlines in national newspapers like 'Islamist school can segregate boys and girls' (*The Times*, November 2016); 'SECRET I.S. SAFE: Half of British Muslims would not go to cops if they knew someone with ISIS links' (*The Sun* website, December 2016); and 'Isolated British Muslims are so cut off from the rest of society that they see the UK as 75 per cent Islamic, shock report reveals' (*The Mail on Sunday*, December 2016).[11] In 2012, researchers at the University of Leeds studying the depiction of British Muslims in the media found that Muslims were 'almost always constructed as belonging "outside" the nation' and were frequently represented in the media in ways that were 'hostile and strongly Islamophobic', fomenting 'hysteria' and an 'overwhelming sense of fear by insisting that terrorists are lurking on the streets of Britain, as well as beyond national borders'.[12]

'One of the big problems is that editors, and some journalists, don't see what they are doing as Islamophobic, or that their stories could cause harm,' Miqdaad Versi, the assistant secretary general of the Muslim Council of Britain, told me in 2018. Like many others I spoke to, Miqdaad was dismayed by the biased media representation of British Muslims, but what particularly incensed him was the level of inaccuracy in much of the coverage. 'In the internet age it poses a much greater danger,' he said, 'because inaccurate stories can end up going viral in a short amount of time, and the people who share those stories can end up getting angry. And it only takes one angry person to cause damage in the real world.'

At the MCB, one of the things Miqdaad is most known for is his diligent tracking of stories about Muslims in the mainstream media, which he organises into columns on a spreadsheet, commenting on both their tone towards Muslims and their accuracy. 'It started by accident,' he laughed. 'It was just a way to keep tabs on stories that might require a response from [the MCB] ... but I realised that the more I kept looking, the more stories I found being published, particularly online, that had reported stories about Muslims inaccurately.' Those inaccuracies can range from attributing certain imams and speakers to mosques with which they have no affiliation, to more sinister cases.

On 28 August 2017, *The Times* ran a story with the headline 'Christian child forced into Muslim foster care', about a five-year-old girl whose Muslim foster parents allegedly spoke no English, tried to teach the child Arabic, removed her crucifix, and stopped her from eating pork.[13] Later that week, on 30 August, the same newspaper reported that a court had ruled against Tower Hamlets council and ordered that the girl be removed from the care of the Muslim family and placed instead with her grandmother. The case was picked up by other national media outlets. However, after complaints were made to the Independent Press Standards Organisation (IPSO), it was revealed that the *Times* account was one-sided (it had omitted that the child's grandmother was also a Muslim) and, according to IPSO, contained 'distortion' of the facts—in fact, Tower Hamlets council had itself requested that the child be moved to stay with her grandmother.[14] Regarding claims made in the first article, *The Observer* and *The Guardian* also reported that the child's Muslim foster family could speak English; that the crucifix was removed for safekeeping; and that there was no evidence of a forced halal diet.[15] IPSO compelled *The Times* to publish a correction citing inaccuracies in the 30 August article. However, the original story—'Christian child forced into Muslim foster care'—is still available online.

For people like Miqdaad Versi, the foster child story is one of many that demonstrate the importance of holding the press to account. 'Working with regulators, with press bodies, even with editors and journalists themselves, can bring about a healthier, long-term change,' he said. He believed the prevalence of misleading content was partly a symptom of 'religiously illiterate' newsrooms, with few Muslims on their staff. (Muslims make up 0.4 per cent of the UK's journalists, despite comprising 5 per cent of the population.[16]) He also acknowledged that there are 'high demands to churn out content that isn't properly checked until a complaint is made'.

I asked Miqdaad whether his strategy for tackling false and misleading reportage by filing complaints one article at a time was too slow, especially when anti-Muslim media now spreads online faster than corrections can be issued. He agreed this was a problem, but said that lodging complaints to press regulators still had an important effect on media outlets. 'If they have to issue corrections, or pay damages, then that also takes a hit on their reputation.' This, he hoped, would lead to broader changes in the media's rhetoric about Muslims, as journalists and editors would take greater care to be accurate. 'It means that a change in language can be normalised—things like "Muslim terrorist" becoming "Islamist terrorist", or even getting them to correct terms like "Muslim cleric" when the person isn't even a preacher. The small things matter if we want any kind of long-term change.'

* * *

Of course, not everyone is so hopeful, and for young Muslims whose main access to news is through social media, the impact of these negative stories can feel much more direct. From online Islamophobia to the rise in anti-Muslim hate crime, some Muslims believe that their negative portrayal in mainstream media is far too entrenched in British culture to change. In response, some have concluded that the only way to challenge these stereotypes is to create their own news outlets.

'We wanted to provide space for British Muslims to express their opinions and their voices, but to do it in a way that was professional. With professional journalists, who knew how the media works,' says thirty-year-old Dilly Hussain. Dilly is the deputy editor and public face of 5Pillars, an independent Muslim news website whose stories range from coverage of Middle East politics and foreign affairs, to reports about the work of local mosques in Britain.[17]

Sara Khan, the lead commissioner for the Home Office's Commission for Countering Extremism, has referred to 5Pillars as a 'media arm' of the 'Salafi-Islamist jigsaw', and asserts that its content 'is devoted to deriding the Government's Prevent counter-terrorism agenda and adopting a critical tone toward those British-Muslim civil society groups that work with it'.[18] When we speak about these accusations, Dilly says that 5Pillars is not sectarian and reports on events related to all Muslims—but he doesn't deny Khan's latter claim.

'Part of the reason 5Pillars exists is to challenge the government's policies that discriminate against Muslims, and Prevent is absolutely one of them,' he tells me, referring to the government's counter-extremism strategy that requires teachers, doctors, social workers and others to report those they believe are vulnerable to radicalisation. '5Pillars was designed to be a place that advocates and supports things that are in the best interest of Muslims. We have an editorial process, where I discuss with my other editor about what stories we should cover and whether they fit our guidelines. And of course, one of those that ticks all our boxes is resistance against Prevent, which we feel unfairly targets Muslims, even those without "normative"[19] [conservative] views.'

5Pillars is one of the most popular Muslim media outlets, with over 300,000 likes on Facebook.[20] Dilly says that nearly 8,000 unique readers visit the site every day, and that some of its pieces have been shared more than 250,000 times. 'We're a small site, funded by individual donors, activists, students, and every so often we fundraise through Ramadan appeals on TV channels,' Dilly tells me. 'So we rely on social media engagement to get our message out. For us, our online community is important because it's the way we keep the site running. In that way, we make sure that all our news is as accurate as possible, and that it serves the Muslim community who hold us accountable.'

In that way, Dilly adds, 5Pillars can posit itself as an 'authentic' voice, which he believes helps build trust in the platform. 'We aren't beholden to a big funder, or a particular sheikh, or even a country. Working through small donations means that we're accountable only to our readers, and it's our sole duty to provide them with the best possible journalism as we can. Sometimes that will mean going abroad to report on an issue affecting Muslims in Palestine, or in Bangladesh. Other times it will mean making sure we are on the scene when something happens in a mosque or a big Muslim community that we know no one else is covering.'

Crucially, Dilly says, being an online platform 'keeps us ahead of everyone else'. 'We see our competitors as Islamic TV channels, which don't do much news and are mostly focused on theology and *da'wah*. Being online means that we can be in direct contact with people in the community—people know who Roshan and I are, and we can build trust with them. All of that is important when you want to tell the best possible story about Muslims.'

5Pillars isn't the only Muslim news website to have emerged in a climate of hostile news reportage. The Muslim Vibe, a news and entertainment website, describes its birth in a context in which 'hateful discrimination against Muslims and Islam has become a tool by both mainstream media and politics'. In response, it declares, 'Our mission is to inspire, inform and empower young Muslims in the West to reclaim their narrative, by providing a grassroots platform to share their ideas, views and experiences.'[21]

Much like 5Pillars, The Muslim Vibe covers British and international news stories. But it also features lifestyle articles, which range from parenting advice,[22] personal finance tips,[23] and ideas for budget 'Halal Holidays'.[24] Since it was founded in 2014, TMV says that it has reached 420 million people worldwide and has amassed a following of 650,000 people across its social media platforms.[25]

The site has strong branding, with rich purple banners, large picture-led and search-engine-optimised headlines, and a website that is easy to navigate on both mobiles and computers. Salim Kassam, the website's founder, told me that this was a deliberate strategy. 'We noticed that there wasn't a lot of websites for Muslim news available, and the things that there were just didn't look like modern websites. They were hard to navigate—too much information on the page—and they wouldn't work well on mobile devices, which is how nearly half of all people now read their news. Our thinking was, if mainstream news websites are optimising their platforms for mobile technology, then we should do that too.'

TMV isn't just unique because it has an up-to-date website. Being run by two Shi'a Muslims in North London, the site posts articles debunking popular misconceptions about Shi'a Islam believed by many non-Muslims and Muslims alike.[26] Some of its pieces include '10 lessons from the day of Ashura',[27] and 'Dear Shia Muslims, Hussain ibn Ali is my Imam too', an article about how Imam Hussain, revered among Shi'a Muslims, also occupies a holy space in Sunni tradition.[28]

To Salim, these articles are some of 'the best examples of what we're trying to accomplish'. 'The Muslim Vibe is a platform for all Muslims,' he said. 'We want as many voices expressing them- selves here as we can, because we also want to show Muslims that you don't need to be sectarian, that the things that divide us in our belief can co-exist, and that what unites us is much greater.' Though Salim says that TMV will always have a discernible Shi'a identity, reflective of the beliefs of its founders and its core read- ership, there is no intention to let that dominate or direct the site's content. 'We want to represent the Muslim experience as accurately as we can,' said Salim. 'For us, it's about publishing positive, uniting Islamic content that is accessible for Muslims and non-Muslims, for those who are practising, as well as for those who are not.'

* * *

Arguably, no website has done more to capture the intersection between current affairs and Muslim lifestyle content than Amaliah, which describes itself as 'a media company that centres the voices of Muslim women' as 'a powerful tool for cultural change'.[29]

'We wanted to build a media platform where women wouldn't be afraid or discouraged to express themselves,' says Nafisa Bakkar, a co-founder, with her sister Selina, of Amaliah, an online media company built by and for Muslim women.

The project began on the kitchen table of the Bakkar sisters' parents' house. In 2016, when Nafisa, then twenty-five, first began writing code for the website, its aim was simple: to curate 'modest' fashion and create a destination for Muslim women who 'found it difficult to find clothes that they liked that also would be in accordance to their religious values'. Within a couple of years, interest in Amaliah grew, as more women began asking to contribute essays and comment pieces to the site. This was an exciting and welcome development; as Nafisa told me in the café of the East London start-up space where Amaliah is based, 'I wanted to make sure that Amaliah wasn't just about fashion. Clothing is still a big part of it, but we wanted Amaliah to also be the place where unheard voices from Muslim communities could speak.'

Amaliah now gets over 30,000 page views a month, and has a staff of five. The website layout is clean-cut; on its homepage, high-quality images accompany each piece, presented in a grid against a white background. In fact, at first glance, Amaliah looks less like a traditional 'Muslim publication' in the traditional sense, than it does the website of a high-end fashion magazine like *Vogue* or *Elle*.

Since its soft launch in January 2016, Amaliah has been featured in larger publications including *The Telegraph* and *Wired*. And while the platform still focuses on modest fashion, it is becoming increasingly known for the original, light-hearted, and at times irreverent style of its daily articles. Popular articles on the site include 'Beekeeping: My Interest in Nature Brought Me Closer to

Allah', 'How the Quran and Sunnah Taught Me to Go Vegan', and 'A Woman's Right to Orgasm: Feminism in the Bedroom & Sexual Liberation Through Islam Not Despite It'.[30] Next to lifestyle and fashion columns, Amaliah also publishes content on world affairs, such as the ongoing plight of Uyghur Muslims in China and dispatches from a Rohingya refugee camp.[31]

For Nafisa, publishing such a vast range of content is a conscious decision. 'Before we started Amaliah there wasn't a destination where Muslim women were being taken seriously,' she told me. 'There wasn't a lot out there online for Muslim women. I knew that these conversations were happening in private, or on social media, but there wasn't a place where you could go and read things that spoke to the experiences of Muslim women.'

Nafisa knows that Amaliah can't 'represent Muslim women' in their entirety, and, more importantly, said that the site was still 'learning about the unique experiences of Muslim women and their place in their communities.' Still, she hopes that Amaliah can become a platform where they can express themselves freely and openly. 'Amaliah should be a place where people can discuss the big issues our communities face, but in a way that is true to themselves.'

'Ultimately,' she added, 'we want young Muslims, and even non-Muslims, to know that there is a place out there that will allow them to simply exist as they wish.'

Meeting the Islamophobes

In 2017, I started to receive messages from a Twitter user who called themself 'True Brit', telling me that my religion was 'Satanic', 'barbaric' and 'evil'. Bearing a profile image of the St George's Cross and a biography that simply read 'Anti-Islam, stop Islamic immigration now', True Brit often spammed me with pictures taken from anti-Muslim websites, blogs and

Facebook groups. Sometimes they would be cartoons depicting the Prophet Muhammad as a sexual deviant. Other times, I would be sent memes I'd seen circulating right-wing communities online, depicting groups of South Asian men who had been arrested for child sexual grooming, or alleged Syrian refugees who were, supposedly, secret members of ISIS. One meme showed a man with a long beard, in battle camouflage, brandishing a pistol in one hand and holding the hand of a woman wearing niqab. In bold white writing below the image were the words 'EUROPE IN 2020'.

True Brit never said anything directly to me to begin with. I had seen social media profiles like theirs, and much worse, for years. Like those accounts, True Brit had few followers, sixty-five in total. Their activity on Twitter predominantly consisted of retweets from right-wing news sites like Breitbart and Fox News. They frequently posted videos of online celebrities who were popular on anti-Muslim forums and Facebook groups, including Milo Yiannopoulos, a right-wing 'provocateur' who has referred to Islam as 'the real rape culture', and Paul Joseph Watson, a UK-based YouTuber and editor of the far-right fake news website Infowars.com who produces weekly videos about the 'dangers of Islam' in the West, with titles like 'The Truth About Islamophobia' and 'Dear Gays: The Left Betrayed You For Islam'. True Brit was also a fan of the British right-wing commentator Katie Hopkins, who in 2015 likened Syrian refugees to cockroaches, and who currently produces videos about the 'Islamisation of the west' for Canadian far-right outlet The Rebel Media.

Their feed might have been homogeneous and their followers few, but True Brit was a very active Twitter user. They would post at least ten times a day, often attacking members of the UK Labour Party, in particular Shadow Home Secretary Diane Abbott, branding her a 'disgusting bitch', and Mayor of London

Sadiq Khan, accusing him of being 'anti-white' and 'pro-Sharia law' after he participated in a campaign against hate speech.

Accounts like True Brit's aren't uncommon on Twitter. Thousands like it exist, with names like 'Patriot Princess', 'FREEDOM OF SPEECH UK' and 'THE GREAT AWAKENING: MAKE BRITAIN GREAT AGAIN'. Although there's no exact figure for how many accounts on the platform could be classified as anti-Islam or anti-Muslim, the cross-party think tank Demos recorded 215,246 Islamophobic tweets sent in English alone in July 2016—nearly 7,000 a day.[32] In an analysis of over 100,000 tweets sent between March 2016 and August 2018 from forty-five right-wing Twitter accounts, researchers at the University of Oxford found that nearly half contained Islamophobic messaging.[33]

When True Brit first messaged me on Twitter, I assumed they were a bot account. 'Bots'—automated accounts that don't belong to real humans—have long been a common feature of social media. Twitter bots, which are estimated to number in the tens of millions, are programmed to like tweets, retweet, and follow accounts.[34] Bots tend to be used by commercial brands to share their adverts with real users on Twitter. In other cases, companies dedicated to programming thousands of bots sell the accounts to customers who want to artificially boost their number of followers. Social media companies tend to consider bots harmless and do relatively little to regulate them, other than restrict the privileges on accounts that seem to be spamming or breaking rules on privacy and data protection.

Bots can, of course, be used in more sinister ways, and have become a common feature of anti-Muslim social media communities. In 2017, *The Observer* reported that popular right-wing and far-right figures were actively employing bots to retweet and 'signal boost' their anti-Muslim content, based on findings by the anti-racist think tank Hope Not Hate.[35] In a study into

113

Islamophobic content on Twitter, Hope Not Hate found that Pamela Geller, whose blog 'The Geller Report' regularly posts anti-Muslim news and warns about the 'Shariafication of the West', had more than 100 accounts that automatically retweeted every one of her posts, on top of her audience of hundreds of thousands of loyal readers. The study also found an average 117 per cent increase in followers of anti-Muslim Twitter accounts over a period of nine months. 'The growth among Twitter accounts and websites spreading anti-Muslim hate is alarming,' said Patrik Hermansson, a researcher at Hope Not Hate. 'In such a key area of public interest, it is an indication of increased interest in these views and, as each account or site grows, more people are exposed to deeply prejudiced anti-Muslim views.'

* * *

By late June 2017, the direct messages from True Brit had become incessant. What started as a few random stabs of abuse had become a regular onslaught of DMs twice a day, asking why I was part of an 'evil religion' and whether I really wanted to follow the Prophet Muhammad—'the worst person history has ever known'—who had 'killed, enslaved and raped'. True Brit sent me links from the anti-Islam website 'The Religion of Peace', which posts articles, blogs and how-to guides for debating Islam online and 'proving the evil roots of Mohammed'.

When True Brit tired of me not replying to their private messages, they made them public. Under tweets I posted—most of which had nothing to do with Islam or Muslims at all—they relentlessly posted anti-Muslim memes, and shared links to videos of Muslim preachers in Pakistan calling for gays and lesbians to be killed. It was when they replied to one of my tweets with an ISIS video, showing jihadist fighters publicly hanging a man they accused of being a thief, that I finally responded.

'Why do you keep posting this shit to me?' I wrote. 'Why do you think any of this would change my mind about anything?'

Half an hour later, True Brit responded.

'It's not just you,' they said. 'I send it to everyone who follows Islam that I see.'

'Why?' I asked. 'Have you convinced anyone to turn away from Islam because of it?'

After a while, True Brit responded. 'No ... I believe Islam is an evil cult, and people should turn away from it. I don't hate Muslims, I hate Islam.'

'Don't you think that by hating Islam, you also hate the followers of the religion?' I asked. 'How can you convince someone they are following something evil, when you attack the things that make them who they are?'

'No,' they responded. 'I just want them to know they are following evil.'

After our first back-and-forth, I started speaking to True Brit on a near daily basis. Most of our conversations tended to tread similar ground, covering topics that were popular on right-wing social media—we talked about what True Brit referred to as 'Pakistani Muslim grooming gangs' and how they were, in True Brit's words, 'just following the commands of their prophet'. True Brit talked to me about how Muslims were 'taking over towns and schools' and 'encouraging non-Muslim children to wear headscarves', information they had gleaned from a Breitbart article about schoolchildren in Leicester visiting a mosque. And though True Brit evaded my questions about who they were, they were keen to ask me personal questions: why wasn't I married yet, did I intend to circumcise my future children, and would I kill my future child if they were gay?

But our conversations weren't just about religion. True Brit supported Aston Villa, and they'd often talk about the team's performance against rival teams like Norwich and Sunderland. We would talk about what Netflix series we were watching, and whether the British version of *House of Cards* was better than the

American adaptation. True Brit even tried to get me into their favourite band, AC/DC.

After weeks of talking, True Brit agreed to meet me at their home.

* * *

I stood in front of a house on a quiet, suburban road just a few miles outside of Birmingham city centre, finally about to meet my anonymous online interlocutor. A middle-aged man opened the door, wearing a pair of three-quarter-length khaki shorts and a plain blue T-shirt with two yellow stains on the front.

True Brit immediately shook my hand and welcomed me into his home, warning me not to take off my shoes in case I accidentally stepped in cat poo. He introduced himself as Phil Lyons.

Phil was forty-eight-years-old, around 5′7″, with broad shoulders that rolled forward as he moved into his default slouch. In harsh light, a slight paunch was visible. He had thin wisps of light brown hair that barely cover his receding hairline, and uneven stubble covering his face.

Phil lived on his own. On the stained beige walls of his kitchen were drawings by his five-year-old daughter, and photographs of them together at theme parks, restaurants and outside Cardiff Castle. Since Phil's divorce a year ago, his daughter had moved to a different area of Birmingham with her mother. Phil told me that his marriage ending 'broke me emotionally'.

He didn't want to talk about it much, but told me that since then, he spent most of his time alone and at his computer, watching YouTube videos, reading articles and spending hours on message boards. 'I started off just wanting to read about politics,' he said as he made us tea. 'I voted for Brexit—the first time I'd ever properly voted—so I used to spend my time reading about the whole process, how the government would negotiate with the EU. I wasn't really that political, but it was just seeing everything that happened during the referendum. All the fighting, name-calling, and the hypocrisy from the media—how they were insulting anyone who voted Leave, but they just don't understand what we go through.'

Phil told me how he'd been let go from a steady, decently paid job at a plumbing and repairs company in 2015, and had struggled to get back on his feet as a self-employed handyman. During one period of that transition, he had had to claim benefits, a process that had made him embarrassed, as if he 'had lost all dignity', as he was made to fill out endless forms at the local Jobcentre and attend countless interviews for jobs he didn't want, just so he could claim the little money we was eligible to receive.

Around the same time, in the midst of marital trouble, Phil began spending more and more of his free time browsing websites that 'weren't the mainstream media or the biased BBC'. He started off reading obscure blogs he found on Google, including 'Truthseekers.org', which posted about the Illuminati and accused 'elites'—politicians, celebrities and journalists—of having secret meetings where they ultimately planned to 'control' the British population. From these blogs Phil moved on to reading about the 'great replacement', a right-wing conspiracy theory claiming that white British people are deliberately being wiped out—discouraged from getting married and having children to be systematically replaced by non-white Muslim migrants and refugees.

It wasn't long before he switched from blogs to more active communities on sites like Facebook and YouTube, where he found abundant videos about the 'great replacement' from YouTubers like Lauren Southern and Stefan Molyneux, both of whom amassed followings of hundreds of thousands of pro-Trump supporters during the 2016 election campaign. Phil told me that he spent 'hours on YouTube, researching the imminent demographic change'. From these videos, he had learnt that

'Islam is taking over the UK by stealth', and that 'their followers are being encouraged to have lots of children and outbreed non-Muslims'. They were all statements I'd heard before, on conspiracy websites and YouTube's largest right-wing channels.

What was strange to me was just how much time Phil was actually spending online. He spent most of the day in his small, untidy bedroom, where bright-green paint was peeling off the wall and a thin sheet lay crumpled on his single bed. His cabinets bore thick layers of dust, some of which had fallen onto the carpet. On his table lay several cups of days-old tea, one of which was beginning to show white spots of mould. But what immediately caught my eye when I entered his room was an unfurled Union Jack flag taped to the edge of his desk.

This was the table where Phil, under his 'True Brit' alias, would sit before his computer to talk to me. Now as I sat with him, he showed me that he spent his time messaging tens of others on Twitter with the same kind of content. I saw that his direct messages had all been sent to notable Muslim and left-wing figures, and it was clear that he used Twitter for little else. 'Most of the time, they just block me,' he said. 'Some of them swear at me, call me names or accuse me of being [an internet] troll.' Phil retweeted almost every anti-Islam post he saw, often without even reading the links. He said that for him, retweeting 'doesn't mean I agree with it', but rather that he wanted 'to make the debate about Islam open to the public'. He also found that as he continued to retweet anti-Muslim accounts, he would amass more followers, especially if a big right-wing figure retweeted him in turn. 'One of my tweets was favourited by Katie Hopkins a while back,' he told me. 'I ended up getting twenty new followers off that—imagine if she had retweeted it to her followers!'

When I asked Phil if anyone had influenced him while he was developing his views about Islam, he claimed that he'd come up with his 'own views based on my own research', and that he wasn't against Muslims. Nor was he racist, because 'Islam isn't a race—it's a set of ideas'. He said he hadn't deliberately searched for material on Islam. Rather, 'I'd go on YouTube, and I would just see a new video every day showing [male] Muslim migrants attacking women, or robbing a shop, or burning a car. It happens all the time, and you can find it quite easily.' He showed me his YouTube homepage, replete with recommendations—based on what he had watched previously—of footage from EDL marches, clips from the right-wing US programme *The Alex Jones Show*, and videos from alt-right YouTube personalities who have expressed anti-Muslim views like Brittany Pettibone and Martin Sellner. These videos appeared in YouTube's recommended side-bar too; Phil had autoplay on, so they would run on from each other. On the whole, he estimated that he watched at least an hour of these videos every morning, 'just because they were there'.

* * *

YouTube's algorithm for 'recommended videos' has come under fire, particularly after the election of Donald Trump, when it was accused of promoting fake news that incited racial and religious hatred, and even violence. In *The New York Times*, Zeynep Tufekci called YouTube 'the Great Radicalizer', after finding that simply watching a few Donald Trump rallies led the site to recommend videos to her that denied the Holocaust and called for Muslims to be forcibly deported from the West.[36] Tufekci argued that though YouTube was not deliberately directing its users to extremist material, its recommendations algorithm, designed to keep users on the site for as long as possible, naturally brought up more graphic, 'hard core' material. 'What keeps people glued to YouTube?' she asked. 'Its algorithm seems to have concluded that people are drawn to content that is more extreme than what they started with—or to incendiary content in general.' And this didn't just go for Trump supporters. Tufekci cited an investigation by *The Wall Street Journal*, which found that even users who watched mainstream news on YouTube were 'fed far-right or far-left videos'.[37] 'If you searched for information on the flu vaccine,' she commented, 'you were recommended anti-vaccination conspiracy videos.'

In a number of public statements since the 2016 US presidential election, Google has claimed to be clamping down on extremist material on its YouTube platform.[38] But critics have accused YouTube, like other social media companies, of acting too late, and doing too little. Indeed, even when extremist accounts do get restricted or banned, users can easily set up a new account, upload their old videos, and, within a matter of weeks, get their followers back.

* * *

One such person was a YouTuber called 'World2Awaken', whose channel Phil had subscribed to. When I contacted World2Awaken, he told me his name was Mike, but wouldn't disclose any personal details, like his age or where he lived. He told me that two of his previous YouTube accounts had been deleted after he had posted material that was deemed harmful by the site's standards.

Mike's YouTube following was modest, but he uploaded videos at least once a week. All his videos were anti-Islam and anti-Muslim, with titles like 'Muslims demand Sharia law in Britain!' and 'Muslims attack Christians in UK streets "we're taking over" "we hate you"'. Most of his content was ripped from other, larger YouTube channels, like Infowars, RT (formerly Russia Today) and The Rebel Media.

Mike also posted old videos of speakers who were well known for saying negative things about Islam, and who sometimes appeared on mainstream news channels: people like Tommy Robinson, prominent critic of Islam Ayaan Hirsi Ali, and her husband, historian Niall Ferguson. 'Usually,' he told me by email, 'I upload videos of Douglas Murray because I know that they will get a lot of views.' Shortly before his channel was deleted for violation of YouTube's terms and conditions, World2Awaken shared a video of Murray, a political commentator and columnist for *The Spectator*, talking at an Intelligence Squared debate about how 'Islam is not a religion of peace'. The original video has over a million views on YouTube since it was first broadcast in 2011.[39]

'I was getting a good thousand views a day at least,' Mike recounted with pride. 'Usually from people who would search for names of particular speakers, and would come across my videos.' For Mike, there was a thrill in seeing more and more people visit his channel, a belief that 'I wasn't alone in my fear about Islam in Britain and the need to do something about it'. He told me that people had emailed him after coming across his channel to 'thank me for opening their eyes to the problem', and said that over the year he was operating his channel, he had amassed over 2,000 subscribers—a sizeable number for a channel that didn't produce original content.

Mike's explanation for this was that people were 'coming to YouTube to find out the truth about immigration and Islam in their country', because the site was a good place to find material and digest it in a short period of time. 'You can listen to a video when you're at work, on your way home, you don't have to read anything—that's one reason we are more effective at spreading our message than lefty newspapers,' Mike explained. He also argued that YouTube was 'more transparent' than other forms of media, because 'you can't lie when you're making a video'. Mike did admit that he sometimes uploaded videos he found without knowing the full context of the clip.

Once, he uploaded a video of predominantly black football fans in Paris shouting after a match in 2014, titling it 'Muslims attack bus after Ramadan'. Another time, he posted a clip of Abu Haleema, a UK-based Muslim vlogger whose passport was seized by the Home Office under suspicion of plans to engage in terror-ism. Mike had taken the video from a Channel 4 documentary about countering fringe extremists online, and reposted it with the title 'UK Imam says Sharia will take over Britain by force', despite the fact that Abu Haleema wasn't an imam. For Mike, these aren't big issues, and he dismissed the inaccuracies as unim-portant when I asked why I had seen the videos on his channel just before it was shut down. 'Even if it was wrong that time,' he said, 'there is plenty of evidence that shows that Muslims are causing problems everywhere they immigrate. They only respect Sharia law and they will not stop until Sharia takes over.' Mike went offline, and refused to answer any more of my questions.

* * *

When I asked Phil about YouTube videos that were uploaded either with a false synopsis or without context, he brushed it off and told me, 'The news lies all the time, and you don't call them up on that.' He wasn't convinced that videos falsely depicting Muslims as criminals, rapists and violent attackers perpetuated a narrative that could be destructive and alienating for Muslims living in the UK, including those he had worked with, and the small Muslim community that lived only a stone's throw away from his house. 'I don't think all Muslims are evil,' he repeated. 'I only think their ideology is evil.'

For Phil, the veracity of individual incidents was irrelevant. 'You don't know what's true or not these days anyway,' he shrugged. 'But I know that whenever I see a terrorist attack or a shooting happen, and the culprit always has a Muslim name ... I know that the problem is bigger.'

He paused, and scrolled down his worn iPhone 6. Sadiq Khan had just tweeted about reducing hate crime—the kind of tweet that trolls routinely responded to with hundreds of abusive, anti-Muslim comments. 'I've got a meme for this,' Phil sniggered, showing me a picture of a poorly drawn caricature of Khan's head transplanted onto the body of a pig, the Arabic word *haram* written on its side.

'Mayor Khan wants to ban this,' Phil tweeted. 'Would be a shame if it got retweeted.'

The Muslim Alt-Right

In his small, dark, cramped bedroom in West London, leaning over his desk, twenty-eight-year-old Ahmed Miah was watching a lecture on YouTube about the meaning of life. In the video, a tall, lanky man with greying hair, wearing a blue checked shirt and a black sports jacket, was urging men to 'take responsibility for your life'. He had just related the Biblical story of 'the fall of man'—the transition of Adam and Eve from a state of pure innocence to one of corruption and disobedience to God. 'Responsibility, struggle, that's what gives life meaning,' the speaker said confidently. 'Young men are so hungry for that ... we need to sell responsibility.'

Ahmed, a tall and skinny Bengali man who, when we met, wore a pair of loose jogging bottoms and a stained, white Adidas T-shirt, had heard this all before. He had heard it in madrassa when he was first studying Islam, and given reminders of his obligation to his parents. He had heard it from his father, a Bengali restaurant owner, who worked long hours each day to provide for his family and had spent a good portion of Ahmed's teenage years berating him for not working hard enough at school or in the kitchen. And he had heard it from imams for years—whenever he went to *jumu'ah* prayer; every Ramadan; and, of course, during weddings, when the imam would talk about the 'roles and responsibilities husbands are obligated to perform for their wives'. But where Ahmed was concerned, most of this had fallen on deaf ears. He found those lectures boring, repetitive and lacking in substance—lines and tropes repeated by the same relatives and community leaders that, at best, seemed like empty conversation filler, and, at worst, sounded completely condescending. In his words, their words 'made me feel useless, pointless, basically like I was shit'.

Watching the video now, Ahmed was transfixed to his screen. In a small blue notebook, he jotted down key points from the lecture. He ignored an incoming phone call. It was clear he was hanging on to every word from this charismatic speaker—a Canadian professor turned viral internet star, Jordan Peterson.

For most people in Britain, the Canadian psychologist entered the public conversation after he appeared on Channel 4 News in 2018, partaking in a heated debate with anchor Cathy Newman over the existence of the gender pay gap.[40] Online, however, Peterson rose to prominence in 2016, after a video was shared in which he declared that he would refuse to use the preferred gender pronouns of trans students.[41] For some, this was evidence of Peterson's transphobia, but for others, particularly online groups affiliated to the right, Peterson became a champion, if not a martyr, of 'free expression'.

Ever since the clip went viral, Peterson has embraced YouTube as a medium for posting his lectures, discussions and interviews. They range from subjects about the 'dangers of Marxism' on university campuses, to warnings about the 'destabilising nature' of modern feminism. Other popular videos fall into the self-help category, providing advice, particularly for young men, on everyday issues like setting up a schedule, maintaining good physical health, and getting a meaningful career. Each of Peterson's videos, published on his Facebook and YouTube channels, garners hundreds of thousands of views.[42] He reportedly makes over $60,000 per month from his fans and followers via the subscription content website Patreon, and his book *12 Rules For Life* has sold millions of copies.

* * *

On the surface, Ahmed's fawning over Peterson isn't particularly abnormal. He's a young man, around the age of Peterson's target audience, who are attracted to the professor's messages and strategies for self-improvement. But while Peterson and his provocative claims attract much attention and ire, there is just as much controversy around his army of loyal fans, many of whom are part of online communities linked to hard-right, socially conservative internet personalities, who are vehemently anti-Muslim.

Though Peterson does not identify as politically right-wing, nor claimed to be 'anti-Islam', his videos, particularly on feminism, transgender issues and 'social justice' culture, have found resounding support in more extreme parts of the right-wing internet, including from open neo-Nazi groups, ethno-nationalists and the alt-right communities that still thrive on community message boards like Reddit and 4chan. On the Jordan Peterson subreddit, users frequently talk about the 'evils of Islam' and its role in 'destroying Western civilisation'.[43] Some users refer to Islam as a 'violent religion' and the Prophet Muhammad as a 'warlord'.[44]

More explicit attacks on Islam and Muslims are found on other social media platforms. Under a fan-made YouTube video titled 'Jordan Peterson Destroys Islam in 15 Seconds', one user wrote, 'ISLAM IS INTRINSICALLY MISOGYNISTIC AND UNSCIENTIFIC. If Mohammed is wrong about the intelligence of women (and he is), then he is a false prophet.'[45] The comment was upvoted more than 100 times. Meanwhile the comments under a live-streamed Peterson video in 2018 about alcohol addiction, which had nothing to do with Islam at all, quickly descended into anti-Muslim commentary, as users referred to Muslims as 'pond scum' and 'disgusting paedophile worshippers'.

Ahmed is used to these comments. He has seen Peterson fans on YouTube make explicitly racist statements about Muslims, and visits the 500,000-strong Peterson subreddit page where similar comments are made. While people have different views about who Peterson is and what he stands for, most who venture into his online orbit, Ahmed included, can probably agree that it's not the most welcome space for Muslims. And yet, Ahmed describes himself as a 'die-hard' Peterson fan.

Ahmed discovered Peterson on YouTube after the professor's confrontation with transgender students at a protest in the University of Toronto, a moment which, to Ahmed, showed that 'he was against political corruption and moral correctness'. 'He is very wise and knows the dangers that ideas like feminism and social justice can do to communities,' Ahmed told me, referring to videos of Peterson warning about the 'threats of postmodernism' in the West. For Ahmed, Peterson's message is personal to him. 'He's not just referring to white communities. I've seen it in my own Muslim community. When liberals take over and Islam becomes less important, it leads to corruption. Peterson can see that. He knows how to articulate it too.'

Ahmed's defence of Peterson's message wasn't unlike other defences I'd heard before. But I'd heard them from his more predictable fans, mostly white, atheist men whose views on Islam were openly derogatory and demeaning. Some described Muslims as 'culturally backward' and 'a threat to the Western way of life', and were fans of famous alt-right YouTubers like Lauren Southern, Brittany Pettibone and Stefan Molyneux.

Ahmed describes himself as a 'quiet Peterson fan', in part because he's aware of the suspicion his active support, as a Muslim, would provoke from other fans. He only participates in the Peterson subreddit rarely, and when he does, he doesn't use his real name. Nor does he bring up Islam or Muslims.

To Ahmed, Peterson's popularity offered some hope. As a religious and socially conservative Muslim, he had felt isolated online.

'There was all the Islamophobia, all the anti-Muslim hate on most forums I was part of,' he says. 'On the other hand, Muslim forums would be filled with liberals who condoned things like [same-sex] marriage, transgenderism, feminism—things that I knew were wrong. But whenever I brought it up, I would be attacked, sent hate messages and even banned from groups.' Peterson's ascent as one of the internet's most well-known and influential figures meant that for the first time, Ahmed came across communities that held values which were, by and large, in tune with his.

'I know that Peterson's fans are hostile to Islam,' Ahmed says, 'but the messages he is spreading are, at the core, very Islamic. He promotes studying and acquiring knowledge, being respectful to your parents, the importance of marriage and monogamy. They are all Islamic values.' Ahmed even credits the professor with bringing him closer to Islam. 'When I saw how these Islamic teachings could be applied into your life, and that Peterson, a non-Muslim, was advocating them, I was more certain in my *iman* [faith].'

* * *

Ahmed isn't the only Muslim to call himself a 'quiet fan' of Jordan Peterson. The Canadian professor appeals to a number of Muslims—especially men—because of his combination of practical life advice, theological knowledge and conservative values.

Through Peterson's Reddit page, I spoke to five men, all in their late twenties and early thirties, who thought of themselves as practising Muslims and who, like Ahmed, had discovered Peterson online. They were attracted to his message for similar reasons to Ahmed, namely, because he represented the possibility that 'socially conservative ideas had a place in 2018' and signalled a way for Muslims to 'follow a path closer to the ways of Islam than to the ways of *haram* and *shirk* [idolatry]'.

'His fans can be nuts, and they can be racist, anti-Islam, but I don't think Dr Peterson is Islamophobic. I don't think he knows enough about Islam,' said thirty-year-old Kareem. I met Kareem through the Peterson Reddit group, and he agreed to meet me in July 2018 at a café near the Hammersmith Apollo, where he had tickets to see Jordan Peterson's live show.

Kareem didn't want his surname to be published, because he hadn't told any of his Muslim friends he was going to the show. Many of them considered Peterson to be 'racist' and 'alt-right', and he was worried his relationship with them would deteriorate if they found out he had paid more than £100 to see him live.

Like Ahmed, Kareem was aware of the problems that come with being a Peterson fan and a Muslim. But he felt strongly that Peterson's YouTube lectures had changed his life. 'I was unemployed for years. I used to spend every day on the computer playing games, wasting time on Facebook, just aimlessly going through life.' When he discovered Peterson on YouTube, by chance, he 'saw a man who genuinely understood pain, struggle and what it's like to feel like a failure'.

That was something, he said, that no imam or religious speaker he had grown up listening to had been able to articulate. 'When you're at the mosque, you're supposed to revere the imam,' Kareem told me. 'He is considered to be the community leader, the person of knowledge. Your relationship with the imam is one of respect. That's fine, but it also means it's difficult to open up about your issues, your struggles with him. And even if you do, it would be difficult to find an imam who could relate to that.' Peterson's advice comes across as 'more authentic'. Even without having met him in person, Kareem feels that hours watching the professor's videos have helped him to develop a deeper insight into life. 'His advice isn't condescending and patronising, like so many *da'wah* people [preaching Islam] on the internet,' Kareem says. 'It's actually useful ... it doesn't matter if he isn't Muslim, if the advice can help, and it won't lead me astray from Islam, then I believe it is valuable.'

* * *

As I continued to seek out Muslim members of Peterson's fan base, I discovered some Muslims gravitating toward more extremist corners of the right-wing internet, sharing content from creators who were not just overtly Islamophobic—they had essentially built their entire online brands around taking down Islam.

Such was the case with the Facebook page 'United Muslim Brothers UK'.

By late 2016, the obscure page with only eighty likes, which had until then largely focused on posting Islamic reminders and prayers, was beginning to put out more cultural and political content on its page. Sometimes, these posts were from news outlets like Al Jazeera and the Turkish broadcaster TRT, showing scenes of the ongoing Syrian civil war, or humanitarian crises in parts of West Africa. But in January 2017, the group attracted attention, after it posted a video of British 'provocateur' Milo Yiannopoulos, former Breitbart News editor, who courted the alt-right and built his online brand in America through deliberate offence, usually toward Muslims, transgender people and feminists.

Yiannopoulos, then at the height of his popularity, had shared a video clip on Facebook from his 2016 lecture at the University of Wisconsin-Milwaukee, in which he referred to a transgender student, who was in the audience at the time,[46] as 'just a man in a dress', and said that her transition was 'failing'.[47] It was a fairly typical video for Milo at the time, of the kind I had become accustomed to seeing on right-wing news blogs and social media.

But when United Muslim Brothers UK shared the clip, it was the first time I, and many other Muslims online, had seen overtly far-right content in a Muslim online space. People started posting criticism. 'Why would you post something made by Milo?

Do you know he hates Muslims?' one commenter wrote. 'Why are you sharing videos made by this man? Do you understand what he stands for? I do not want to be part of this group if you are going to post videos from this Islamophobe,' said another.

Despite criticism from some, the post also received a positive reaction. More than 100 people liked the video, and it was shared more than fifty times—more engagement than any post on the page since it had been set up in late 2015. Plenty of people expressed their approval; most had no idea who Milo Yiannopoulos was, but shared his disdain for transgender people.

'*Astaghfirullah* [I seek Allah's forgiveness],' one person wrote. 'I do not want my children to see this disgusting peoples [*sic*]'. 'Allah s.w.t [Glory to Him, the Exalted] warned that men would act like women, and women would act like men,' said another. 'It is a sign of *Qiyamah* [the Day of Judgement].'

Muslim Brothers UK eventually deleted the original video, but its admin, who did not want to be named, told me that he didn't regret putting the video up, even if it did come from Milo. The admin's name on Facebook was 'Kha Led' and his profile picture was the word 'Allah' in gold Arabic calligraphy.

Recalling a conversation with the page's other admin, Kha Led told me that 'our only concern is to publish things that keep Muslims on the right path and that do not lead them astray. It does not matter where that message comes from.' He said that the page regularly posted videos by non-Muslims, from self-help videos from motivational speakers like Jay Shetty and Tony Robbins, to cooking videos from Jamie Oliver and Gordon Ramsay.

The admins of United Muslim Brothers UK had originally seen Milo's video in a Muslim WhatsApp group, as part of a discussion about 'the influence of transgender and LGBT [*sic*] in schools'. 'Many Muslims are very worried about this,' Kha Led told me. 'But also, many non-Muslim parents are worried too.

We all want our children to have a good education and to stay in Islam, and we are worried that this agenda will stop that.'

When I asked Kha Led how transgender people were threatening the education of children, he said that nothing had happened yet, but that this video was 'a warning sign of [where] society is going'. 'It is already in America—there are transgenders [sic] teaching children that they are not boys and girls. They do not need to learn that,' he said. 'It does not matter who is saying the message—as long as parents can see the danger and can protect their children, that is the most important thing.'

Neither of the admins say they endorse or support Milo Yiannopoulos. Kha Led told me he wasn't aware of the beliefs of most alt-right figures online, and said he and United Muslim Brothers UK would disavow anyone who called for the abuse of Muslims, or who spoke ill of Islam generally. For them, sharing the video wasn't an attempt to amplify Yiannopoulos' personal profile. Rather, they had simply come across the video and found it resonated with them, just as Peterson's videos resonate with so many.

'The reason it reached so far is that so many people see the same warning signs as we do,' Kha Led said. This makes him optimistic. 'If people are worried about all these issues, then it means that they already accept some Islamic values, even if they aren't aware of it. ... In the long term, it's an opportunity to bring more people into the *deen*,' he says hopefully. 'Only Allah knows best.'

Red Pill: Entering the Muslim Manosphere

Abu Muawiyah was laughing at me. A thirty-something-year-old man with a thick Northern accent, and a messy black beard, dressed in a white *thawb*, he chuckled as he claimed that I was too emasculated to get married to a 'good Muslim woman'.

Over a grainy video chat, speaking to me and a small group of students who had signed up for his online marriage workshop, Abu Muawiyah said that I, like other Muslim men living in the West, had 'forgotten what being a Muslim man means'. 'You have given into liberalism, feminism, all these ideologies that undermine the traditional Islamic family,' he told me.

According to him, I was not alone in this. 'There is a problem with Muslim men today!' he proclaimed to the group. 'They complain that they can't get married to good Muslim women, but they have allowed the women, their sisters in Islam, to be corrupted by Western ideals, and, as a result, to belittle them as men.'

* * *

Abu Muawiyah—a *kunya*, or Arabic nickname (he would not disclose his real name in the interview)—gave lectures like this semi-frequently through videos he posted on Facebook or to smaller groups of Muslim men on Google Hangouts and Instagram.

In October 2016, when I first reported on his marriage workshops for *MEL* Magazine, he had a modest following: around 500 people on Facebook, and just over 200 on Instagram.[48] The public videos he posted online tended to receive a small amount of traffic, usually garnering around 100 views. On his social media pages—where his profile picture is a photograph of the Al-Aqsa Mosque in Jerusalem—he posted Islamic reminders, Qur'an recitation videos and advertisements for various Islamic events around the UK.

Upon first glance, Abu Muawiyah's online activity wasn't remarkable. Like many others, he posted a lot of Islamic content. But in some groups he was part of—where he would advertise his 'marriage and advice videos for brothers'—he also uploaded things that weren't purely religious in nature. In Facebook groups like 'Muslim Men', a 900-member group aimed at

Muslim husbands, fathers and male newlyweds, he would post links to YouTube videos produced by popular right-wing accounts, from people like Stefan Molyneux, Hunter Avallone and Gavin McInnes, warning about the 'dangers' posed by transgender students in schools, or talks by provocative speakers like Milo Yiannopoulos with names like 'FEMINISM IS CANCER'. In one post, Abu Muawiyah shared a screenshot of a picture of a hijab-wearing woman who identified as 'LGBTQI'.

'Wow, the *ummah* has really gone astray,' Abu Muawiyah wrote underneath the picture. He went on to warn that the image was a sign of the coming of *Al-Masih ad-Dajjal*— the 'false messiah' who, in Islamic eschatology, is symbolic of the end times and the approach of the Day of Judgement.

This kind of queerphobia and moral panic is not uncommon in online spaces dominated by the alt-right, for whom a return to 'traditionalist' conservative values is central to their ideology of Western revivalism. But these are also communities that tend to be hostile toward Islam; some have called for the forced expatriation of Muslims from the West.

While Muslims like Abu Muawiyah are more than aware of this, they are nonetheless attracted to the strict social conservatism endorsed by the alt-right. 'Even though they are not Muslim—and *inshallah*, one day they will be—the values they are advocating and supporting are not that different from those that most Muslims should be supporting,' Abu Muawiyah told me. 'They believe that marriage is between a man and a woman; they believe that men and women have different roles—that it is the role of the man to provide for his family, and the role for the woman to uphold the household. These are all things that Islam already teaches. All I am doing is using a modern language to communicate what is already in the religion.'

Abu Muawiyah realised that this kind of language wouldn't work with older generations, whom he blamed for 'leading the youth astray' and 'making them doubt their belief and their place in Islam'. Frustrated by their lack of guidance, he had started making his own videos and running workshops specifically targeting young Muslim men. Most people in his audience, he said, were in their late teens to their late twenties—an age at which they were thinking about getting married but 'don't feel they have the correct support or guidance from their families, communities or *masjids*'. This was something he had experienced first-hand, he told me, when he was trying to get married after graduating from university in Manchester in 2014.

'We are told, when looking for spouses, that religion must come first ... So I went to meet many [Muslim] women and their parents, in a completely halal way. I didn't have a job when I first started looking, and my family is not wealthy. But I told them that I am a practising Muslim, I want to raise practising children, and I want to ideally move to an Islamic country in future.' Despite this, he had no luck; no prospective wife returned his calls. To this day, he still blames this on the 'Western standards placed on Muslim men', which, in his view, are valued more than Islamic belief and practice.

Further frustrated by the sense that imams at the mosques he attended were of little use in helping him find a partner, Abu Muawiyah found solace on Islamic forums like Ummah.com and Salafitalk.net, where he found that he wasn't the only man struggling to find what he considered a practising Muslim wife. In these forums, and later in private Facebook chats, Abu Muawiyah and other men would spend countless hours posting Islamic lectures about the roles of men in society, the ways that modern life was 'corrupting the spiritual life desired by Allah', and how Muslim men could best fulfil their religious duties, even as they struggled to get married and thereby 'complete their *deen*'.

At that time, Abu Muawiyah had started to share content of a different genre, which marked him as distinct from the tens of

Islamic speakers and commentators making the same points as him. 'It was like the start of a kind of Muslim MGTOW movement,' he recalled.

MGTOW stands for 'Men Going Their Own Way'.[49] It refers to an online subculture of straight men who believe pursuing romantic relationships with women is detrimental, and who have therefore vowed to stay single. On Reddit, where MGTOW has its largest base, there are well over 72,000 members from all over the world. Reddit MGTOW forums largely consist of anti-feminist memes and discussions about the ways feminism has unfairly disadvantaged men.[50] The debates range from wondering whether sex robots will make having sex with women unnecessary, to whether women fake orgasms in order to make men subservient to them.[51]

But MGTOW groups only scrape at the surface of the internet's male-dominated communities. Alongside groups like 'incels', or 'involuntary celibates'—men who blame women for unfairly denying them sex—and Men's Rights Activists (MRAs)—who believe that men are discriminated against by both the law and the government in comparison to women—MGTOW is part of a broader online space known as the 'Red Pill' movement, or the manosphere.

A community named after a scene in the sci-fi film *The Matrix*, in which Neo is presented with a choice between uncomfortable knowledge and blissful ignorance, the Red Pill movement is based on the notion that most men are yet to 'wake up to the reality of feminism', which they say has such a strong hold over politics and pop culture that men have become the more oppressed gender. In 2015, when the group was still in its infancy, *Business Insider* wrote that the Red Pill is founded on:

an ideology that revolves almost exclusively around gender. Those who 'swallow the pill' maintain that it's *men*, not women, who have been socially disenfranchised. Feminism is considered a damaging ideology and Red Pillers are quick to cite examples that bolster their points, some going so far as to argue that society is outright anti-male.[52]

When I asked Abu Muawiyah if he, or any of his fans, identified with these movements, he was evasive. 'I don't subscribe to ideologies that aren't from Islam,' he told me. 'But,' he added, 'groups like the Red Pill and MGTOW represent the alienation of men in our society, which many men feel, whether they are Muslim or non-Muslim.' For Abu Muawiyah, Red Pillers desired the same things that many Muslim men wanted—traditional marriages, stable homes and children brought up with 'the right values'—things that they felt were 'impossible to obtain'. To Abu Muawiyah, this was because 'liberal society' no longer values men. 'They want to empower women everywhere. They want to give them more wealth, higher status, independence—but that comes at a cost, which is the denigration of the family, and the denigration of communities.'

To Abu Muawiyah's mind, more and more Muslim men are feeling frustrated at what they see as a pervasive erosion of strict gender roles, something he argued was 'also evident in the *masjids*, where barriers between men and women are being taken down, where women are being told that they can lead prayers, and where girls are marrying later, and more often to non-Muslim men.' He saw himself as an advocate of 'traditional Islamic values', someone who told 'young brothers that they don't need Red Pill' to restore their masculinity, because 'Islam already teaches the things these men want to have'.

* * *

While Abu Muawiyah didn't self-identify as a Red Piller, he and others have adopted the language of the online men's rights movement to promote socially conservative Islamic values. In fact, some Muslim figures have become so well-known in the manosphere that they have even been able to build profitable brands from it.

One such figure is Nabeel Azeez. Possibly the manosphere's most visible Muslim, he is a Dubai-based copywriter who also runs a website called 'Becoming the Alpha Muslim',[53] which caters its articles and at-home courses to Muslim men.

Nabeel told me he set up the website 'to tell millennial Muslim men, "It's okay to be a masculine, Muslim man. Embrace it. Revel in it. It is God's decree."' He also wanted to 'synthesise a culture that is unapologetically Islamic, not watered-down to appease non-Muslims.'

According to Nabeel, the dominance of feminism and secularism in countries where Muslims live negatively affects the way they practise Islam. His website offers what he sees as a much-needed corrective. 'Most websites for Muslims living in the West are run and maintained by women ... and with women comes feminism.' He wouldn't provide any examples, and simply maintained that this was a 'well-known' fact.

To Nabeel, feminism is a liberal scourge that clashes completely with Islam. 'Feminism denies what we Muslims call *fitrah*, man's innate disposition. Not only is it not compatible with Islam on an ideological basis, it doesn't even make sense according to biological or sociological fact.' Becoming the 'Alpha Muslim' means combating feminism using 'classical, authentic Islamic teachings'.

Though his teachings may dovetail with MRA ideology, Nabeel explicitly rejects the anti-Muslim strains of the manosphere. He thinks Red Pill Islamophobia comes from being threatened by Muslim masculinity. 'Part of the anti-Muslim sentiment comes from the fact that Western, white Red Pillers are afraid of Muslim men. We are the personification of "alpha", conquering their weak, feminised "beta" societies.' What's more, according to Nabeel, 'Muslims don't need Red Pill to tell us that men and women are a certain way and should behave in a certain way for society to function properly. We have the Qur'an, the words of the Prophet Muhammad, and sacred tradition.'

* * *

To some Muslim men, the Red Pill's broad anti-Islam leanings don't stop them from identifying with its values or with those of the men's rights movement. Most of the Muslim Red Pillers I tried to contact refused to be interviewed, even under pseudonyms. They suggested that as a journalist, I would deliberately misrepresent them or write with a liberal, feminist bias. While it's hard to know how many Muslims subscribe to this ideology, on platforms like Twitter, sentiments that align with Red Pill values are becoming more visible. Muslim women have coined the term 'Akh Twitter'[54] (Bro Twitter) to refer to Muslim men who tweet misogynistic statements under the guise of religious piety.

The women I spoke to about the uniqueness of Akh Twitter did not want to be identified, fearing that anything they said would result in online harassment and abuse. One woman, a university student based in London, told me: 'Akh Twitter basically refers to young Muslim men on social media who are constantly going on about how Muslim women aren't like the wives of the Prophet Muhammad. They say Muslim women aren't pious enough, while they secretly go out drinking, smoking hookah, flirting with girls in clubs—all while pretending that they're religious online.'

Another woman, Saba, told me that the ethos of Akh Twitter had less to do with religion than it had to do with a brand of 'toxic masculinity' that pervades some Muslim male communities. 'The men act like they're religious police,' she told me on Twitter. 'They are usually guys who wedge themselves into conversations that are about Muslim women and their experiences, to tell them what they should do, or what is prescribed in the

Sunnah of the Prophet. Then, when they are shut down by Muslim women, they get angry about it and openly question the devotion and faith of women they were referring to as "sister" ten minutes before.'

'I don't believe that everyone on Akh Twitter is a misogynist,' she clarified. Rather, she believed that this kind of attitude is an inevitable result of being a young Muslim man online who doesn't know much about the experiences of Muslim women, and who doesn't know about what feminism means. 'They end up getting exposed to toxic parts of the internet that tell them that Muslim women are being corrupted.'

Saba added that while Akh Twitter wasn't any more toxic than other male-dominated online spaces, the difference was that Muslim bros making these statements believed that they were doing so out of religious sincerity.

'They believe that when they're telling Muslim women they should wear hijab, or that they shouldn't be wearing make-up ... that they are doing this with the best intentions, and because of their faith. I'm sure that in many cases that's true, but at the same time these [men's] online communities aren't encouraging them to think about the experiences and environments these women live in, or the online contexts they exist in. Or even how women express their faith in different ways that men won't be able to understand. It encourages a black-and-white kind of thinking ... where you either follow Islam the "correct" way, or you don't.'

* * *

Despite these men's ideas or intentions, the attraction they feel to Red Pill cultures might have less to do with Islamic belief than with the many ways the internet allows men to express their masculinity without being checked. 'It's likely that there are a lot more men like this who really only talk about their vulnerabilities, especially when it comes to their masculinity, on the internet,' says Professor Amanullah De Sondy, author of *The Crisis in Islamic Masculinity*.

'Emerging ideas of feminism and gender rights are being incorporated into the discourse around British Muslim identity, which you can see on social media. But on the other side, there are men who will feel like their identities—personal, cultural and religious identities—are under threat because they're considered to be outdated, or less relevant ... So when they see online movements that reinforce their ideas, their stereotypes, it's completely natural for them to be attracted to that.'

De Sondy explains that this wider sense of male alienation is likely to be ingrained further in young Muslim men living in Britain, as they come to terms with how they can blend their religious and social identities as men with an environment in which more women are becoming educated, taking up white-collar jobs and, in some cases, becoming the breadwinner for their families.

'Women are becoming more visible, and the internet is a big factor in how they form their own social groups, having their own conversations that don't involve men,' he tells me. 'So, emerging men's rights groups may be a reaction felt by those who feel insecure about their position in society—including Muslim men, who, maybe felt they had fixed patriarchal positions that are now on the verge of disappearing. That's likely to be really scary for them.'

Abu Muawiyah disagreed with De Sondy's analysis, when I suggested that his workshops might be feeding off or legitimising these kinds of anxieties, which many men share irrespective of their religious beliefs. For Abu Muawiyah, workshops like the one I participated in are a religious duty, designed to keep young Muslims 'on the right path' and away from the 'evils of liberalism and Westernisation'.

He repeated that his views had been vindicated in wider society—through the election of Donald Trump over the 'feminist Hillary Clinton' and through the cult status of strongman leaders worldwide, like Turkey's Recep Tayyip Erdoğan and the Russian president, Vladimir Putin. Abu Muawiyah saw Islam as the answer to the emasculation felt by men living in the West, and hoped that his posts, videos and classes would help Muslims attracted by Red Pill to see their religion as the best way to 'combat feminism' and 'bring a better society for everyone'.

Laughing, he told me, 'Islam is the ultimate red pill.'

4

INFLUENCERS, GAMERS AND TROLLS

The Instapoets

It was a Wednesday evening in April 2017, and in the campus of the School of Oriental and African Studies, a constituent college of the University of London, I was sitting in a dimly lit lecture hall, in a room filled with students—mostly of black and South Asian descent—as they took to the front of the class to read poetry.

This on-campus open mic night ran once a term, and anyone who had written poetry or pieces of spoken word could come and perform. These events have always been staples of university life, but the atmosphere in the room tonight was electric. Every seat of the auditorium was filled. There was an enthusiastic hum of chatter between performances as pieces of poetry were commented on.

The woman sitting next to me was wearing a red-and-gold hijab, a bright-green Nike puffer jacket and a clean white pair of Yeezy shoes. 'Wasn't that just gorgeous, and so powerful?' she asked me. 'Are you reciting poetry too?' I told her I was not, and that I was here to interview a poet called Abdi Ahmad, a student at Westminster University, a few miles away from campus, who was performing tonight. I had come across his poetry not in a book or at a performance in a seedy East London bar, but rather on Instagram, where he posted screenshots of poems he was working on, and occasional videos in which he would perform, either directly to his phone's front camera, or while being filmed in a park or shopping centre.

* * *

Abdi isn't a well-known poet—at least, not yet. Of Somali origin, he was born and raised in Finchley, North London, where he lives with his parents. He is short—around 5′4″—and skinny, with a slender face and strong cheekbones. He has frizzy, black hair that he rarely combs, and his usual attire consists of black jeans, beat-up blue Converses and plain coloured T-shirts, over which he wears his favourite piece of clothing, an oversized, matte black North Face jacket. '£200! The most expensive jacket I've ever bought. My mum still doesn't know how much I paid for it.'

Abdi's poetry derives from a combination of Somali poetic traditions—his grandfather was a poet and used to perform in Mogadishu before moving to the UK—stories from the Holy Qur'an, and old-school hip-hop artists, like KRS-One, Rakim and Jeru the Damaja. When we met, he had been writing his own poetry for just under a year. Though he read poetry voraciously as a young man, and grew up in a household where music was always playing—his father remains a big fan of the legendary Somali musician and poet Abdullahi Qarshe—Abdi never thought he would write material of his own. 'I always liked reading at school, but not enough to think I could write things, you know? I always assumed I would go and study business, open my own shop, and that would be it.' Abdi did have a short stint as an MC in his teens, but it only went as far as 'one freestyle night at a club I snuck out of the house for.' He laughed. 'Other than that it was just rapping on the bus, or pretending I was a rapper from New York or something.'

But at the beginning of 2017, Abdi found himself wanting to try his hand at writing. The moment was a defining one—not just for him and his craft, but also for other young Somalis in the UK. Beyoncé, one of the world's greatest living musicians, had just released *Lemonade*—a grittier, more experimental and more confessional album than any of her previous full-length works. *Lemonade* was long awaited by fans and music critics, and when Beyoncé released a teaser video for the project, essays and think pieces flooded social media, expounding the messages their authors felt Beyoncé was attempting to convey. At the same time, attention had been directed at the twenty-seven-year-old British Somali poet Warsan Shire, the Young People's Poet Laureate for London, whose poetry is interlaced throughout *Lemonade*. CNN described her work as '[weaving] together the frictions and contradictions of diasporic life and the pain of leaving your roots behind'.[1]

Abdi had been familiar with Shire's poetry since before she became an internationally recognised name. Shire was just one of many young Somali Muslim poets whose work reached tens of thousands of people through social media. On WhatsApp groups, Abdi would often be sent links to Shire's poetry, from family and friends who were in awe of her talent.

Another British Somali poet who had become famous was Farah Gabdon, who performed a poem about women's rights and the horrific practice of Female Genital Mutilation (FGM) to thousands at an event for the Finnish League for Human Rights in 2016.[2] Another of her poems, called *This Poem Is All Woman*, has reached more than 37,000 people on YouTube since it was published online.[3] Other poets use Instagram, like twenty-four-year-old Faisal Salah, who has over 8,000 followers and who uses the platform to showcase his work and promote events and charitable causes. Zain Haider Awan, a British Pakistani, uses Instagram's 'stories' function to share his poetry, reflecting on Muslim identity and experiences to an audience of nearly 4,000.

For Abdi, and other young Muslim poets, using social media is more a necessity than a choice. 'A lot of us know from the outset that poetry is a very white environment,' he told me. 'Poets like me don't usually have agents. We don't know how to navigate the publishing world—even with our parents and family, the poetry was kept within our family. There wasn't any obvious way ... any idea that the poetry we grew up with could be published in a book and sold at Waterstones.' But the proliferation of social media meant a new, free self-publishing platform, with the potential for reach. Poets were starting to make names for themselves—crucially, on their own terms. Poets like Rupi Kaur and Nayyirah Waheed, initially dubbed 'Instapoets' because of their use of Instagram to publish and curate their own poetry, amassed millions of fans on social media—online followings which could then be fuelled into book sales.

Instapoets were 'responsible for poetry going viral at a time when the genre was alleged to be all but dead', *Bustle* magazine wrote in 2018, in a piece looking at whether new social media poets were undermining or reviving the art and traditions of literary poetry.[4] Meanwhile, *The Washington Post* considered the advent of Instapoetry to be a turning point for the art form— this was a new genre of poetry created for a global, online audience, and its legacy would be contingent on virality: 'Social media is upending what it means to consume poetry and what it means to create it. It has birthed a new cohort of bards known as "Instapoets" who share on Instagram tidy compositions that have the feel of literary selfies.'[5]

* * *

Abdi wouldn't describe his work as solely serving an online audience. But social media did offer important, direct connections with young, often Muslim, communities, who related to his poetry and who sometimes wrote their own. One such example is London-based Suhaiymah Manzoor-Khan, also known as 'The Brown Hijabi', whose poem *This Is Not a Humanising Poem* went viral in 2017,[6] racking up more than 60,000 views on YouTube and leading to numerous articles with titles like 'Why You Should Listen To This 22-Year-Old Poet Perfectly Slaying Islamophobia'. The poem's popularity made sense. It took on the concept of the 'Good Muslim', the idea that silence equated to integration, and the fact that mainstream media often portrays Muslims through simplistic, black-and-white frames. Manzoor-Khan recites:

> *This will not be a 'Muslims are like us' poem,*
> *I refuse to be respectable.*
> *Instead, love us when we're lazy, love us when we're poor …*
> *Love us high as kites, unemployed, joyriding, time-wasting, failing at school, love us filthy,*
> *Without the right-colour passports, without the right-sounding English.*[7]

Speaking to the American website 'Muslim Girl', Manzoor-Khan explained that her motivation for writing the poem came from a sense of frustration about the portrayal of British Muslim identity:

> I was sick of writing, or at least reading, about Muslims in this dichotomy where we're either suspicious and criminal, or 'victims too' and heroes. That's not a dichotomy that allows for all the nuances of life. And it's just as dehumanising to only ever be recognised when you contribute something deemed 'valuable' to society, and to only ever be applauded when you're publicly condemning and proving you're 'against' the 'Bad Muslims.'

She went on to say:

I, and other Muslims, don't exist in those binaries and I don't believe anyone really does unless they've allowed the state to co-opt them to its own ends—primarily the vilification and policing of Muslims. ... So that's why I was compelled to write it, really—the final push was the London Bridge [terrorist] incident and a tweet about how Muslim taxi drivers were giving free rides home. Of course they were. The fact it had to be stated was heart-breaking and dehumanising and understandable all at once. That's what I wanted to capture in this poem. That we're human even when you don't notice us.[8]

Most of the poets I spoke to expressed similar sentiments to Manzoor-Khan; while their poetry wasn't limited to Muslim issues, the presence of their religious identity in their work existed to challenge binaries around identity that they had little control over in any other medium or space. This was also why so many Muslim poets were turning to social media to push out their messages—here, they could finally express their identities on their own terms.

'With social media, there is a sense of ownership,' said twenty-five-year-old Mohamed Mohamed, a London-based poet and the founder of Muslim Poets UK.[9] 'For most people,' he remarked, 'their first interaction with poetry will come from a school environment, where they've been taught that certain things are poetry, and certain things are not. What young Muslim poets are doing when they use social media is sharing their work unapologetically and without regret.'

Started in 2016, Muslim Poets UK is a network that connects Muslim poets with each other, raises awareness of local writing workshops and performance opportunities, and helps new poets to make their mark on the poetry scene. 'Poetry is one of Islam's creative centrepieces,' the website states. For Mohamed, it is a much-needed organisation.

'The number of Muslim poets across different backgrounds is growing massively, and has been over the past five years,' he told me. 'In mainstream poetry spaces, there isn't a big emphasis on religion, and the main barriers are ones to do with class.' Muslim Poets UK hoped to create more offline spaces that Muslims from all walks of life could access, and where they would feel comfortable performing. 'For many Muslim poets, there are limits to what they can do and where they can perform—for example, many Muslim poets we work with won't perform at venues where alcohol is being served, or at nightclubs. Part of what we do is try to establish good open nights that are accessible to them. We also try to encourage larger poetry organisations and arts organisations to work with Muslim creatives they might not know about.

'The poetry space is a unique one for Muslim communities in the UK, and it's a really special one too,' Mohamed added. 'It's one of the few places where Muslims are actually allowed to be daring and creative, without compromising on their faith. We've had brothers and sisters who come to poetry nights because it aligns with their spiritual values, in a way that, for example, going to a music event wouldn't.'

For Mohamed, inclusivity and accessibility were key. 'Because poetry environments have a history of being warm and welcoming, and very accepting of people, it means for Muslims who feel they were excluded from some white-dominated cultural spaces, they know that they can freely express their faith at our poetry nights.'

* * *

For hours after we left the SOAS campus, Abdi repeatedly checked his phone, eager to know how his poem had gone down on social media. He had gained a couple of new Instagram followers—enough, he said, to warrant putting up a new video to test out some material he's working on. He planned on doing a few more open poetry nights to get his face out there, and hoped that, upon graduation, he might be able to pursue a part-time postgraduate course in poetry.

'I don't know how my parents would react to that,' he laughed. 'I guess it really is just a family tradition.'

The Gamers

Most days, in the early hours of the morning after he has finished *fajr* prayer, Amar Salim, twenty-four, fires up his custom-built home computer, complete with three electric-blue rimmed monitors, and puts on his Bose soundproof headphones. He stretches his arms, cracks his fingers and then places them around his fluorescent-green Xbox One controller.

This is a precious time for Amar. In a few hours, his parents will wake up. Both have severe disabilities, meaning that Amar needs to help them get up and get dressed, and make them breakfast. Later, he'll go to his local Sainsbury's supermarket, where he usually works evening shifts, stacking shelves and managing the stockroom. Often, he doesn't finish work until midnight.

In 2015, Amar had moved from his home in Burnley to London to study law. He had big dreams: to become a barrister, but also to experience life in the big city. Before moving, he had scarcely left his hometown for more than a few days, largely because he looked after his mother, who suffers from arthritis, while his father worked as a mechanic and moonlighted as a taxi driver. After his father injured his back, making him unable to stand for more than a few minutes at a time, Amar had had little choice but to leave his friends and classmates to move back home.

'I didn't have many friends when I came back, because most of them had left to go to uni or to work in other cities,' Amar says. 'So I was really only talking to friends of my parents, or the carer that came a couple of times a week.'

Amar ended up spending more time online, especially on YouTube. Initially he watched videos about football, but he soon became interested in gaming streams and playthroughs—videos that gamers record of themselves playing entire games in one sitting, usually providing commentary, not just on the game itself, but also on varied issues ranging from sports to current affairs. Sometimes, these streams consist of one player walking viewers through a game and discussing its merits and flaws. But most of YouTube's most popular gaming streams involve multiple players from across the world playing role-playing games, like *Fortnite*, *Call of Duty*, and *Dark Souls*, and having conversations with each other in the process. Sometimes, these streams can go on for more than twelve hours, and the format has become so popular that gamers can make millions in advertising and sponsorship revenue.

Gaming streams are one of the most avidly consumed forms of online content, not just on YouTube but across the entire internet.[10] Popular streams on YouTube regularly garner millions of views, while on Twitch, a video-streaming platform designed specifically for gamers, that number can be even higher, and indeed, more profitable. Steven Bonnell, a US-based gamer who made his name on Twitch playing *League of Legends* under the username 'Destiny', claimed he made $5,000 a month directly from Twitch subscribers, not even accounting for the extra revenue he made from advertisements on the platform.[11] Meanwhile, as competitive gaming becomes more established and backed by corporate sponsors, professional gamers, particularly those who play multi-player battle games like *Overwatch*, can make over $15,000 a month in international competitions.[12]

* * *

But for most people, gaming isn't about making money. Streams can also offer a sense of community for many amateur players and enthusiasts like Amar. Gaming culture has offered a range of new instant chat services and forums like Discord, the biggest social network for gamers. Launched in 2015, the service is now host to over 130 million users.[13] Its popularity comes partly from how easy it is to use, and the fact that users can host their own communities and chat groups. Some groups are huge and open for anyone to join, but most are much smaller and invite-only. As a result, there are now thousands of Discord communities on the platform, ranging from general discussion groups, like those that specialise in world politics, to more niche subcultural communities, home to lengthy discussions about obscure movies, to groups that only communicate with each other through Seinfeld memes.

When he first started gaming, Amar joined Discord's larger groups, which were hosted on big servers and consisted of thousands of players. They centred around his general interests. He was part of a group for Manchester United supporters, and another for fans of the TV series *Breaking Bad*. When the 2015 UK general election came around, he was part of a few groups where members casually talked about politics while they played games. Most players, Amar said, tended to be apathetic toward parties and politicians. 'They would say things like "fuck all politicians", while they were in the middle of shooting one of their opponents, or a monster or whatever,' Amar remembers.

Yet, those groups soon became darker. Soon, people were discussing the UK's European Union membership referendum and Donald Trump's presidential election campaign in America. In both cases, the winning campaigns had employed anti-immigrant, xenophobic rhetoric and fanned the flames of Islamophobia.[14] Scores of users identifying with the growing 'alt-right' movement, some of whom openly espoused violent, racist and 'ethno-nationalist' views, started to join Discord groups that Amar was a part of, including a group that was originally supposed to be for discussing the Premier League. With usernames like 'Deus Vult', an eleventh-century battle-cry used by Christian Crusaders, and 'Atomwaffen Division', a reference to the

US-based neo-Nazi terrorist organisation, these users would join gaming streams and openly talk about 'removing blacks and Muslims from the West', and how the election of Trump would 'make all good whites rise again'. They used racial slurs openly, and insulted Muslims in particular. Amar remembers the first time an Islamophobic slur was ever directed at him. His profile picture had been a photo of the Prophet's Mosque in Medina. 'There's a sand nigger here?' a fellow gamer had said. 'Deport him out of here now!'

Suddenly, the gaming communities that Amar had for so long felt he belonged to, and the part of the day he looked forward to the most, felt closed off to him. He stopped playing games for months, fearing that he would be subject to more anti-Muslim abuse, including physical threats.

Amar wasn't the only person to experience this fear. Black, Asian and minority ethnic gamers have frequently complained about the problems of racism, anti-Semitism and Islamophobia in gaming communities, and the tardiness of website administrators to respond.

Only recently have operators of gaming community forums shut down servers and groups because of hate speech and incitement of violence. After white nationalists marched in Charlottesville, Virginia in August 2017, killing one person and injuring dozens of others,[15] Discord shut down a number of alt-right servers, and promised to do more to tackle racially motivated hate speech on its platform and permanently ban users who espoused violent and exclusionary views.[16]

Despite this crackdown, however, anti-Muslim comments are still common on the main servers, Amar says. 'I haven't ever played on a normal server without hearing something anti-Muslim,' he laments. 'Players will say things like "kill all the fucking Muslims" when we're playing a shooting game, or they'll call every player who has a Muslim name a terrorist. Sometimes, even when you're playing a regular [non-violent] multi-player game like *Portal*, people will casually talk about killing Muslims, or say that they're all ISIS fighters. Some of it is really awful too, like they will talk about tearing off the heads of Muslims—stuff that you definitely wouldn't say out loud, but people feel they are protected when they say it online.'

* * *

It's for this reason that Amar decided not to play on big servers anymore. In 2017, he decided to become a member of the Discord group 'The Ikhwan', a small group of fewer than 1,000 members, open only to male Muslim gamers. Its terms and conditions were simple: members agreed to be respectful to each other, not to engage in hate speech, and to abide by Islamic rules and etiquette. That meant no swearing or foul language, no misogyny, and no racist abuse.

Any violation of these rules would result in being banned from the group by the admin, who went by the username 'Ibn Salah'. According to Amar, Ibn Salah, whom he had met on a Reddit thread, had faced the same issues as him as a Muslim gamer. He had set up The Ikhwan—meaning 'brotherhood' in Arabic—because he felt that mainstream gaming spaces were actively harmful for young Muslims. 'Not only because of the Islamophobia and racism,' Amar says. 'Also because these mainstream groups spread material that could lead to *kabirah* [major sins].'

Ibn Salah believed that as gaming became more popular and widespread, young men in particular would be exposed to gambling and sexually explicit advertising, both of which are prohibited in Islam. Furthermore, he warned that mainstream gaming communities promoted lifestyles that 'encouraged alcohol, drugs and pre-marital sex,' especially if they were promoted by professional gamers on YouTube. The purpose of The Ikhwan was to create a 'safe environment' for young Muslims to 'stay on the *deen* while knowing that they can have fun'.

The Ikhwan isn't the only Discord gaming room set up specifically for Muslims. 'Muslim Gamers', set up in 2017, has over 500 members. It is an active community, where users not only talk about games, but also have in-depth conversations about other aspects of their daily lives, ranging from seeking advice about marriage, to talking about interview techniques for jobs. 'We're open to all kinds of Muslims,' says admin Salman Mirza, a twenty-three-year-old graduate student based in North Carolina. Though he's not sure of the exact breakdown of users, he thinks that Muslim Gamers is 'probably the most international Muslim server on Discord'. 'Our members come from different backgrounds, different opinions,' he says. 'Some of us pray; others don't. The thing that unites us is that we're all Muslim, and that our Muslim identities have been attacked relentlessly, both in gaming and in our online experiences more generally.'

Other Muslim-orientated servers are much more religiously minded, and more selective about who gets to join. The 'Slaves of Allah' group, which has 700 members, describes itself as a 'server whose members are only servants to Allah'. The server is administered according to 'traditional Islamic roles'. For the admins, that means that Muslims are given priority over non-Muslims when it comes to leading discussions, that men are given a higher ranking in chat groups than women—meaning men's posts are shown above women's—and that private messaging between male and female members on the group is strictly forbidden. The long list of rules include:

Support of any obvious terrorist organization will result in a ban.

This server shall not be used as a platform to commit sins.

Maintain modesty at all times; especially with the opposite gender. There may not be giggling, unnecessary talk, usage of emojis, or shamelessness in a mixed company.

Do not make statements, in which you will have no gain if they are correct, but will lose much if they are not.

What happens in private messages will be as if it happened in this server as soon as it is brought to our attention.

In terms of music only *nasheeds* [Islamic songs] are allowed.

Profile pic. and usernames must be appropriate and *Awrah* [private parts] must not be shown.

'The rules are in place to keep the community as halal as possible,' explained 'Al Hanafi', one of the administrators of Slaves of Allah. Like every other Muslim gamer I spoke to, he had experienced anti-Muslim abuse online since he started gaming over a decade ago.

'It was rare to find other gamers who were Muslim in the past, but now there are more,' he told me. 'Most of them are younger, and it's important that they have spaces like this—ones that don't compromise their *deen*, where they are in the hands of good brothers and sisters when they are online.'

Al Hanafi wouldn't tell me his real name. His avatar on Discord was an image of Muhammad Ali training, and his user bio simply read 'In the name of Allah, the Most Gracious, the Most Merciful' in Arabic. He told me he was in his thirties and lived in New York City, where he worked in the Financial District. Gaming was his way to relax when his colleagues would go out drinking and clubbing after work. While he enjoyed playing games, he disliked the kind of content that was shared in most gaming communities. 'Even back in 2010, when everyone was hooking up their consoles to the internet, you'd hear filthy language—disgusting, sexual things. Lots of *haram*. And because you would hear it in your headphones, no one would know. Even people who lived in Muslim countries were saying this while they were playing games. I felt it was a big problem, right from the start.'

In 2014, Al Hanafi decided to make space in his apartment to host his own server, which he still stores in a cabinet under his oven. 'There wasn't any kind of Muslim-dedicated server back then,' he remembered. 'I had the choice of either forgetting about it, or doing something. I could ignore the filthy things being said, but I worried about our youth—how easily they can get influenced, and the fact their parents didn't know about it. So if I can at least make an halal environment, *inshallah*, Allah will reward me.'

By mid-2015, he began sending invites to Muslim gamers to join his server on Facebook groups and Twitter, amassing 'at least 200 in a single day'. To him, the rate of subscriptions showed that 'Muslims were desperate for a space online where they could be themselves'.

'The problem is that on social media—Facebook, Twitter, Instagram—even if you're a practising Muslim, you have to set limits on yourself because you're aware that people are watching. Like, if you have a beard, then people will assume things about you, like you're a Salafi or an extremist. Or if you wear niqab, then you must be oppressed. I wanted to make an environment where practising Muslims can be themselves, they can be in a place where they know Islamic rules will be followed. ... They know they won't have to give up parts of their Islam here.'

To Al Hanafi, Slaves of Allah is more than just a server to host Muslim gamers. It also represents the drive of young Muslims to create their own spaces in an environment that's increasingly hostile to their religious identity—what he calls a 'secular internet', which makes it difficult for 'practising Muslims to follow their *deen* while remaining connected to the rest of the world'.

It's a challenge that he believes affects every young Muslim who has an online social media profile, and a problem that few mosques, imams or community leaders are equipped to handle.

'Imams warn that the youth are exposed to *fitnah* [temptation]. They are right, but most of that *fitnah* is online!' he said. 'Online porn, gambling, drugs, everything you can imagine. And just because the youth are at home rather than on the streets, parents think they are fine. But they are in danger. I hope that groups like mine can attract them to a place that is safe, where they don't have to compromise who they are, and at the same time they can make friends in a healthy, halal environment.'

For Al Hanafi, creating that halal environment doesn't just mean forbidding particular images or discussions. It also means using his server to provide Islamic educational resources. 'We have a library in our Discord group, which has digital copies of the Qur'an, *hadiths*, commentary. Lots of books that are difficult to find, but that you can download instantly.' He also promotes Islamic conversations on the server. Each week, he or another administrator posts a section of the Qur'an on the discussion forum, which its members can discuss, either while chatting to each other, or while in the midst of playing a game. 'Last week, we spoke about an *ayah* [verse] in *Surat al-Baqarah*, which was all about being respectful to parents and caring for them. We were playing *Fortnite* at the same time!'

To Al Hanafi, though this type of conversation style might be unconventional, it is one that encourages members to discuss and engage with their faith. 'I've found that the youth will be more likely to talk and engage with Islam when you take the conversation to them. We could do the same thing but all sitting down in a *masjid*, or in a Facebook group, and most of them wouldn't speak, or they wouldn't say much, because they'd be intimidated by other people, how they look, if they're older than them,' he said. 'But in the game, everyone has an avatar, and it makes them feel like they're the same. Like they are on the same level. That's the beauty about the games *alhamdulillah* [praise be to Allah]. They provide a way of following the *deen* for the young people of today, without losing any of the traditions set by the Prophet Muhammad and his companions.'

* * *

Amar agrees. Since joining The Ikhwan, not only has he been gaming more, but he also believes he's more engaged with practising Islam than he used to be.

'The brothers and I will usually talk about Islam when we play,' he says. 'We talk about different aspects of Islam ... how you should behave, things like taking out loans and permissibility of interest, what charities you should pay *zakat* to. Other times, it's just chill—we just talk about football.'

To Amar, The Ikhwan is more than just a gaming community—it's part of his Muslim community too. He refers to other users as 'brothers', and when he speaks to them as he plays, he usually calls them *akhi* and bro. He says that he has had deep and intimate conversations with some, about difficulties in their marriages, relationships with their parents, and even when they struggle with following some parts of their religion. 'We are always there for each other as Muslim brothers, and as friends,' Amar says.

'We've been through a lot together, you know?' he adds. 'Even if we don't meet in this life, I am sure that I will be with them in the *akhirah* [afterlife].'

The YouTubers

'*Asssssalamu alaikum* guys, it's Faisal, and welcome to today's vlog!'

At twenty-three years old, Faisal Choudhry is one of the most popular Muslim YouTube personalities. His name kept cropping up in my interviews with young Muslims about their online experiences. Since he started uploading vlogs in 2016, Choudhry's YouTube page has amassed over 25,000 subscribers.

He uses his channel to promote Izaha, his Arabic-themed clothing brand, as well as *Freshly Grounded*, a podcast he hosts that focuses on contemporary Islamic issues, Muslim youth culture and current affairs.

At first glance, Choudhry's channel looks like that of any other YouTuber. His slickly shot and edited videos—anywhere between five and fifteen minutes long—document his days working from his west London office, hanging out with friends and going to the gym.[17] Other videos are more Islam-orientated, focusing on his daily routine during Ramadan, or on providing advice to Muslim teenagers at school or university. He uses similar video formats to other YouTubers, and has made videos trying out candy from Dubai,[18] recorded face-to-camera Q&As answering questions from his followers,[19] interviewed other well-known Muslims, and taken part in popular 'challenges', such as 'eating the world's spiciest noodles'—a stunt that became a YouTube trend in 2017. The thumbnails on Choudhry's videos also match the style and branding of other popular YouTubers; he titles his videos in all capitals, adding bold typefaces and emojis to his promo images for maximum attention and appeal.

At its most basic level, a YouTuber is someone who creates content for YouTube. According to YouTube's data, there were more than 1 billion active users on the platform in 2018,[20] about a third of whom create and upload videos.[21] But in reality, very few of these users would count as 'YouTubers' in the way that the term is used in contemporary discourse, to denote a specific cultural phenomenon: YouTube celebrities, video-makers who have achieved fame. 'The top YouTube stars aren't just popular: they are genuinely influential figures for their young fans,' wrote Stuart Dredge for *The Guardian* in 2016, when beauty and fashion YouTuber Zoella hit 10 million subscribers.[22]

Since then, YouTuber culture has expanded to span genres. YouTuber megastars range from PewDiePie, a Swedish gamer with millions of subscribers, to JJ Olatunji, known as 'KSI', a British comedian and prankster, to Tanya Burr, a British make-up artist whose channel has nearly 4 million subscribers, one of the highest followings on YouTube. With the platform's popularity comes big money too. Mainstream YouTubers can make millions, like Jake and Logan Paul, LA-based actors known mainly for their daily vlogs, who receive millions of views—usually from young children—and reportedly make over $10 million each from their YouTube videos alone. Such is the power of YouTube that the most prominent celebrities on the platform can work with established corporate brands as 'influencers'—a marketing strategy whereby companies advertise their products through people with a large online following, often in the form of review videos. Influencers' power is so strong that they can be paid to affect their viewers' purchase decisions.

Understanding the culture around YouTube influencers requires going back to the sociological theories set out by Richard Wohl and Donald Horton in 1956, when shared access to television was emerging. Wohl and Horton argued that when people watched TV, they were prone to forming deep-seated personal attachments to television celebrities, and investing immense emotional energy in them—a 'one sided affection ... in which they develop a kind of one-sided kinship and intimacy that makes them believe they know the celebrity, even though the celebrity has no idea they even exist.'[23] In the digital age, modern sociologists have expanded on this theory, arguing that not only are these relationships forming much faster through the normalisation of on-demand video across multiple social media platforms, but also that the emphasis influencers place on presenting themselves in ways that make them seem as 'real' and 'authentic' as possible means that one-sided relationships based on familiarity are likely to become much more personalised.

Furthermore, YouTubers can encourage hyper-personalised relationships by allowing their audiences to send them questions and requests for future content, name-dropping them on their videos, and even providing them with mailing addresses for fans to send them letters and gifts. Speaking to The Verge in 2018, Arienne Ferchaud described YouTubers' relationships with their audiences as '[blurring] the line between creator and viewer [in a way] that hasn't been possible before.'[24]

* * *

Most analysis of YouTube influencers tend to be focused on the impact of the commercial transactions that continue to shape the internet. And while parts of the Muslim online world have seeped into mainstream commercial spaces, most notably in the genres of 'modest fashion' and 'hijabi make-up' tutorials, channels like Choudhry's exist in a different space, one that navigates between conventional YouTube-based pop culture and orthodox teachings of Islam.

Choudhry provides content geared toward a demographic of young, urban British Muslims who express their religiosity through deep commitment to Islamic practices in real life, as well as in their online activities. For example, in one video, Choudhry addresses his 'Muslim followers' with advice on when to buy Apple products without accruing interest, something that many orthodox Muslims believe is prohibited in Islam. In another, he encourages his followers not to engage in '*haram* relationships', but rather to opt for a halal marriage, 'for the sake of Allah'. Of course, this argument has been made by numerous Islamic preachers and scholars who draw from theology to make their claims. Choudhry, on the other hand, makes his case without turning to scholarship. 'Marrying for the sake of Allah is such an amazing thing,' he says in a face-to-camera video on his channel, adding:

> You will be scared about getting married, definitely, yeah. But you have to remind yourself, I'm doing it for the sake of Allah. ... Just plunge into it, like if you've ticked all the boxes and you're at the

point now where you're asking 'should I get my *nikah*' ... all you're gonna be doing is prolonging it ... and potentially falling into sin by not having your *nikah*. So if any of you guys are thinking about getting your *nikah* ... but you're scared, this is me, saying to you guys, even I was scared and it was the best decision I ever made.[25]

Speaking to the Muslim lifestyle website Bahath, Choudhry said that the motivation for setting up his YouTube channel was because he felt there was a dearth of Muslim role models in the UK, beyond people like London Mayor Sadiq Khan and superstar baker Nadiya Hussain. For Choudhry, this was particularly a problem for young practising Muslim men, who felt they were at a disadvantage when it came to media representation. 'I [wanted to] show people that you can be a practising Muslim and also a regular part of society,' he said, adding, 'I am not trying to say I want to be a role model, and I guess that's one of the challenges of putting yourself out there on YouTube but, the Muslim youth need to see Muslim role models.'[26]

Choudhry's fans say his message resonates with them. 'He's really inspiring,' said one Muslim in his early twenties, whom I contacted on Instagram. 'I started watching his videos in 2017 when someone recommended me to check out his beard conditioning routine ... I'm a practising Muslim and I would say that I'm orthodox in my belief, and the truth is that it's rare to find people in the mainstream media or culture that reflect that. Usually, the people who are promoted in Western media are liberal Muslims or people who just have Muslim names or backgrounds, but they don't practise—they don't understand the world that I come from. Faisal is the first person I've come across who, I think, shows what a positive and fulfilling life you can have, while also following Islam properly.'

Other young Muslims, all between the ages of sixteen and twenty-five, expressed similar sentiments. As Rabbil Shams, nineteen, from Manchester said, 'When you're in school or college it can be tempting to not follow Islam properly, even if your friends are Muslim, because they don't always follow the religion in the right way, or they will do things that are *haram*, like going drinking or partying in mixed-gender environments. ... I think Faisal's videos are important because they can reach people like that. Since I started watching [his videos] I have been more conscious about the way I practise Islam and mindful of my intentions, *inshallah*. I started studying the *deen* more when I saw that he was doing it, and also balancing it with his work and social life—before then I always assumed you had to be proper religious to do that.'

* * *

Choudhry isn't the only person to create online content geared toward young, practising Muslims, and in the past few years, several young people have used YouTube as a way to convey similar messages. 'Yarimi', a channel hosted by the nineteen-year-old London-based YouTuber Nasser al-Yarimi, features videos like 'BRITISH TRYING JAPANESE CANDY!' and 'GREEN HAIR PRANK ON ARAB MUM!' along with videos of al-Yarimi reciting verses of the Qur'an and giving Islamic lectures, like 'I'm a sinner and Allah won't forgive me', in which he describes his journey from being a rapper in a London gang to a practising Muslim who doesn't listen to music.[27] Diya Eddine, another British Muslim YouTuber, with over 53,000 followers, has uploaded videos that jump on more recent trends, combining YouTube's prank and stunt culture with specific referential points of Muslim youth culture.[28] These videos have names like 'GIRLFRIEND PRANK ON MY MUSLIM FRIENDS!!', while other popular videos on his channel include daily vlogs from *umrah* pilgrimage and Islamic-themed spoken-word videos.

'Social media has made it easier to spread Islamic messages to more people, and there are different ways you can do that. ...

What you're seeing on YouTube, and [with] these young creators, is that they understand their audience and their Muslim experiences,' said Zeeshan Ali, a thirty-something London-based YouTuber who runs the channel 'Simle2Jannah'. Zeeshan has been running the channel, where he uploads halal parody videos, skits and comedy—sometimes with other Muslim influencers—for a few years, amassing over 100,000 followers in the process.

Zeeshan and I met at a café near his house. He was wearing a light-blue jacket over his *thawb* and had a mid-sized, roughly combed beard. He described himself as an 'earlier adopter' of technology. 'I remember when dial-up [internet] first came out, I was always interested in how I could put all our *nasheeds* and Islamic prayers in one place.' Zeeshan spent much of the '90s and early 2000s extracting audio from tapes he and his family had collected, initially transferring them to CD-ROMs, before eventually uploading them directly to Islamic websites for anyone to download. 'When YouTube first emerged in the mid-2000s, I had a big channel where I would upload prayers, *naat*, *nasheeds*, where anyone could listen to it. I had listeners from all over the world on my channel, sending me messages and requests for uploads. And at the time, I was one of the only people doing it.'

Though Zeeshan now focuses on his comedy skits, which range from satirising groups like the English Defence League (EDL), to commenting on football teams, to making fun of western stereotypes of Muslims, he attributes the rise of more orthodox Muslim YouTubers to a market gap. 'Muslims have Western used [the internet] a lot—they've used it to share details of events, or to send Islamic reminders or prayers to each other ... so it is natural that there is a big audience for Islamic material. The problem is that there is a portion of the Muslim community that don't feel represented, or they don't feel they can connect with what mainstream [less orthodox] Muslim culture on YouTube is,' he said.

Young Muslim YouTubers are important for addressing this lack of representation, Zeeshan argued, because 'they are able to connect with the youth in a way that many *masjids* can't'. 'That isn't to say that the *masjids* are irrelevant, or that they aren't important,' he added, noting that YouTube had its limits. He said that many Muslim YouTubers recognised their duty to remind their followers that they 'aren't scholars, and they shouldn't be the ones giving out Islamic rulings', and encouraged their viewers to go to the mosque.

For Zeeshan, Islamic content on YouTube has even helped to bring some Muslims closer to their religion, and away from activities that he believes go against Islam's teachings—something that he said was 'a risk for any Muslim growing up on the internet'. Online, he warned, young Muslims 'can be influenced by so many people who show off their riches, their cars, their girls—all of which they got through *haram* activities, like music, drugs, alcohol.'

Ultimately, for Zeeshan, the best thing about Muslim YouTubers was that they helped young people to see that having an Islamic lifestyle can be positive and fulfilling—and not as difficult as they might believe. 'What they are able to do is present Islam in a way that is more relatable,' he said. 'On YouTube you can show young Muslims, especially those who might be questioning their faith ... that you can stay on the right path and be funny, that you can have a good time. All the things that mainstream media says you can't do if you are a religious Muslim.'

Memes, Trolls and Shitposters

Every few minutes, Azad Khan, nineteen, dressed in a light-grey tracksuit, his black hair messy, refreshed the Facebook app on his phone and belted out a slightly raspy, low-pitched laugh. He was particularly proud today, he told me in a coffee shop near his house in East London. 'I made them proper furious, innit!' he laughed. He started scrolling again, only half-attentive to my questions. 'They're going mad on here, you know!'

Azad, a student studying electrical engineering, was telling me about his favourite pastime: posting memes on various Muslim Facebook and Instagram groups, with the sole intention of making members of these groups as angry as possible.

He had just received more than fifty angry responses to a meme he posted in the 8,000-strong Facebook group 'Halal Memes for Sunni Teens', showing a made-up Muslim woman wearing a black hijab and holding a bottle of Jack Daniel's whiskey. The caption under the meme read 'Liberal Muslims'. The meme was supposed to be offensive, implying that people who identified as 'liberal' Muslims openly contravene the rules of Islam.

Since then, Azad's meme has got over 1,000 likes and 200 shares, and been reposted on other platforms like Snapchat and Instagram. But it has also received a fair amount of criticism. 'You don't have a right to judge people's *iman* [faith], that's not what this group is here for,' one person wrote. 'Just another bro on this page trying to stir shit,' said another. 'Tired of these guys pretending they're righteous but probably secretly drink,' reads another retort.

Azad is indifferent to the criticism he receives. 'It's just trolling,' he said, a reference to the practice of making 'random unsolicited and/or controversial comments on various internet forums with the intent to provoke an emotional knee jerk reaction from unsuspecting readers to engage in a fight or argument'.[29]

For as long as message boards have existed, so have people who troll. And while in many cases, the consequences of trolling can be fairly minor—provoking online arguments, and maybe causing a comment thread to be shut down—in other cases, trolling can have severe costs, leading to cyberbullying, harassment and even real-life casualties. Fears over the physical safety of individuals as a result of trolling have even led the UK to reassess the law; certain forms of online harassment now constitute a prosecutable offence—a huge reversal after years of laissez-faire approaches to social media safety.[30]

Azad, of course, doesn't feel that his trolling will ever really harm anyone. He tells me that he tries to keep it as funny as he can, and that when he 'shitposts'—a term used to describe the kind of aggressive, troll-like memes he's known for—he does so with the intent of getting a few laughs, and 'just causing a mess'. 'I don't really care about how other people are practising Islam, or if they are even practising at all—it's irrelevant to me,' he told me, adding, 'I just do it for fun, or if I'm bored.'

But at the same time, for Azad, Halal Memes for Sunni Teens and the other Muslim meme groups he belongs to, also offer something rare to young Muslims: spaces to explore Muslim identity in a way that would be impossible in more regulated settings, whether on Islam-specific forums and message boards, or in the mosque.

* * *

There are dozens of Muslim meme groups on Facebook—'Top Rated Muslim Memes', 'Implying We Can Discuss Pan-Islamism', 'The Shariah Compliant Islamic Meme Bank'—most of which comprise thousands of members from across the world, who use references to politics, pop culture and trends within internet culture to discuss Islamic issues. Some groups cater toward more specific sets of Muslims, like the Shi'a-centred 'Shi'a Memes for Twelver Teens', and 'Sufileaks', a page that posts both memes and long discussions about the Sufi spiritual path.

One of the most popular Muslim meme groups is the 160,000-strong 'Halal Memes for Jannah Minded Teens', which posts humorous and often absurd memes to reflect the experiences of Muslims living in the West. One shows an advertisement for 'halal' pork chops in a supermarket catalogue, while another uses an image of Homer from *The Simpsons* kneeling on a prayer mat to show how Muslims prepare for exams. One post, which has been shared more than 4,000 times, is a video of the musician DJ Khaled making incomprehensible sounds to his baby son, with the caption, 'When you're told to recite in the mosque but can't speak Arabic.' A common theme in the group is mockery of debates around manners and modesty. One of its most popular posts shows a picture of two lollipops, one without a wrapper and covered in insects, and the other in its wrapper— an analogy sometimes used by conservative Muslims to indicate the importance of wearing hijab to ward off harassment. At the bottom of the picture reads the caption: 'That face when you don't know if insects are Halal'.

Speaking to *HuffPost*, Halal Memes for Jannah Minded Teens founder Abdirahman Osman, a twenty-one-year-old student at Vanderbilt University, said he was inspired by other meme groups he'd seen on Facebook and Tumblr, and the way they encouraged people to express their views and perspectives. 'Memes are a way that young people nowadays talk about the world around them and talk about social issues,' he said. 'Religion is no different from that, and people see that this page is a safe space for them and that they can find people who relate to them.' Osman added that the popularity of meme groups showed how young Muslims were generally more 'open-minded and willing to learn'. He hoped the groups like his would help young Muslims to 'find ways to connect with one another and share experiences and tackle the issues in the Muslim community'.[31]

Memes are considered to be part and parcel of the modern online experience, and while for the most part, they simply serve as momentary, humorous distractions for bored office workers and commuters, meme groups can also produce niche communities, 'fandoms' and subcultures, who communicate through a common online language. Muslim meme groups are no different, adapting and partaking in broader internet culture, while adding an extra layer of shared identity. Writing for *Wired* magazine in 2017, Rahat Ahmed describes Islamic meme groups as 'sharing many of the influences familiar to western audiences, but serving a completely different set of values'.[32] He argues that these spaces reveal 'a more playful side of Islam that isn't as public as the violent side that is widespread in media'. They also show a wide variety of Muslim beliefs, experiences and practices, and different levels of engagement with mainstream culture. 'Many of these images can be interpreted as devout attempts to play within the bounds of Islamic law while stretching it gently to meet pop culture at the edge. Others go much further, offering more forceful attempts to bring Islamic thoughts and beliefs into a Western frame of reference, and revealing a much stranger relationship between the two in the process.'

* * *

Most of the people I spoke to who visited Muslim meme pages were between the ages of fifteen and thirty. And while each had their own unique experiences of being part of these groups, nearly all agreed that what the groups offered was an easy-to-access online space where they could express themselves, away from the eyes of their parents and other community elders, and from individuals and groups who are hostile to Islam. Facebook groups like Halal Memes for Jannah Minded Teens are private, which allows their members to feel they can be relaxed and open when talking about their faith, and that they don't have to compromise their Muslim identity in order to fit in.

'You can talk about Islamic issues in a way that you can't in a mosque,' says Sara Adel, a nineteen-year-old university student based in Birmingham, and a member of several Muslim meme groups. 'Obviously, it's a place to go when you want to have a laugh, and people tend to post memes that are really about Muslim culture—so things like sneaking out of the house to go dating, or the hypocrisy of Muslim men having sex before marriage, but demanding virgin women when they get married. That type of [content] is funny to us, but at the same time it's a very real experience for most young Muslims living in the UK. And when you can't talk about things like sex outside of marriage, or relationships, or even challenging parts of being a Muslim living in 2018, when it comes to having doubts or questions about the faith, the internet is the place you end up going to. I know that I myself am more comfortable talking about more serious cultural issues in a Facebook group, than I would be talking to my family or talking to an imam.'

Sara describes how the growth of these groups has meant that some Muslims are being forced to meet others who practise the religion differently, or who have different lived experiences to themselves. 'I think these groups have been good in presenting a wider range of Muslim experiences, especially to Muslims who come from communities that are insular, or where people have only known other Muslims in their own communities.' She mentions a video she saw in 2016 of Muslims who identified as queer being interviewed in the run-up to the Pride festival in the United States. 'Initially, the comments under the video were derogatory. You know, the usual stuff about how being gay isn't permitted in Islam and how it was an abomination,' she says. 'But then, members of the group who hadn't ever really posted before started talking about how they were both practising Muslims and LGBTQ, basically telling them that [others] had no right to determine if they were or weren't Muslim ... Of course, it caused a big scene, and I think eventually the moderators had to shut the conversation down. But the fact that these straight Muslim men had to actually debate LGBTQ members in the group was a new thing for them. It just goes to show that it wasn't really the mosque that forces Muslims to interrogate their views, but a group that largely consists of cartoons and memes!'

While Islamic meme groups open up spaces for young Muslims to explore their faith, the existence of these lightly regulated communities can pose challenges, especially for those whose job it is to moderate the groups and enforce the rules of conduct. For these mods, this doesn't just mean ensuring that members follow Facebook's guidelines about harassment, safety and protecting user data; it also means making sure that the community abides by certain Islamic principles.

Munira Bouramann, twenty-two, a former moderator of the Facebook group 'Implying We Can Discuss Pan-Islamism', which had over 5,000 members before closing in April 2017, told me that this was often more difficult to enforce than she had assumed. 'You tend to think that because the people joining these groups are Muslim, that they will practise their Islam online as well as offline,' she said. 'But I would usually get at least one direct message a week, usually from a woman, telling me that she was being harassed by a male member, or she was being abused online for not wearing a hijab, or for showing her face in her profile picture, and being called things like a slut or a prostitute. All this was being done outside of the public threads, through direct messages,' she added.

'Usually we screened people who wanted to join the group. We would ask them questions about their *niyyah* [intention] when joining the group. Did they want to pursue knowledge? Or have a community? But we can't stop people from being disingenuous. So you would have people who would join our group and pass the screening, only to then harass members and make them feel uncomfortable.'

Despite these issues, Munira, who now works in IT consulting in the Midlands, believed that the Islamic meme groups 'genuinely do show the positive future for young Muslims across the world', adding that while there were people who broke the rules, and people who, like Azad Khan, would deliberately troll and cause mischief, the majority of conversations and debates were well-intentioned and carried out in good faith. Moreover, she said that the Islamic meme groups were visual evidence of the diversity of the Muslim community.

'If you look at the media, they tend to report on Muslims living in ghettos, or being backward, or [living] like they never left their homelands, but they never actually ask young Muslims what their lives are like. And young Muslims, like the ones in our group, have always felt silenced or like their voices don't matter. But the group had so many interesting conversations, and so much humour and wit as well. The point of the group was to create a space where people could discuss Islam without being told they weren't qualified to do it, or that they should just shut up and pray.'

Munira told me that the group was a place 'where a lot of Muslims could feel less alone'. This was especially true for converts to Islam, known amongst Muslims as 'reverts'. 'In many cases, reverts lived isolated lives, because they were too shy to go to a mosque, but also they were ostracised by their families for their decision to be a Muslim,' Munira said. 'We made sure our group was welcoming by providing advice, but also providing communities they could depend on.' Munira told me that during her tenure as a moderator of the group, at least three reverts had joined and had used the group to find other Muslims living nearby, because they had been kicked out of their family homes. 'Without the group, they probably wouldn't have found places they could stay in until they were back on their feet,' she told me. 'Regardless of all the drama that went on in the group, there was a strong community, and I'm proud I was able to help build that.'

* * *

Azad Khan also feels that the meme groups offer a unique and valuable sense of community to young Muslims like him, even if his contribution is mainly to troll. 'It's difficult to be funny when you're in a mosque, or even in a setting where it's like, really religious,' he said. 'And I don't want to be the guy who does dirty humour, or stuff that goes against my religion. So these groups at least allow me to be me, a funny guy, while also keeping in line with the teachings of Allah and the Prophet Muhammad, peace be upon him.'

Azad knows that sometimes he goes too far, and doesn't mind being called out whenever he does cross the line. 'Ultimately I just want to be the best Muslim I can be, you know? And I would rather be told in the group that what I'm doing goes against an Islamic teaching, than to try to be funny outside that setting and then head toward things that are un-Islamic.'

He paused and scrolled on his phone. 'Can you wait a second?' he asked me. 'There's this chat that's about to pop off, and I want to post a meme.'

5

EXTREMISM, COUNTER-EXTREMISM

The ISIS Propagandist

On a Thursday night in February 2016, I was scouring a dimly lit housing estate in East London for a man called Abu Muntasir for one of my last assignments as a reporter at BuzzFeed News. I had heard that Abu Muntasir was using Twitter to find vulnerable young Muslims and draw them into private conversations on apps like Telegram, attempting to convince them to join ISIS. No one knew who the man was. Like in most cases, Abu Muntasir was a *kunya*, an Arabic alias used on social media to protect someone's identity while also playing into the fantasy of emulating the companions of the Prophet Muhammad.

When I went searching for Abu Muntasir, the UK was in a state of crisis. In 2015, it was estimated that around 600 British people had travelled to Syria to join ISIS, most of whom were young and British-born, and were said to have been manipulated through social media platforms into pledging allegiance to Abu Bakr al-Baghdadi, the self-styled 'caliph' of ISIS.[1]

At the time, most of these young people were able to use social media to find the fixers and handlers needed to get them into Raqqa, then ISIS HQ, who provided them with money, shelter, transport and, upon their arrival, spouses. Instructions on how to enter the self-styled caliphate were distributed using JustPaste.it links through virtual private networks, largely undetectable to authorities or internet service providers who might report suspicious activities to them.[2]

There had been some high-profile cases of young British Muslims leaving the UK to travel to Syria that still loomed large in public memory. In February 2015, three teenage girls left their homes in Bethnal Green, East London, to travel via Istanbul to Raqqa, where they married ISIS fighters.[3] Just a couple of years before, the twenty-two-year-old Ifthekar Jaman left his home in Portsmouth, South-West England, to go to Raqqa, having made contact with ISIS commanders on social media. Jaman eventually became instrumental in ISIS's recruitment of Western foreign fighters.[4] A proficient computer hacker, he was able to set up secure communication lines with other British fighters including Asad Uzzaman, Muhammad Hamidur Rahman and Muhammad Mehdi Hassan, all from Portsmouth, who referred to themselves as the 'Al-Britani Brigade Bangladeshi Bad Boys'.[5]

With hundreds of young people considered vulnerable to radicalisation, social media companies came under scrutiny for their lax approach to the threat, and were accused of themselves aiding and abetting Islamist extremist activity. In August 2016, Keith Vaz, then chairman of the Home Affairs Select Committee—a cross-party group of British MPs who work together to make policy recommendations to the Home Office—accused large social media companies of 'consciously failing' to fight terrorism and extremism:

> We are engaged in a war for hearts and minds in the fight against terrorism. The modern front line is the internet. Its forums, message boards and social media platforms are the lifeblood of Daesh [ISIS] and other terrorist groups ... Huge corporations like Google,

Facebook and Twitter, with their billion-dollar incomes, are consciously failing to tackle this threat and passing the buck by hiding behind their supranational legal status, despite knowing that their sites are being used by the instigators of terror.[6]

MPs and security services were starting to ask what responsibility—and capability—social media giants had to prevent the distribution of extremist content. These were questions that few pundits, let alone politicians, had any real answers to.

* * *

Abu Muntasir, I had been told, was one of those harnessing social media in order to radicalise young Muslims. On Twitter, where he was followed by over 2,000 people, he distributed ISIS-related material—videos, Tumblr blogs, links to private networks where people could interact with '*mujahideen* fighting in Shaam [the Levant]'. Those who told me about him had reported him to Twitter for sharing such content, but said that their attempts to shut down his account hadn't worked. At the time of writing, his account no longer exists, but in 2016, he was freely distributing material—including videos of beheadings, battles, and speeches from ISIS fighters—to people in *Dar al-Kufr*, or the land of disbelief.

As I approached the worn, sunburnt red door of the apartment, I realised I was nervous and that my hands were shaking. None of my editors knew I was meeting Abu Muntasir, or that I had been in contact with him. In fact, I didn't even know if I had a story, or whether it would ever be published. I had no idea whether British authorities knew about Abu Muntasir. I knocked on the door, and took a couple of steps back. Could this man, a guy who lived a few tube stops away from my central London office, be one of the biggest threats facing the British Muslim community, and the British state?

Abu Muntasir was a small, plump man. He wore a white skullcap, grey Nike sweatpants and a plain black T-shirt that was slightly too small for him and hugged his belly. He had a short, scruffy black beard, framed by a thin, pencil moustache that touched his upper lip. His chubby cheeks were marked by red patches of acne, some of which was hidden by his curly dark-brown hair. '*Assalamu alaikum, akhi*,' he said, with a slight smile on his face. 'Glad you could make it, *alhamdulillah*.'

The flat was cramped. Before he let me in, Abu Muntasir went over the rules for the interview. I wasn't allowed to talk about his family, and I wasn't allowed to disclose personal details of his life, like his occupation. I certainly wasn't allowed to say that he was a 'supporter of ISIS'—something he said 'is a problem with media people like you—you always see things in black and white'.

Abu Muntasir spent most of his free time online, on a desktop computer that took up most of the space in his living room. I sat down on a small, black leather couch in the corner, taking out my Dictaphone and notepad, while he took a seat at his computer desk and turned on both of his large external LCD monitors. On the left monitor was Abu Muntasir's Twitter feed—a stream of posts in Arabic and English, with plenty of news clips from Syria and Iraq, peppered with Qur'an recitation videos and occasional tweets about football matches from Sky Sports and PaddyPower, a UK-based betting company. On the right monitor was a live video stream from Al Jazeera Arabic, which tended to cover the Syrian civil war around the clock. The desk was clean, and above the wall was a passage from *Surat al-Baqarah*, printed in black on a background of gold and mounted in a chestnut-coloured frame.

When I asked Abu Muntasir about the allegations I had heard that he was using Twitter to link young British people with ISIS, he laughed. 'This is a fantasy!' he said. 'It is not my job to do this. I put out material I see from Syria, that I see the *mujahideen* fighting against Bashar al-Assad, and everyone who sees it can make their own decision, *inshallah*.' According to Abu Muntasir, all he was doing was 'showing the atrocities of what is happening in Syria, to our Muslim brothers and sisters', whose plight, he claimed, Muslims living in the West were not paying enough attention to. He said they were 'more preoccupied with their own lives, making money, buying expensive houses and fast cars'.

Abu Muntasir told me he believed that the best society is one that practises what he calls 'normative Islamic values', and said that true justice can only be achieved under Sharia. He emphasised that this was 'not an uncommon belief' among Muslims. 'We believe that Allah's rule is the best rule, that Allah is the most mighty and just. So why would we not want to live under Allah's laws?' He said he couldn't comment on whether ISIS or Al-Baghdadi were living up to those principles. 'Allah knows best. If he decides that ISIS are correct, then *alhamdulillah*, I will believe this.'

Abu Muntasir didn't deny that he knew people who were in ISIS; nor did he deny that people had sent him direct messages on the platform asking about making *hijrah*—a migration—to Syria. When this happened, 'I tell them that I do not know how to get to Syria, but there are other people online that do.' He denied directly encouraging young and impressionable Muslims to join ISIS, and maintained that if his content did lead people to make that decision, 'there are more complicated reasonings behind it'. But, at the same time as eschewing responsibility, Abu Muntasir also said, 'If what I do is helping people realise that we are a global *ummah* of Muslims, and that *ummah* is suffering, then *inshallah*, Allah will reward me for that. But I do not have any other motives other than to watch what is happening, and to wake Muslims up to what is happening to our community.'

Abu Muntasir ended the interview on that note, telling me that he needed to pray *isha* before it was too late. He did not accept any of my subsequent requests for follow-up interviews.

* * *

Of course, what Abu Muntasir was doing wasn't unique. The Twitter account 'ShamiWitness', run by the twenty-four-year-old Indian ISIS propagandist Mehdi Biswas, had over 17,700 followers before it was shut down in 2014.[7] Biswas was also spreading ISIS-related content, under the guise of documenting the Syrian civil war as a citizen journalist.

Other Twitter, Facebook and Instagram accounts acted in similar ways, scraping together ISIS-related video, audio and pictures from social media and republishing them to their audiences, many of whom were supportive of ISIS and other Islamist militia groups.[8] When ShamiWitness was shut down, ISIS supporters even came out to defend Biswas using arguments that would now be associated with reactionaries and even the alt-right. 'I disapprove of what you say but I will defend to the death your right to say it. #shamiwitness', one supporter tweeted, citing the famous defence of free speech often misattributed to Voltaire.[9]

'These kind of accounts were important in the way that they were distributing information across the internet,' said Shiraz Maher, director at the International Centre for the Study of Radicalisation and Political Violence at King's College London, and one of the first academics to research the process of online radicalisation in militant Islamist spaces. I met him at his office in the King's Strand campus in London. On the walls of the room were numerous charts, detailing all the foreign ISIS fighters that the institute had managed to track through social media networks. The times and dates that these fighters had made contact with researchers at the institute were meticulously recorded.

'It's not necessarily the case that the internet or social media have caused radicalisation,' Shiraz explained. 'Many of these guys already had grievances or motivations to go, regardless of whether the internet existed or not. The key thing about social media is how fast propaganda can be sent around, and how easily they can be seen and replicated.

'Social media companies have been better at responding to warnings of extremist content, and, thanks to governmental and social pressure, they've been able to detect content that could be dangerous or that promotes harm. But the issue is that it still might not be fast enough—especially when, as a piece of content gets taken down, it can get replicated multiple times and then distributed, without social media platforms even knowing.'

That said, the internet alone wasn't usually enough to motivate violent radical behaviour. 'The internet plays an important role in terms of disseminating information and building the brand of organisations such as the Islamic State,' Shiraz told me. 'But it's recruiters offline—people who can build human networks—that are almost always the most effective in getting someone from being a passive supporter who might be intrigued by online content to being an active participant who is willing to fight and die for the cause.' In that sense, men like Abu Muntasir have a limited influence in recruiting people to travel to fight.

'Social media is an effective tool for making the process happen faster, at least faster than the authorities can keep up with,' said Shiraz, 'but there isn't much evidence to suggest that the platforms are the root cause behind people making those decisions to begin with.'

Despite this, the British government still believes that when it comes to radicalisation, social media companies should bear the brunt of the responsibility. Security Minister Ben Wallace referred to large tech companies as 'ruthless profiteers' who refused to work with the government to combat extremism, and threatened to tax the industry because of its alleged inaction.[10] In 2019, Digital and Culture Minister Margot James said she wanted the government to bring in legislation forcing social media platforms to remove illegal content, in order to 'prioritise the protection of users, especially children, young people and vulnerable adults'.[11] The aim is commendable, and such measures might indeed help to curb the problem. But, if men like Abu Muntasir show anything, it's that violent online material is quickly replicated, and spreads across platforms faster than regulations can control. That means that social media companies will always be a few steps behind, and that many of those who are most vulnerable to radicalisation—whom regulations are supposed to protect—are often only found when it's far too late.

Prevent Strategy

It was a cold night in February 2016, and in a packed-out community centre in Walthamstow, North-East London, a woman wearing a large winter jacket, boots and a black-and-silver hijab was speaking about the time her son had been questioned by his teachers about whether he supported the Islamic State. 'He was so frightened, and was completely on his own,' she told the audience. 'He was taken aside by teachers because of hearsay and rumours ... there wasn't any evidence to even show he had been looking at material from ISIS,' she said. 'It just proves that Prevent is targeting and singling out Muslims, especially ones that are practising. And now, because of the statutory duty placed on teachers, even more of our children will be at risk of becoming criminals, just because they are Muslim.' A number of people in the audience shook their heads in agreement. Some stood up to applaud her.

I heard several stories that night about the government's counter-extremism 'Prevent' strategy, which places a statutory duty on teachers, religious leaders, doctors, social workers and others working in public institutions to report anyone they suspect of vulnerability to radicalisation.[12] Tonight was one of several community events held by Prevent Watch, an organisation that tries to support people impacted by Prevent, and raise awareness of the programme's failings and overreach. At the time, Prevent Watch was a fairly new organisation set up by Walthamstow resident Haras Ahmed. It mainly communicated through Facebook and Twitter, either with news stories about the Prevent strategy, or highlighting cases that people brought forward about being subjected to interrogation or questioning under Prevent.

Other speakers at the event spoke about teenage students who said they had been referred to the counter-extremism programme on spurious grounds, including being involved in pro-Palestine activism, and gaining 'sudden interests' in politics and worldwide current affairs. Some mothers and fathers claimed that their children were being questioned under Prevent measures because they had become more religious, growing out their beards, or adopting the hijab. A few absurd cases had even made national news, such as the four-year-old boy whose nursery teachers nearly reported him because he had drawn a 'cooker bomb'—actually a cucumber—or a fourteen-year-old questioned by teachers over his use of the word 'eco-terrorist' in a French class.[13] As one parent told me that night, 'It's created a culture of fear in our schools and our communities. We're British, and we should be treated like other British people. Why are we being targeted, and our children being made to feel afraid, by policies that target us because of our religion?'

* * *

Throughout my time covering Muslim affairs as a reporter, and in the course of writing this book, the UK government's Prevent strategy was the most common subject that came up in interviews. Like the parent who spoke to me in Walthamstow, most of my interviewees argued that the initiative had demonised Muslim communities, both online and offline. Prevent is part of the British government's 'Contest' programme, set up in 2003 to combat the threat of violent, and, more importantly, unorganised extremism, in response to the threat of radicalisation and international terrorism from groups like Al-Qaeda following the 11 September 2001 attacks.[14] Contest centres around the 'four Ps', of which Prevent is one component, the others being Pursue, Protect, and Prepare.

The Contest counter-terrorism strategy was largely a step into uncharted territory. The threats that the UK faced were no longer from organised, centralised groups like the Irish Republican Army, or geopolitical entities like the Soviet Union. Al-Qaeda was a decentralised militant group; its reach spanned various countries, and it didn't recognise the nation-state or its sovereignty.[15] 'We'd never done anything like it before ... Al-Qaeda was a new kind of terrorist outfit, where there was no possibility of negotiation, and it appeared bent on causing maximum destruction,' said Sir David Omand, former director of GCHQ and the person who spearheaded Contest.[16]

In its original iteration, Contest was a small network of localised projects, working primarily within the Department of Communities and Local Government. It involved encouraging mosques to hire English-speaking imams and to be more aware of vulnerable members of the congregation who might be susceptible to extremist narratives. After the 7 July 2005 bombings in London, Contest was expanded. Local authorities were given responsibility to allocate funding to community groups, such as boxing gyms and football clubs, who could deliver projects to vulnerable young people, the idea being that providing activities and support networks would prevent young people from falling into the hands of extremist groups.[17]

Most Prevent coordinators and advisors I spoke to told me that the Prevent arm of Contest was 'messy' during this period, and that its implementation and chances of success were largely dependent on each local authority, how much money they had been allocated, and who had been receiving money. 'Prevent was all about politics,' one project coordinator based in West London told me. 'It ended up putting Muslim groups against each other … some were courting local government for more funds by telling decision-makers that other projects weren't effective, or that the people running them were themselves extremists or extremist sympathisers.' She wished to remain anonymous, and told me that even though Prevent's structure had changed and most of these local groups were no longer involved, animosity between those competing for money was still rife.

'There are a lot of people who you see today, online, who rail against Prevent,' she said. 'The ones who spearhead the campaign to end Prevent, who say the programme spies on Muslims—they're the same ones who, just a decade ago, were singing its praises so they could be at the front line when grants were being given out.'

It's a sentiment that other local Prevent project coordinators agreed with. 'Prevent was difficult to execute, partly because of the suspicions that Muslim communities had about being monitored for acts that they weren't responsible for … but they were also suspicious of the people running programmes, and whether or not they were experienced,' said Ismael Lea South, who worked on Prevent projects in South London focused on countering extremism and gang violence. Having left Prevent in 2008, in 2016 he was now running the Salam Project, an organisation that aims to combat gang violence and prevent people from joining gangs by organising workshops, seminars, urban poetry events, motivational talks, film showcases and conferences around the UK.

Ismael told me that on a wider scale, Prevent's objective wasn't made clear. 'The government said that Prevent was about winning hearts and minds … but there was no evidence it was trying to do that. There was no real outreach, there was no attempt to understand why some [Muslim] communities were sceptical towards it. There was just money flying around, and big expectations of what should be achieved, without any assistance or planning how you would achieve them.'

Prevent was focused on local communities up to 2011. When the Conservative–Liberal Democrat coalition came into office, Prevent underwent its first major overhaul, moving from the jurisdiction of the DCLG to the Home Office under the then home secretary Theresa May.[18] May's decision to change the structure of Prevent was in part justified by groups like Islam4UK, an Islamist radical group led by the self-styled 'radical' cleric Anjem Choudary, who was formerly a senior figure in the extremist group Al-Muhajiroun, which had carried out a number of demonstrations against the British Armed Forces at memorials for deceased soldiers.

Under the new structure, Prevent became less informal. Fewer organisations would be involved in producing counter-extremism materials and developing policies to counter radicalisation, and those that did get a seat at the table tended to be think tanks like the Quilliam Foundation, academic departments like the International Centre for the Study of Radicalisation at King's College London, and non-governmental organisations like the Active Change Foundation. The focus moved from fostering community cohesion to preventing the spread of 'radical' and 'Islamist ideas'.[19] The most significant change was Prevent's sharper focus on 'non-violent extremism'—an ambiguous term even to people who are bound by the programme's statutory duty, including people I spoke to who have been working on the project as coordinators, advisors and private-sector consultants.

In part, this new emphasis on non-violent extremism came as the result of the growth of social media as the dominant medium by which ideas could be distributed and exchanged. In 2013, research conducted by the RAND corporation in conjunction with the UK Association of Chief Police Officers and UK

Counter Terrorism Units found that 'the internet may enhance opportunities to become radicalised and provide a greater opportunity than offline interactions to confirm existing beliefs'.[20] Although it didn't go as far as to say that the internet was radicalising people, it did suggest that the existence of social media allowed the 'radicalisation process' to accelerate. In 2015, more than 800 Britons were estimated to have travelled to Syria to fight with the Islamic State. In the government's counter-extremism strategy report that year, Home Secretary Theresa May declared, 'When non-violent extremism goes unchallenged, the values that bind our society together fragment.'[21]

* * *

Little is publicly available about how Prevent's annual budget of around £40 million has been distributed and spent.[22] In the course of my years as a reporter, all of my requests under the Freedom of Information Act 2000 for details about Prevent spending have been denied, either for not being specific enough, or for reasons of national security.

We do know that the Home Office conducts some of its Prevent work through its Research, Information and Communications Unit, which, according to documents seen by *The Guardian* in 2016, attempts to employ 'strategic communications to effect behavioural and attitudinal change'.[23] RICU's staff consists of psychologists, linguists and anthropologists. Funded by part of Prevent's overall budget, it not only monitors online activity in 'extremist' spheres, but also helps to create counter-narrative propaganda to challenge it—some of which is developed by organisations like Breakthrough Media, a London-based PR agency that creates websites and social media content for carefully vetted Muslim civil groups, in order to 'influence online conversations by being embedded within target communities via a network of moderate organisations that are supportive of it's [*sic*] goals'.[24]

Gradual radicalisation, sometimes referred to as the 'conveyor belt theory', is a relatively new concept in counter-terrorism, and some critics of Prevent argue that allowing the theory to shape government policy on radicalisation and extremism has been misguided. Fahid Qurashi, a sociology lecturer at Staffordshire University, argues that the Prevent strategy 'attempts to control the future by acting in the present' and that it has built a 'surveillance infrastructure, embedded into Muslim communities'— in terms of both policing offline, and monitoring online by security services and private internet service providers.[25]

Others worry that aspects of Prevent that aim to combat non-violent extremism risk targeting people based on their views, even if they pose no risk of violence. 'There is no evidence to prove that extremist views graduate into violence,' said Rizwaan Sabir, a lecturer at Liverpool John Moores University. 'Ideas may justify violence but they do not cause them.'[26]

An open letter published in *The Independent* in 2015 argued that Prevent's markers for radicalisation, such as 'growing a beard, wearing a hijab or mixing with those who believe Islam has a comprehensive political philosophy' serve to reinforce 'a prejudicial worldview that perceives Islam to be a retrograde and oppressive religion that threatens the West'. It also said that:

> The way that PREVENT conceptualises 'radicalisation' and 'extremism' is based on the unsubstantiated view that religious ideology is the primary driving factor for terrorism. Academic research suggests that social, economic and political factors, as well as social exclusion, play a more central role in driving political violence than ideology. Indeed, ideology only becomes appealing when social, economic and political grievances give it legitimacy. Therefore, addressing these issues would lessen the appeal of ideology.[27]

These arguments have been criticised, not just for their hostility to Prevent, but also for the ways they have used the internet and social media, as one Prevent project manager told me, 'to disseminate falsehoods into their networks, and misrepresent what the programme is supposed to achieve'. He claimed that others who work on Prevent felt the same way, and said that claims that the strategy unfairly targets Muslims 'hinders the work we do to help vulnerable people'. 'They're not all Muslims, and we're actually very careful to ensure local communities, and parents, know that this isn't about targeting. It's about making sure people are aware of the dangers both online and offline, and it's about making sure that vulnerable people are protected before it's too late.'

This sentiment is echoed throughout the book *The Battle for British Islam: Reclaiming Muslim Identity from Extremism*, written by Sara Khan, the former head of the counter-extremism charity Inspire, who was appointed to the post of lead commissioner for the Home Office's Commission for Countering Extremism in 2018. Khan argues that the reality of Prevent is far from the 'scare stories' narrated by groups like Prevent Watch and the grassroots advocacy organisation CAGE. A prototypical Prevent intervention, Khan says, is multi-faceted. No cases have ever resulted in convictions or prison time, but rather they consist of a series of 'safeguarding measures', which can include being referred to counsellors and mental health specialists, or being connected to mentorship schemes.

One response to this defence is that there has been little public information about how Prevent and its affiliate programmes actually work. To Khan, this is because 'Prevent does not aim to publicise cases, as the aim is to ensure that individuals resume their lives without any stigma or punishment.'[28] In contrast, she argues, groups that lobby against Prevent are 'less reticent' about making known details of individual cases. She also says that they ignore that Prevent isn't just about stopping terrorism; it is also about 'safeguarding children at risk of being influenced by extremist rhetoric' or stepping in when 'abuse is actually taking place'. While Khan does say that there have been 'unfortunate cases' of referrals that have turned out to be based on specious evidence, this is more indicative of the need for better training than reason to dismiss the programme entirely. 'Those questioning the need to safeguard need to ask themselves ... has the Government invented a problem to criminalise Muslim kids, or is there a real threat of children being radicalised online and offline by terrorist and extremist far-right groups?'[29]

Prevent is also polarising among ordinary British Muslims. While many Muslims spoke to me openly about Prevent's problems, those who supported the programme were more wary of expressing their opinions on record, out of fear that they would be labelled 'coconuts' ('brown on the outside but white on the inside'), supporters of 'British imperialism', or even *munafiqs* (hypocrites in Islam). One Muslim woman, a mother of two living in East London, told me she was in favour of the government's counter-extremism strategy, particularly after hearing about the notorious 'Bethnal Green girls' case in 2015.

'As a mother of two girls, I was horrified when I had heard that,' she told me when I went to visit her in her home, not far from the school that the Bethnal Green trio had attended. 'These were girls who wore hijab, they were practising Muslims, and yet they joined this horrible group, without anyone knowing it was happening.' Her own daughters had just started secondary school. 'As a parent,' she said, 'it's my responsibility to protect my children at all costs. In places where I can't be there for them, the government I pay taxes to has a duty to ensure that they aren't put in danger. If Prevent is what does that, then I will support it, but I expect it to work.'

The Muslim mother knew that this wasn't a popular opinion, and said she had rarely voiced it outside of private WhatsApp groups. 'I do think that Prevent probably has more support from Muslims—especially Muslim women—than you would expect,' she told me. 'But you wouldn't put that up on the internet unless you really wanted to fight with Muslim men who think they know better. At the end of the day, I am a mother and a parent, and we want what is best for our children. And for me, the biggest danger isn't about my daughter not being able to practise her religion, *alhamdulillah*—she wears hijab and can practise freely. My fear is that she might get influenced by some bloke who tells her that she isn't a proper Muslim unless she goes to Syria and gets married. That sounds crazy, until you remember that it actually happened just a couple of years ago.'

* * *

It is true that Prevent has successfully stopped some vulnerable young people from joining extremist groups and organisations.[30] In fact, it's likely that Contest has saved lives. But one of the problems restated by Prevent's critics is that it's next to impossible for laypeople—particularly those who might be targeted by Prevent—to assess the strategy's success, especially when access to information is difficult to obtain and requires requesting information from multiple government and police departments. To some critics, it then comes as little surprise that many Muslims are distrustful of Prevent, and this itself makes the programme ineffectual, even counterproductive. In a letter to *The Guardian* in 2019, Jenny Jones, a Green Party peer in the House of Lords, wrote:

> The safeguarding of vulnerable people and vulnerable communities will only work if we have the cooperation of those communities and Prevent is simply not trusted by many whom the authorities need to work with them. Prevent has become discredited because it has thrown the net so wide that it includes many thousands who have committed no serious crimes, but are seen by the police as subversives and domestic extremists.[31]

What is clear is that the state's counter-terrorism surveillance powers are unlikely to shrink in the near future. Following a succession of ISIS-inspired terrorist attacks in both Manchester and London in 2017, Prime Minister Theresa May said that the government would be putting more pressure on social media companies themselves to restrict extremist material and to shut down accounts and groups that distributed such content. In a speech following the attacks on London Bridge in 2017, May said: 'We cannot allow this ideology the safe space it needs to breed. Yet that is precisely what the internet—and the big companies that provide internet-based services—provide.'[32] That year, Amber Rudd, then home secretary, advocated both government access to encrypted messaging services like WhatsApp and prison sentences of up to fifteen years for individuals who repeatedly viewed extremist material online.[33] Since those attacks, concerns about online extremism have only heightened—not only because of the ongoing threat from militant Islamist organisations, but also because of ever-growing far-right groups, emboldened by the Trump presidency and the ascendance of right-wing populist movements in Europe and worldwide.

A 2018 report from the anti-extremist group 'Hope Not Hate' showed that while offline membership of far-right organisations was still relatively low, right-wing identitarian groups were increasingly turning to the internet to recruit younger people, often finding them on public forums and social media sites like Facebook. These movements enticed new recruits using anti-Muslim and anti-refugee memes, and then invited people to private chats for further grooming. The report added that incidents like the 2016 murder of Labour MP Jo Cox by a white supremacist, as well as the terrorist attack on Finsbury Park Mosque in North London in 2017, had also illustrated the growing threat of far-right individuals exposed to extremist material on the internet. 'The right-wing terrorist threat is more significant and more challenging than perhaps public debate gives it credit for,' Mark Rowley, then assistant commissioner of

London's Metropolitan Police, said in February 2018. 'There are many Western countries that have extreme right-wing challenges and in quite a number of those the groups we are worried about here are making connections with them and networking.'[34]

While some Muslims welcome Prevent's efforts to clamp down on extremism of all varieties, the strategy is still perceived by many as 'anti-Muslim'. Part of that probably has to do with the programme's development being correlated to the growth of militant Islamist groups, both in the UK and overseas. Many British Muslims feel judged, by both their own communities and public authorities, under pressure to prove the veracity of their faith, their patriotism, and ultimately whether they pose a security risk. At the same time, Prevent's lack of transparency—a point raised by both its supporters and its detractors—means that debates on the programme's effectiveness tend not to lead to any practical resolution.

Many public sector workers, such as university lecturers, have criticised the statutory duty to report those at risk of radicalisation, arguing that it is not their job to police their students or co-workers, and that in the absence of training, people have been left to their own devices to decide for themselves what constitutes a potential extremist. 'Thanks to the government's policies that aim to transform academic staff into counterterrorism police, openness, tolerance and freedom of expression in UK universities are under threat,' said Imran Awan, a sociology lecturer at Birmingham City University in an article for Al Jazeera. 'Academic staff are being encouraged to report their students for reasons like discussing certain "sensitive" topics, asking certain questions or even reading "suspicious" textbooks.' He went on to say that:

> With the 'Prevent' guidelines, the government is trying to incorporate academic staff into a state surveillance programme. Lecturers are being forced to monitor and judge their students against an ambigu-

193

ous, all-inclusive framework that few found helpful. These types of measures can never counter terror threats, and can only lead to an Orwellian society in which the police and the state have broad and intrusive powers and academic debate is silenced.[35]

It's this question that is likely to guide the future of Prevent over the next decade. The programme faces new challenges from extremist groups outside of the militant Islamist framework, and will need to find ways to tackle 'internationalised' national security threats, sometimes organised in impenetrable spaces like the dark web, which the government has little or no access to. Journalists like Jamie Bartlett believe that the challenge for those working in Prevent will be how it deals with other kinds of radicals—whether anarchists, libertarians or environmental activists—who decide to pursue direct, if not violent, action, to protest against crises like climate change.[36] Soon, arguments about Prevent will no longer just be part of the discourse around surveillance of Muslims, but will inform the difference between a 'free citizen' and an 'enemy of the state'.

#TraditionallySubmissive

In January 2016, Prime Minister David Cameron wrote in *The Times* that Muslim women should be taught English in order to combat radicalisation in their communities. He argued that language barriers between Muslim boys and their mothers had 'an important connection to extremism', and that not speaking English prevented Muslim women from speaking out against the 'backward attitudes' of some Muslim men, who were themselves attempting to 'stop their partners from integrating'. 'If you don't improve your fluency, that could affect your ability to stay in the UK,' he wrote.[37] Cameron was also reported to have privately suggested that the vulnerability of young Muslim men to radicalisation was partly due to the 'traditional submissiveness of Muslim women'.[38] It was a controversial declaration.

A government source told *The Telegraph*:

> David knows that the traditional submissiveness of Muslim women
> is a sensitive issue, but the problems of young people being attracted
> by extremism will not be tackled without an element of cultural
> change within the community. At the moment, too many Muslim
> women are treated like second-class citizens who may speak only
> basic English at best, and have no jobs or independent financial
> standing. It means they are in no position to speak out against the
> influence of the radical Imams, however strongly they feel about it.[39]

Outrage over the prime minister's statements came almost
immediately, as Muslim women went to their social media pages
to express their anger. Using the hashtag #TraditionallySubmissive,
hundreds of Muslim women detailed their achievements, qualifica-
tions, skills and abilities in response to Cameron's statements. 'A
television presenter and public speaker while raising two sons.
Working full time. Am I #TraditionallySubmissive?' tweeted Zahra
al-Alawi.[40] 'Columbia grad, BBC journo, Pilates instructor, sport
enthusiast and mummy. Yes, Cameron #TraditionallySubmissive,'
wrote Zahra Khimji.[41]

What was remarkable about the #TraditionallySubmissive
hashtag was how fast the campaign came together. 'I heard about
it through a WhatsApp group I was in,' said Sara Ahmed, a law-
yer, mother of two and a devout Muslim who wears hijab. When
I met Sara in her office just outside of London, she told me that
the prime minister's statements had shown 'what the government
and this country' thought of British Muslim women. 'A statement
like that? What does it even mean?' she asked. 'Cameron never
defined what it meant to be traditionally submissive, and for many
of us, it didn't speak to our experience, you know?

'My dad died when I was very young, so I was raised by my
mum, who was working and looking after us at the same time.
She could barely speak English but she provided for us in every
way possible, and without any help from any of our extended

family. She was so strong because it was the only way to survive. That's far from submissive, and I think when I saw those statements, something inside of me sparked. It felt like he was attacking my mum.'

Sara said that someone in the WhatsApp group had recommended trying to get the hashtag trending on Twitter, so it would get picked up by the media and force the government to respond.

One of those who helped launch the campaign was author Shelina Janmohamed. When I spoke to her in 2015, Shelina said, 'Muslim women face huge amounts of racism and Islamophobia, and they face big challenges in the jobs market.' She added, 'By making a statement like that, [Cameron] is ignoring the huge diversity of Muslim women in Britain that already contribute to public life, and the level of talent among Muslim women living in the UK. A lot of people who participated in the campaign were incensed by his comments.'[42]

To Shelina, #TraditionallySubmissive wasn't just a response to Cameron, or the Conservative government. It was an attempt to fight back against years of anti-Muslim messages—especially about women—in the British media. In her words, 'preconceived images of oppressed Muslim women end up shaping policies that harm our communities'. Research has shown that women do bear the brunt of this harm; according to a 2018 report by Tell MAMA, a project monitoring Islamophobic incidents, 'most victims of anti-Muslim hatred are women.'[43]

* * *

The #TraditionallySubmissive hashtag was also indicative of a more telling truth: that the government was so removed from the country's Muslim communities that such an alienating statement from the prime minister hadn't been prevented, and that Muslims themselves felt that taking to Twitter was the only way they might break through to their elected representatives.

Baroness Sayeeda Warsi, the former chairman of the Conservative party and the most senior Muslim politician under David Cameron, who had resigned in 2014 over the government's stance on the Israel–Gaza conflict,[44] said of the prime minister's statements:

> To threaten women and say to them that 'unless you are of X standard [in English] we will send you back, even if you have children in the UK who are British and your spouse is British' is, for me, a very unusual way of empowering and emboldening women.[45]

Warsi warned that the Conservatives were at risk of losing the vast majority of their Muslim supporters if they continued to ignore the concerns and voices of Muslim communities.

The advice came again in 2017, in the 'Missing Muslims' report by the Citizens Commission on Islam, Participation and Public Life, launched by community organising charity Citizens UK. The report urged the government 'to reassess the way in which it engages with the UK's Muslim communities', saying that 'there is a broken relationship that needs to be resolved'. While the Commission cited findings by Policy Exchange that 72 per cent of British Muslims had voted in an election, compared to 54 per cent of the general population (per the control group), many Muslims told the report's authors that they felt alienated from politics. 'Discrimination, and fears of being discriminated against, are actively discouraging participation and contributing to disillusionment with the political process amongst young British Muslims,' the report stated.[46]

In the years since the #TraditionallySubmissive hashtag trended, there has been little to suggest that the ruling Conservative Party has made efforts to reach out to the nation's Muslims. Meanwhile, under Jeremy Corbyn, the Labour Party has become more vocal about the issue of Islamophobia.[47] Writing in *The Guardian*, Miqdaad Versi, the assistant secretary general of the Muslim Council of Britain, reasoned that part of the Labour Party's somewhat unexpected good performance in the 2017 general election may have been due to support from young Muslim voters—not only because of 'the pull of Jeremy Corbyn's broader anti-austerity message' which resonated with 'many Muslims for whom public services and decreasing inequality are key priorities', but also because Muslims were being pushed away from the Conservative Party. 'On the key issue of Islamophobia, the party appears to have ignored the huge increase in hate crime against Muslims on its watch.'[48]

Today, Islamophobia in British politics—especially directed toward women—is still rife. So much so that in 2018, the then foreign secretary Boris Johnson, who many speculated might be a potential prime minister, writing in *The Telegraph*, referred to Muslim women who wore veils as 'letter boxes' and compared them to 'bank robbers'.[49] Not only does it seem that Islamophobia has become further entrenched in the Conservative Party since #TraditionallySubmissive went viral, but it has also become even nastier. Prominent British Muslim Tory politicians, like Baroness Warsi and Lord Sheikh, have called for an independent inquiry into Islamophobia in their party.[50] 'The danger of further isolating Muslims and other ethnic minority voters as well—not to mention how corrosive Islamophobia is to the party's moral core—is of [great] concern,' wrote Conservative councillor Hashim Bhatti in *The Guardian* in August 2018. 'If we become a party that is hostile to the Muslim community,' he added, 'it will be through choice.'[51]

For Versi, Muslims will continue to be disenfranchised so long as they are seen by government officials 'almost entirely through the prism of extremism'. Until the government proves itself willing to reassess its 'widely castigated counter-extremism strategy', including by addressing widespread concerns about Prevent 'unfairly targeting Muslim communities', the Conservative Party will have difficulty restoring the faith of British Muslim voters.

'It won't happen overnight, and it won't happen through super-ficial platitudes such as visiting mosques,' he wrote. 'But change can happen. For the good of the country, I hope it does.'[52]

6

SPACES FOR MINORITIES

Ahmadis

In March 2016, I received news through WhatsApp of a murder that had taken place in Glasgow. Messages on the group, which I was a member of during my time as a religion reporter, came through in English, Urdu, and sometimes Arabic. One phrase abounded: '*inna lillahi wa inna ilayhi raji'un*'—to Allah we belong and to Him we return—recited by Muslims on news of a death. Other people expressed their outrage. 'We always knew that this time would come, Allah has warned us that we would see our brothers killed in front of us as we near *Qiyamah* [the Day of Judgement],' read one message.

I eventually learned that a shopkeeper named Asad Shah, an Ahmadi Muslim who lived in Shawlands, a few miles from Glasgow's city centre, had been brutally stabbed to death while at work in his store.

Like most people in the WhatsApp group, my first instinct was that this was an Islamophobic attack—one that, as the son of a shopkeeper, I had often feared would happen to my own family. It wasn't uncommon for shopkeepers to be racially abused while doing their jobs. I had grown up hearing stories about threats my family had received at their store in the 1980s from white nationalist groups like the National Front. Moreover, only months after terror attacks on the Bataclan theatre in Paris, where 137 people had been killed by ISIS-linked gunmen, anti-Muslim sentiment across Europe was at an all-time high, making a 'revenge' attack on Muslims all the more plausible. My presumption was reinforced when Shah's photograph was posted in the WhatsApp group. It showed a small, dark-skinned man with sleepy eyes, wearing a formal suit and tie, sporting a trimmed but messy black beard and, on his crown, a dark-red, gold-laced *kufi*. In other words, he was visibly Muslim.

What happened to Asad Shah, however, turned out to be more complicated, and, in some ways, a lot darker.[1] As more details of the murder spread, not just through mainstream media but also through WhatsApp networks, Facebook posts and Twitter feeds, it emerged that Shah had been killed by another Muslim of Pakistani origin, Tanveer Ahmed, a taxi driver from Bradford who, according to court documents, had travelled over 200 miles to confront Shah about videos he had uploaded on Facebook.[2] Shah had regularly used social media to upload videos of himself speaking about his faith, and religion generally.[3] His last video, uploaded days before his murder, was a clip in which he wished his online friends 'a very happy Easter'—an innocuous act that some conservative Muslims nonetheless believed amounted to *shirk*, or idolatry. Some reporters and commentators, myself included, concluded that that video was what had prompted the murder.[4]

A few weeks after the attack, it was revealed by BBC *Newsnight* that the murder was, in fact, motivated by other videos, which Shah recorded in his shop and uploaded on YouTube. He often spoke about his spiritual beliefs, spreading a message of peace, love and unity.[5] In one video, Shah allegedly even likened himself to a prophet.[6] That video was shared across Urdu-language Facebook groups and private WhatsApp groups—not just based in the UK, but also in Pakistan—among communities that have openly expressed hatred and vitriol and even advocated violence against the minority Ahmadi sect.

* * *

The Ahmadiyyah sect was founded in the nineteenth century in the Punjab region of British India by Mirza Ghulam Ahmad of Qadian, whom Ahmadis believe was a 'renewer of Islam', chosen by Allah after the death of the Prophet Muhammad to spread the messages of Islam in society, which had 'deteriorated to the point where divinely inspired reforms were needed'.[7]

While Ahmadis insist that Mirza Ghulam Ahmad was not himself a prophet, and that the sect does not challenge the orthodox belief that Muhammad was the last prophet, this didn't stop larger Sunni and Shi'a sects from labelling the Ahmadis as heretics. Some groups, such as the Pakistan-based Sunni Barelvi organisation Khatme Nubuwwat, have gone as far as to call for Ahmadis who refuse to renounce their beliefs to be killed.[8] It was unsurprising, then, that in the aftermath of Asad Shah's murder, conversations about the rising threat of violent sectarian attacks were mired with debates about the legitimacy of the Ahmadi community as Muslims at all. Not only do these arguments have a real-life impact on the physical safety of many British Ahmadis, but they also define their day-to-day online experiences.

'I'm constantly aware of being different,' says Tahir, a twenty-four-year-old Ahmadi Muslim from London. 'There's a feeling of not being accepted by wider society who see me as an enemy because I am Muslim, and by zealots in my own community who believe I am a threat to Muslims.'

Tahir and I meet in a café in South London, a few minutes away from the Baitul Futuh Masjid, one of the most prominent

Ahmadi mosques in the UK. Tahir is active within his community. He volunteers regularly, teaches Qur'an and participates in public outreach events like the annual Jalsa Salana, a global gathering of Ahmadis addressed by Hazrat Mirza Masroor Ahmad, the head of the worldwide Ahmadiyya Muslim Community, who is recognised by the Ahmadis as the 'true caliph' of all Muslims.

'I feel Muslim when I'm in my community, as well as when I am praying by myself,' Tahir tells me. 'But expressing my identity as a Muslim online is so much harder—partly because as Ahmadis we are a small community, and we'll always be underrepresented compared to larger sects.' But there are also more pernicious things that make it difficult to be Ahmadi on the internet. 'There are other Muslims online who assert their beliefs and identities purely through attacking us. Even when an Ahmadi or an Ahmadi organisation posts a peaceful message— one that encourages non-violence or dialogue between different faiths—you'll always have commenters who say things like "Hazrat Mirza is a *Dajjal* [false Messiah]" or "Qadiyanis are *kuffar* [disbelievers]".'

Tahir and his community grew up knowing that they weren't just minorities, but ones who would inevitably face abuse because of their beliefs. Many Ahmadis living in the UK and other Western nations are refugees who fled from Pakistan, where they faced physical abuse, vandalism of property and even death threats. Tahir says it was these threats that have made his community 'so grateful to Britain for letting us have a home and opportunities'. He thinks this is why Ahmadis 'are keen to contribute to the UK, to join the British Army, and why the community continue to work with the Royal British Legion's annual poppy appeal to commemorate the British armed services'—one of few Muslim organisations to openly do so.[9]

While Ahmadis have always received abuse from other Muslims, Tahir says that it took the murder of Asad Shah for the threats of sectarian violence to be taken seriously. 'In the days after the murder, I remember there being more security around our mosques, and our social media groups becoming more active and more focused on safety. I was in several WhatsApp groups where families would just be messaging each other to say they had got home safe from the *masjid*, and aunties and uncles warning us not to go out late at night in case something happened. It really was the first time a lot of us, especially [Ahmadis] like me who were born and raised in the UK, realised that we were targets, and that attacks on us could be coordinated from countries we'd never visited in our entire lives.'

This last point was the most important. While Tanveer Ahmed had been pushed to attack Shah after watching his YouTube video, the context in which his murder took place was much broader.

In June 2016, *Newsnight* revealed that Ahmed had been in contact with supporters of Mumtaz Qadri, another Barelvi Muslim from Rawalpindi, Pakistan, who, in 2011, murdered the Pakistani politician Salmaan Taseer.[10] Qadri had accused Taseer of committing acts against Islam when Taseer proposed reforms to Pakistan's blasphemy laws, which often sentenced people to long prison sentences and even the death penalty if they were found guilty of insulting Islam or the Prophet Muhammad. Qadri was sentenced to death by hanging at the end of February 2016, but many in Pakistan held him up as both a hero and a martyr for Islam. Tens of thousands of people attended Qadri's funeral in March 2016.[11] Iconographic venerations of Qadri, showing his face printed next to passages from the Qur'an and from Urdu poetry associated with prominent Islamic figures, continue to circulate across social media.[12]

Newsnight also found that Tanveer Ahmed had been in contact with Qadri's brother, Dilpazeer Awan, in the days leading up to Shah's murder.[13] Awan told the programme that Ahmed claimed to have 'seen Qadri in a dream' and wanted to follow his example. 'Mumtaz Qadri told me that Allah had chosen me to [pursue] a noble duty for my religion,' Ahmed allegedly told Awan on the phone in March.

It was through Urdu-language social media networks—mainly on Facebook and WhatsApp—that Ahmed had not just made contact with Awan, but also found himself in online communities that venerated Qadri, and that regularly posted anti-Ahmadi propaganda, including YouTube videos of speakers calling for the punishment and death of Ahmadis.[14] One such WhatsApp group was called Tawizat-e-Attari, which I joined when I was researching a story about the Ahmadi community for *The Spectator*. I frequently saw members of the 300-strong group sharing anti-Ahmadi videos, as well as posters that depicted Tanveer Ahmed and Mumtaz Qadri together, described in Urdu as 'soldiers of Allah' and 'the righteous martyrs'.

Most people I reached out to in the group declined to be interviewed for either the article or this book. One member, who went by the pseudonym Pir Abbas, told me that while he doesn't 'support the death of innocent people', he did not consider Tanveer Ahmed or Mumtaz Qadri evil, and could understand their motivations. 'They wanted to defend the faith, and defend the honour of the Prophet,' he told me on WhatsApp. 'This is our duty as Muslims, regardless.' He did not answer any of my follow-up questions.

* * *

Many Ahmadi groups worldwide are aware of the internet's potential as a tool for *da'wah*—spreading Islam. For some, there is also an urgent need to counter misinformation online, about both Ahmadis and Islam, by developing their own social media outreach.

In early 2018, for example, the Ahmadiyya Muslim Jama'at Nigeria, ran a social media workshop to help Ahmadis learn how to do *da'wah* online. According to the group's national president, Mashu'ud Fashola, an emphasis was placed on the 'positive application of social media' and how to 'use it to promote harmony ... through the teachings of Islam'. 'Some people use social media to cause chaos, promote terrorism, persecution, thereby sending the wrong ideas about Islam,' he noted. 'So we need to counter this and we need to enlighten our members.'[15]

Ahmadi groups in India have also encouraged their followers to take to social media to spread their message. 'We need to increase our presence on the Internet,' wrote Shahid Badruddin, a member of the Ahmadi community in Bangalore. 'Media plays a very vital part of society ... Whenever a news report/article on Islam Ahmadiyya is put on the Internet we must make use of the opportunity by putting our comments with useful links and at times we may have to remove misconceptions and allegations put by anti-Ahmadiyya forces.'[16]

While many Ahmadis in the UK might be accustomed to using social media in their day-to-day lives, they have also made efforts to equip themselves with the skills they need to use the internet for *da'wah*. Unlike most Muslim organisations in Britain, the Ahmadiyya Muslim Community UK has a professionally trained media team, whose members are in charge of organisation and communications. The group frequently invites members of the press to its events, offers question-and-answer sessions with Ahmadi leader Mirza Masroor Ahmad, and uses Twitter, Instagram and Facebook to post infographics of Masroor Ahmad's speeches and quotes.[17]

As they face ever more pressing dangers, Ahmadi communities around the world have had to be careful to keep their members safe while propagating their messages online. After the death of Asad Shah, the Ahmadiyya Muslim Community UK, whose slogan is 'love for all, hatred for none', launched the 'United Against Extremism' campaign, which was advertised across its social media platforms via videos and infographics, as well as on buses in London and across Scotland.[18]

The year before, in 2015, Ahmadis in the UK also participated in the #IStandWithAhmadis campaign—a 'tweetstorm', in which participants are encouraged to use a hashtag within a certain time frame in order to game Twitter's algorithm and get it trending on the platform.[19] #IStandWithAhmadis began in response to a spate of violent attacks on Ahmadis in Pakistan, including on an Ahmadi mosque. A factory where an Ahmadi man worked was torched because of unverified rumours that the man had burned copies of the Qur'an.[20] Thousands of people tweeted the hashtag in solidarity, alongside messages like 'Ahmadiyya believe in interfaith' and 'Ahmadi community believe in peace and love'.

Though threats to Ahmadis' safety in the UK aren't as severe as those in Pakistan, the Ahmadis I spoke to who express their religious identity on the internet say their online experiences are still permeated with the same sense of fear and a feeling of otherness. Many young Ahmadis feel that even online, there are boundaries for them that don't exist for Muslims belonging to larger sects.

As Rizk Salih, a twenty-two-year-old university student in London, says, 'I don't put Ahmadi in my Twitter bio or across any social media. I just say that I am a Muslim.' Rizk says this makes his online experiences easier, because 'when I talk about things like Islamophobia, or want to react to anti-Muslim news articles, I can make statements without other Muslims questioning whether I have a right to a platform.'

Rizk told me that he had friends who had mentioned being Ahmadi on social media. 'They've received abusive messages, and been told that they are worse than non-believers. A friend of mine was kicked out of a Facebook group for Muslim students because he was Ahmadi and the administrators of the group didn't classify him as a true Muslim. There was nothing he could do to re-join.' Rizk lamented that there was nothing in place to prevent this behaviour online. 'It's crazy, because the administrators were blatantly being discriminatory, right? It's a clear act of sectarianism, but because it doesn't break any of Facebook's terms and conditions—in fact, so much sectarian [discrimation] online don't technically break any rules on social media platforms—anti-Ahmadiyya statements and comments are still allowed to continue.'

While at the time of writing there has been no major attack on Ahmadi Muslims in the UK since Asad Shah's murder, the continued existence of anti-Ahmadi sentiment online worries Ahmadis like Rizk and Tahir. The rife abuse of Ahmadis on the internet makes them think that it wouldn't take much for another attack to happen, without prior detection by authorities.

'Social media companies are just getting to grips with the violent threat of racists who openly say they want to kill black people, Jews and Muslims,' said Rizk, when I asked about what social media companies should be doing to help protect communities like his. 'It would take something really awful to get their attention—and even then, it might be too late.'

Ex-Muslims

On the top floor of the Old Red Lion pub in Holborn, central London, a group of young men and women were chanting the name 'Amir' and rhythmically thumping the oak table they were crowded around. The bangs became louder and faster, shaking the half-drunk pints of lager and glasses of wine on the table, while Amir, a twenty-year-old university student from Birmingham, stared at the sandwich on his plate. His hands trembled as he grasped the French baguette, its bright-red and orange juices dripping onto his hands as he slowly brought it to his lips. He closed his eyes, and took a large bite as the people around him watched in anticipation. 'It's chewier than I thought it'd be,' he laughed, mouth half full, as the crowd applauded and clinked their glasses. After a few bites, Amir stopped and pushed the plate away, claiming that if he ate any more pork cutlet—a meat that he had never before even touched, let alone eaten—he would probably throw up.

This was a moment that Amir had been waiting for his entire life. Though he left Islam when he was sixteen, he had only done so from his computer in the privacy of his bedroom, announcing his rejection of Islam to friends he had met on internet forums and Facebook groups. 'Happy to announce that I have shaved my beard, and I feel like a new man!' he had written on the private Facebook group 'Ex Mooses United UK'—some of whose members were now cheering him on at the Old Red Lion. He had posted before and after pictures of his face to commemorate the change. Underneath the picture, other members had written congratulatory Islamic phrases to applaud his decision. '*Mashallah!*' said one. '*Audhubillah* [I seek Allah's protection (from *Shaitan*)]!' joked another, accompanied by a picture of a bearded Muslim man with his index finger pointed to the sky—the *shahadah* sign, representing the oneness of God.

Like many people who have left Islam, Amir refers to himself as an 'ex-Muslim' rather than an atheist. 'It's an important distinction,' he says, 'because leaving Islam isn't like leaving Christianity, or Judaism—the experience is completely different. So many ex-Muslims have lost everything by giving up their religion and being themselves. It's not just a matter of no longer believing in God.'

Amir tells me that when he left Islam, he wasn't able to tell his family, or anyone he knew within his religious community, out of fear that they might disown him, or—worse—that he would bring shame upon his family, who have lived in

Birmingham for over three decades and are known for voluntary work at the local mosque. Despite his lack of faith in Islam, he had spent the past two years going to the mosque at least once a week, fasted during Ramadan, and observed other holy days alongside the rest of his community. But tonight, with one bite of a pork sandwich lathered in ketchup and brown sauce, he finally felt like he had moved on to another chapter in his life. 'Tonight was the first time I truly felt I was no longer a Muslim ... that I was finally true to myself.' He refers to it as his 'coming out' moment. 'I just feel so much lighter and better about myself,' he says happily. 'It's like this huge burden is finally off my back.'

* * *

Like many ex-Muslims, Amir's transition away from his religion largely took place online. Though he tells me that he wasn't ever as devout as his parents and other family members, and that he was constantly 'questioning tenets of Islam, asking questions in madrassa like whether everything in the Qur'an was actually real', up to the age of seventeen, he still considered himself a Muslim. So much so, in fact, that he would spend countless hours on Facebook threads, Reddit and The Student Room, 'defending Islam against people who were mocking it or mocking Prophet Muhammad', claiming that 'Islam was a perfect religion', and even that, inevitably, 'everyone who is rightfully guided will come to Islam'.

But while Amir was standing up for Islam, he also had doubts about what he was typing, feelings that would flare up as others online—usually atheists—dismissed his statements, or attempted to refute his claims with scientific arguments he hadn't studied or by referencing philosophers he hadn't heard of. 'It was the first time I'd been exposed to people who'd just say I was wrong, or that my reasoning was stupid and unfounded. I wasn't used to it, because I'd grown up in a community where Islamic arguments were just accepted—you would be seen as weird if you strayed away from it.'

It was around that time that Amir decided to research more into the arguments that his online opponents were using to dismiss his defences of Islam, in the hope that he could find holes in them, and prove he was correct. He started reading atheist Western philosophers like Jeremy Bentham, Ludwig Wittgenstein and Friedrich Nietzsche, and watched YouTube videos of Christopher Hitchens, Sam Harris, Richard Dawkins and Daniel Dennett. Known as the 'Four Horsemen', they are the founding fathers of the 'New Atheist' movement, a group who advocate the view that 'religion should not simply be tolerated but should be countered, criticized and exposed by rational argument wherever its influence arises'.[21]

The New Atheists developed a reputation for being the most ardent opponents of religion, and in recent years, particularly Islam. Hitchens, following the 9/11 attacks, claimed that his support for the subsequent Iraq war came from an 'unmistakable confrontation between everything I loved and everything I hated', while Dawkins stated in 2017 that 'it's quite apparent that at present the most evil religion in the world has to be Islam'.[22]

* * *

But Amir's research alone was not enough to lead him to abandon the religion he'd grown up with and the only way of life he'd ever known. Lighting a cigarette, he tells me that leaving Islam had less to do with the counter-arguments posed by popular online atheists—some of whom he calls 'crazy guys with views just as extreme as hardcore Islamists'—than with discovering ex-Muslim communities online.

The friendships he built through those ex-Muslim networks meant that he felt 'emotionally ready' to abandon his faith. In the months leading up to his decision to leave Islam, he spent endless hours at night, while his parents, sisters and aunts were sleeping in their house in suburban Birmingham, reading the discussion forums of the Council of Ex-Muslims in Britain (CEMB). The CEMB is one of the only UK-based organisations that aims to support and represent individuals who have left Islam, many of whom, the organisation says, would be considered 'apostates' and whose lives could be at physical risk if their 'apostasy' were exposed to their families and communities.[23]

Some of the discussions Amir read on the CEMB's forums were centred on philosophical and theological issues concerning Islamic scripture, often set up as guides for countering arguments made by religious Muslims. But a large number of posts that he read, and indeed related to, had to do with the social costs of leaving the faith, and the emotional turmoil beleaguering many of those struggling to do so.

'I read stories about former Muslims being threatened with being kicked out of their houses or being disowned by their families, not knowing what to do or where they would go. Some people would struggle to try and stay Muslim until they were allowed to leave home, and in most cases, that wouldn't be until they got married, or if they got a job overseas.'

Amir related to many of the internal struggles faced by those on the forums. He remembered one thread on Reddit's ex-Muslim page, a subreddit with over 36,000 subscribers from all over the world, about a man struggling to deal with the guilt of leaving his faith and lying to his family. 'I have left Islam and I know in my heart that I am no longer a Muslim in practice,' the man said. 'But I cannot bear to lose my family. Is it okay for me to practise some Islamic rituals, even if I do not believe them?'

The responses were mixed. Some users argued that becoming an ex-Muslim meant making a choice 'to abandon everything Islam commands, so you cannot cherry pick what you want and don't want to believe'. Others took a softer approach, suggesting that being an ex-Muslim is 'different for different people, and OP [original poster] should do what they feel comfortable with'. This thread, Amir says, encapsulated the struggle that he and a large number of ex-Muslims in the UK face when they leave their faith—what Amir describes as 'the choice you have to make about whether you leave Islam for good, or compromise, and end up feeling you haven't left it at all'.

* * *

This all-or-nothing feeling may be part of the reason some former Muslims have allied themselves with right-wing, anti-Islam groups—something I was told had caused a rift in ex-Muslim communities. Some argued that right-wing groups like the English Defence League (EDL), Britain First and the For Britain party routinely exploit ex-Muslim experiences in order to prop up their animosity toward Muslims.

I reached out to a number of ex-Muslims who had been captured on YouTube videos at EDL rallies, and who had spoken highly of anti-Islam figures like the EDL's former leader Tommy Robinson, but none wished to be interviewed. Some, however, have spoken out about leaving Islam on their own social media accounts.

One public figure who caused a stir when they renounced Islam is the fifty-year-old blogger and political commentator Mufassil Islam,[24] based in East London, particularly when a video from 2017 surfaced that showed him speaking about leaving Islam at a conference hosted by Anne-Marie Waters, an anti-Islam campaigner who was then running for leader of the UK Independence Party (UKIP). Speaking to camera on his now deleted YouTube channel 'Jajbarthenomad' in 2016, Islam said 'all religions are bullshit' and claimed that Islam was currently the most intolerant faith.[25]

Islam had been known in the past for his swearing and obscenities in videos, which he records in both English and Bengali. Some Muslims felt especially uncomfortable at his use of foul language while talking about Islamic issues. When he still considered himself a Muslim, he usually addressed extremist and Islamist groups that he accused of hijacking the religion. In one video, posted on Facebook in late 2015, he referred to the Islamic State group as 'bastards' and 'fucking cunts', in response to news that they had captured and raped hundreds of Yazidi women when they took hold of Kobani canton in northern Syria.

Having left the religion, Islam continued to use his YouTube channel to put out provocative videos, but with different targets. He released clips with titles like 'Should we ban the Qur'an in the EU?' and 'How is Islam compatible with the European Convention on Human Rights?' In one video, published in September 2018, Islam referred to the Prophet Muhammad as 'the most ungrateful refugee in history' who 'subdued the hosts who gave him shelter in Medina, and gave way to the worst people in human history'. He said that 'Muhammad was not just an evil man—he was the most treacherous person in human history'.

* * *

'The appeal of that kind of anti-Muslim content usually comes from anger,' says Salman, a twenty-eight-year-old graphic designer, who requested a pseudonym as his family aren't aware that he has left the faith. Salman was also present during Amir's initiation into being an ex-Muslim, but his story was very different.

Salman had decidedly left Islam after a childhood spent in Pakistan, where he saw religion as 'dogmatic' and 'discouraging any form of intellectual debate or challenge'. After moving to the UK, he spent most of his teen years as an ardent atheist and, until a few years ago, openly supported groups like the EDL. He also admitted to being a fan of Tommy Robinson, saying, 'I grew up not too far from Luton,' Robinson's hometown, and the birthplace of the EDL. 'I sympathised with what he was saying, because it is difficult to live in places like that if you aren't a practising Muslim ... I found the place isolating, as if I was back in Pakistan again.'

He became disillusioned with the EDL when he was twenty-five, saying that 'their forums, their online groups were just filled with rampant racism. You would see these horrible cartoons of brown people with bombs strapped to them, or pictures of Muslim-looking men having sex with animals—really disgusting things that showed they didn't actually care about Islam itself, but just wanted an excuse to be racist, and to use the word "Paki" whenever they could.'

Salman didn't post much in these groups. Occasionally, he says, 'I would intervene in a thread to say that users were being racist, or that they were going off topic whenever they went on a rant about Pakistanis or Arabs.' His interventions, however, had little effect, both online and in real life. 'Even when I went to the EDL rally,' he tells me, 'you would hear racism in the crowd. There were people saying "fucking Pakis" and "Pakis out"—it was the same as what was happening online, but in real life.' For him, it was proof that whether or not he had left his religion, it wouldn't matter to the EDL—they would always see him as a Muslim.

* * *

For no one is this more evident than female ex-Muslims, who face the dual challenges of abandoning Islam (and their presumed duties, as future wives and mothers, to pass on their religious and cultural heritage), and Islamophobia, which, according to hate-monitoring group Tell MAMA, has historically had a greater impact on women than on men.[26] While ex-Muslim women might not receive as much anti-Muslim abuse in the street as visibly Muslim hijabi women, their online experiences are very different. Thirty-year-old Halima Begum, a secretary in North London and a member of the UK Ex-Muslim Network Facebook group, tells me about how she had to change her name on Facebook to stop Islamophobic trolls from harassing her online.

'Not being Muslim isn't enough for these people,' she tells me at the pub. 'They'll pounce on you if you simply have a Muslim name. I've had people who are supposed to be my allies—the ones who are anti-Islam, and supposedly fighting for women's rights—tell me to "fuck off back to Saudi Arabia" or ask whether my husband has beat me for using the internet.

'Other times,' she adds, 'I've had anti-Islam images sent to me by email and direct message, showing pictures of women in burqas being stoned to death, or gay people being hung by ISIS terrorists—just by random people on Twitter who write things in their bios about wanting to protect women from Islam.' It's an experience, Halima says, that her female ex-Muslim friends have also faced, and it is particularly challenging because social media is one of the few places those wanting to leave Islam can turn to for support, guidance and community.

Most ex-Muslims I spoke to said they felt more comfortable in private chat rooms, Facebook and WhatsApp groups, and on the tightly moderated ex-Muslim subreddit, than on other, more pub-lic, social media. 'When you leave Islam, there are always dangers,' says Amina, a nineteen-year-old from Birmingham who is at uni-versity in London. 'Even if it isn't from your own community, you'll have other Muslims—men, usually—who will hate you. And you never know what they might do or say that could put you in harm, even if they don't advocate violence themselves.'

Amina formerly wore a hijab before renouncing Islam in 2017, but she has never spoken about her journey outside of small ex-Muslim communities, both online and offline. In fact, her public social media pages, where she occasionally posts YouTube videos of Islamic lectures and Qur'anic verses to reassure her parents she is practising her faith while away from home, show her wearing a dark-red hijab and a long black chador covering her body—a far cry from her current ensemble of skinny jeans, knee-high boots and brown leather jacket.

Amina says that her low profile is the reason why she's never been threatened—a piece of advice given to her by another female ex-Muslim from Canada, whom she met online. After posting a video on her private Facebook account about why she was leaving the religion ('she didn't ever attack Islam at all,' Amina tells me), her Canadian friend found her Facebook inbox filling up with messages from men calling her a *kafir*, accusing her of deception and sending her death threats. 'Eventually she had to get off social media entirely, and change her phone number and everything. She even had to tell her parents about leaving Islam when she didn't want to, for the sake of their protection,' Amina says. 'The intensity of that harassment definitely came because she was a woman,' she adds. 'Her inbox was filled with men who were harassing her—they wanted her to feel weak and afraid.'

* * *

Experiences like Halima's and Amina's—of threats and abuse from Muslims and non-Muslims—have meant that those who create, maintain and moderate online spaces for ex-Muslims are putting more effort into keeping them safe, ensuring that members feel welcome and comfortable regardless of their different journeys leaving Islam, and making sure that such spaces aren't infiltrated by those seeking to exploit ex-Muslim experiences, or to pursue online harassment campaigns against them.

'One of the things we make sure we do is to keep our group as clearly defined as possible. We usually get rid of posts that are

partisan, or about politics, or shitposting [trolling],' says Imtiaz
Shams, a moderator on the ex-Muslims subreddit page.[27] 'The
majority of the time,' he says,' it's easy to moderate the page,
because people come to the Reddit page knowing that it's monitored. And the guidelines for being a member of the group are
strict enough that it will naturally weed out people who are trying to cause trouble, or those who demean the experiences of
other ex-Muslims.'

Imtiaz tells me that on some occasions, he and other moderators have had to report users for online abuse from other members 'from both the right and left wing', as well as for instances
of homophobic and sexist abuse. While their screening process
for new members is thorough and they carry out detailed background checks, there have been occasions when users with bad
motives have unknowingly been allowed into the group—though
they have been removed swiftly.

Imtiaz says that this would happen on any large social media
platform, and notes, 'The advantage of Reddit is that we can
ensure the quality of conversation on the forum is higher,
because of the stricter guidelines for users, and also because we've
made r/exmuslims a community space. It's a place where people
can talk and process everything they've been through, and it's
our responsibility as moderators to ensure that they have the
space to do that comfortably.'

Over the course of our interview, Imtiaz emphasises this point,
about safe spaces online where people can share their experiences
without fear of abuse. It is why, he says, the internet will remain
the most important space for ex-Muslims, not just in the UK,
but across the world.

'What we often forget is that leaving Islam, or faith generally,
and the process by which people do that, is traumatic. And for
the most part, people who are most active in these online spaces
are those who come from practising, high-intensity religious

families.' He continues, 'That trauma can be reinforced over and over again, especially in public forums where they might have to confront religious people who are hostile to them. For groups like ex-Muslims, who are already going through a serious amount of trauma, those kinds of online interactions can make things much worse for them, so the role we play is to create as safe an environment as we can to [process] that anger and fear, and get people who've left Islam into a better emotional place.'

Of course, Imtiaz adds, a big part of that process should happen offline too, which is why in 2015 he co-founded Faith to Faithless, an organisation that assists people across the UK who have left minority religions. Faith to Faithless provides workshops and seminars on university campuses, led by people who have left their religion, as well as organising meet-ups and social events.

'Community is the biggest part of any ex-Muslim's transition, so our organisation is trying to provide a real-life community for people who have left their faith,' he explains. 'Even though there is so much out there online for ex-Muslims, not all of it is good or helpful, and in some cases it can lead people who are still extremely vulnerable into the arms of others who don't have their best interests at heart ... At least if they come to us, they can see that there is a community of people who are like them, who still have struggles, but who are around people who love and care about them.'

It's a sentiment that Amir agrees with, and he credits the other ex-Muslims he knows for helping him with his transition out of Islam and into a better emotional place.

'I consider the other Ex Mooses my best friends,' he tells me with a relaxed laugh. 'They've seen the worst and most erratic sides of me online before we knew each other, and accepted me for that—and now they've seen me in a better state of mind and accepted me for that too. We've all been through the same things, the same processes of leaving Islam and, in most cases, our communities too, so in a way we're all dependent on each other—and supportive.'

'It's rare that you find a community like this,' he adds. 'Even if they don't tell you how weird and spongy pork is.'

LGBTQ Muslims

On a Friday evening in July 2017, I met twenty-one-year-old Abdul in his room in university halls. He was applying strong, rose-tinted blush in front of his steamed-up mirror. On the floor of the cramped room was an array of garments—bright, red and green crop tops, faux-PVC skinny trousers, rainbow-coloured wristbands, and a deep-red *shalwar kameez*, with gold lace stitched around its collar. 'So sorry about the mess!' he shouted, as he applied his eyeliner. 'I'm usually very clean, I just don't know what I should wear!'

Abdul was preparing to attend his first Pride festival in central London that weekend. The event was a big deal for him, and he had been feeling nervous about it for months. At home in Manchester, as a gay teenager growing up in a devout Muslim family, every summer he had been glued to Twitter, to the pictures of the festival taking place in London. Sometimes, he said, he saved photos of Pride events on a secret USB drive—pictures that serve not only as fashion inspiration, but also as a reminder that as both a gay person and a Muslim, he's not alone. Whatever struggles he faces because of his sexuality, Pride reminds him of 'the brave people who fought for LGBTQ rights despite all of society being against them'.

Abdul didn't want to disclose his real name. He hadn't come out to his parents or any other members of his family, because, in his words: 'While I don't think my parents would disown me, or stop loving me, I am afraid that their community will shun them when they find out I am gay ... especially my *ammi* (mother). I know that there will be people in the community, who attend the same *masjid*, who will say that she's the one to blame, like she could have stopped me from being gay.'

Abdul sat on his bed in silence for a moment, as a tear slipped out of his right eye and ran down his cheek. He got up and shook his head. 'Ugh, I've probably ruined the eyeliner,' he joked, and went back to the bathroom.

Abdul knew he was gay from a young age. 'There were some tell-tale signs,' he said. 'I grew up with my cousins, all of whom are boys, and I was never into things like football, or fighting, or anything considered "macho".' When he entered his teens, he started developing crushes on guys from TV and films. 'Robert Pattinson was a big one!' he laughed. 'That was probably the reason I saw the *Twilight* movies so many times.'

In these ways, Abdul had similar experiences growing up to many other young gay men in Britain. But, he said, another aspect of his identity set him apart, and made being a gay teen even harder. 'What was more difficult was obviously the fact that I am a Pakistani Muslim,' he said. 'I come from a culture where LGBTQ issues aren't understood or treated compassionately, and I grew up in an environment where I was told that my sexuality was just wrong—point-blank wrong.'

It was a challenging time for Abdul. He recalls that during his late teens, 'the time when everyone struggles with their identity', his own struggles were 'so intense'. 'I had so many questions— the things that "normal" teenagers have, like "what should I be doing with my life?" or "what kind of career do I want?" At the same time, I was asking myself about whether I could be both gay and a Muslim, whether I could be who I was, and eventually be with someone I love, while being part of the religion that I grew up with, and which I also love very much.'

Abdul said that many Muslims faced this conflict, between their religious or cultural communities and their sexuality. 'Our communities still don't provide answers,' he sighed. 'They have a very black-and-white view of what relationships and marriage should be, so even openly gay Muslims end up having to be Muslim without support from the communities they've grown up in.'

* * *

For Abdul, social media and the internet have been so instrumental in forming and nurturing LGBTQ Muslim communities, helping 'a lot of young Muslims, not just in the UK but across the world'. These were spaces they could go 'when they have the same questions about their sexuality and their faith'. Often, said Abdul, it was reassuring just to know they weren't alone, 'that there are thousands, if not tens of thousands, of gay, lesbian, queer and trans Muslims who can provide support, advice and encouragement'.

It was through these online communities that I first encountered Abdul. He was a moderator of 'Green Bird', a Facebook group for LGBTQ Muslims, whose name was a reference to a *hadith* stating that the souls of martyrs live on as green birds in Paradise.[28] The group had just under 500 members, and was there to help queer Muslims looking for places to stay, job opportunities, and advice about coming out to their family and loved ones.

Groups like Green Bird have to be discreet. They use ambiguous names that avoid raising suspicion among more socially conservative Muslims. In many cases, the groups are private, and access is sometimes invite-only, in order to protect members' identities and the sensitive information they might share.

'My parents want to send me back to Pakistan so they can "cure" my sexuality,' one Green Bird member posted. 'They say that so many "people like me" who "believe in *haram* things" are fixed there, that they find the beauty of Islam there. I don't know what to do—I can't afford to leave and I have no one else who I can trust.'

Other members sought advice from the group about discussing their sexuality to their families. 'How can I come out to my family in a safe environment?' one person asked. Another user wrote: 'My family want me desperately to be married, and they have found a suitor who does not know about my sexuality—I am struggling to know what to do, as I do not want to upset my mom.'

'There are probably a lot of groups like Green Bird out there that even the wider LGBTQ community doesn't know about,' Abdul told me. For him, these groups represent some of the few 'safe spaces' for queer Muslims, who are often erased from mainstream conversations about LGBTQ issues. 'Most of the time, when people talk about gay Muslims, or LGBTQ Muslim communities, they're usually associating us with liberalism, or with atheism and non-belief. It's why so many people from the wider—and mostly white—gay community say to us, "Why don't you leave Islam? It's such a homophobic religion!" And obviously, that's unhelpful, partly because Islam exists for everyone who professes to be Muslim, and also because so many LGBTQ Muslims are exactly that: Muslim. They don't want to lose their faith. They believe in Allah, and the message of the Prophet— sometimes, more so than straight Muslims!'

Online groups like Green Bird provided a rare opportunity for 'LGBTQ Muslims, who are having identity struggles, and struggles with their faith' to 'know they aren't alone, and that they won't be excluded'. 'It's a place where people can know they can be Muslim *and* true to themselves,' Abdul said. And while there is a limit to what these online communities can achieve, considering that the majority are run by part-time volunteers without any funding or external support, to Abdul, they are part and parcel of the modern queer Muslim experience.

'There's definitely a culture change because of social media,' he told me as he finished applying his make-up. 'It wasn't long ago that gay Muslims had nowhere to turn. You'd have to keep it secret, or you'd have to move away from your family to live your life. At least now there are communities there that can support you, that can provide you with health advice and spiritual advice.' For Abdul, these support groups provided a vital service. 'I do think that the existence of LGBTQ Muslim communities online has stopped vulnerable people from going off the rails.'

* * *

Abdul also expressed another fear: that without support, some LGBTQ Muslims might end up suppressing their sexuality in order to appease their families and religious communities.

In 2015, I wrote an article for BuzzFeed about an online support network of Muslim men who, despite acknowledging that they had homosexual desires, believed that the best way to stay true to their religious beliefs was to 'not act on their impulses', and instead to marry women in accordance with traditional Islamic practice.[29] The piece profiled three men who met every few months to discuss how they were managing their sexual urges—in which they claimed to prevent such activity through prayer and fasting.

Over the time I got to know them, the men repeated a phrase that I'd heard many times before, both in madrassa and in the Islamic videos I watched online: 'Allah hates the sin, not the sinner.' They believed that 'there is nothing in Islam that punishes you for having homosexual desires', but that acting on those desires was sinful.

I had decided to write the piece to explore an under-reported element of Western Muslim experiences, to draw attention to the difficulties that some Muslims had in reconciling their sexual identity with their faith, and to illustrate how poor, ill-informed advice from within religious communities could harm not just gay Muslims, but also their families and friends.

The article got a big reaction. For weeks after it was published, my email inbox was flooded with messages from Muslims living both in the UK and around the world who wanted to be part of the support group for Muslims trying to repress homosexual urges. They told me about how they wanted to be 'pious' Muslims while 'trying to resist sexual desires', which they described as temptation by *Shaitan*. From another side, some Muslims, including activists from Imaan, the UK's leading LGBTQ Muslim charity,[30] argued that the article was likely to cause more harm than good—that, rather than exposing the challenges and struggles that LGBTQ Muslims face, it legiti-mised the opinions of those who believed that people could choose not to be gay, or that it was an issue that could be resolved with prayer.

'The problem I had with the article wasn't in the reporting. It was that nobody had pushed back against the choices these gay Muslim men made—to deceive their families, their friends, their wives,' said Taushif Khan, a twenty-eight-year-old gay Muslim who lives in Brighton.

Taushif was one of the people who had criticised the article on Twitter. When I contacted him, he told me that the mentality of the men I interviewed had brought back memories of what his Muslim friends and family had told him when he came out as gay the year before. 'They were the ones who told me that my sexuality was the result of not being stronger in my belief, or that I had turned out the way I did because it was a test from Allah—like, if I suppressed myself enough, if I stayed abstinent, my reward in heaven would be so significant that it would all be worth it.'

He didn't think he was alone. 'It's something that almost every gay Muslim man who comes from a religious household has gone through. When that article was being spread around across social media, all I could think of was, what happens if someone in my situation reads that, and believes that restraining themselves or denying the truth about themselves is not only the best option, but that it could also make them a better Muslim?'

This is a key challenge for LGBTQ Muslims, and the reason for groups like Imaan. Another organisation set up to support queer Muslims in the UK is Hidayah, which campaigns 'to defeat the stigma, taboo and discrimination faced by many within our communities and to give LGBTQI+ Muslims a voice and visibility to gain social acceptance and change.'[31] Named after the Arabic word for guidance, Hidayah organises marches and campaigns to spread awareness that queer Muslims exist, and takes part in big events like the London Pride march and LGBT Awareness Week. It also provides social spaces, educational workshops, and support for Muslims wishing to come out.

The proliferation of social media means that while LGBTQ Muslims may still be marginalised in cisnormative, heteronormative Islamic spaces, they can now create their own communities and safe spaces in which to congregate and worship. Another group, London Queer Muslims, organises social opportunities and private gatherings, while also providing spaces for prayer. On its Meetup page, London Queer Muslims says: 'We are building a spiritual community of critically consciously Muslim LGBTIQ+ people for whom Queerness and Islam are not something to be "reconciled" but which actually empower each other.'[32]

Online, groups like Imaan and Hidayah face different challenges—from providing support and advice, to combatting queerphobia and discrimination, both within Muslim communities and from anti-Muslim groups that use LGBTQ issues to put forward a narrative that Islam is inherently sexually discriminatory. For most of these groups, this means that secrecy and privacy are paramount. While Imaan and Hidayah both have websites and public social media pages, events are often members only, in order to protect members and allow them to feel safe and comfortable. London Queer Muslims events are advertised only to its members, and prayer meeting locations are only visible to those vetted and accepted by the group.

* * *

'The internet has been great for LGBTQ Muslims in so many ways,' Abdul said, reflecting on the work of his own group. 'We've been able to help so many people, and also raise awareness in our own communities that LGBTQ issues aren't just for white people, or non-religious people. LGBTQ communities can so often feel hostile towards religion, because of how religion has negatively impacted so many queer people, so just existing, and being able to tell people they can still be Muslim, they can still love their religion, and they don't have to compromise them-selves—in my view, that's revolutionary.' He looked at his Pride outfit, which was laid out and ready for tomorrow. 'We've always had to fight for our right to exist, and now is such a crucial time to do that,' he added, 'because we have to fight to exist as LGBTQ and we have to fight to exist as Muslims.'

While Abdul was excited about tomorrow's parade and parties, it was the chance to meet other queer Muslims that he was look-ing forward to most. 'It's good that so many Muslims come to seek our support online,' he said. 'But there's a different feeling when they've shown up for Pride, when they unashamedly march and, for a couple of hours, they can truly be themselves without anyone telling them otherwise ... that's a feeling you can't get in a digital world.'

Black Muslims

'The most vivid memory I have from madrassa is being called a nigger.'

Twenty-eight-year-old Daoud Omar is a financial analyst who lives in north London. We met in a coffee shop near his office in Canary Wharf.

Like many British Muslim parents, Daoud's mother, who converted to Islam after getting married, sent her son to Islamic school on weekends to learn the Qur'an. But for Daoud, those formative years of Islamic studies were dominated by his constant awareness of the difference between him and his classmates: his skin colour. Every other person in Daoud's madrassa was of South Asian descent. Most were from middle-class Pakistani families and attended the same *masjid*, primary schools and secondary schools; in many cases, they even belonged to the same extended families.

Daoud, in contrast, is of Ghanaian descent. He doesn't speak Urdu, and unlike his classmates did not come from a family background where children rote learned *surahs* from the Qur'an and well-known *du'ahs*, or prayers, at home. He immediately felt like an outcast.

'I remember being called stupid and dumb by classmates because I found it difficult to read certain sentences in Arabic, or if I didn't know certain things about Islam that my classmates had learnt as children from their parents,' he said, his eyes beginning to water.

The insults got worse and eventually led to Daoud being bullied and racially abused—something that the teachers did nothing about. 'They couldn't understand why it hurt or what impact it was having on me. The only thing my madrassa teachers kept saying was that I should work harder.' With a doleful sigh, he shook his head and started to laugh. 'Then they did what they always do. They brought up the Bilal story.'

'The Bilal story' is a familiar trope among black Muslims online—an inside joke that, for most black Muslims I spoke to, sums up a great deal of their interactions with their South Asian counterparts.

Bilal ibn Rabah was one of the most notable *Sahabah*—the companions of the Prophet. His story is often used by imams today to show how Islam was truly 'against all forms of racism' from its inception. For Bilal was an Abyssinian slave, described by historians as 'of a handsome and impressive stature, dark brown complexion with sparkling eyes, a fine nose and bright skin'.[33] Upon his emancipation he was put in charge of the Bayt al-Mal, or the treasury, in Medina, and was chosen by the Prophet to call the early Muslims to prayer as the first muezzin. Citing the Prophet Muhammad's reverence for Bilal, the Birmingham-based Shakyh Zahir Mahmood said in a speech uploaded to YouTube in 2014, 'You see, 1,400 years ago, the Prophet [peace be upon him] dealt with the issue of racism', adding that 'to be racist is as *haram* as eating a pork sandwich'.[34]

Yet, to young black Muslims like Daoud, the Bilal story has almost become a meme, used in bad faith to justify and white-wash issues around racism in Muslim communities, while at the same time promoting myths of a 'united *ummah*' in which Muslims of all races are treated equally as part of a global community. When asked a question about how to address discrimination in the American Muslim community against black Muslims, Sheikh Siraj Wahhaj, an African American imam based in New York, responded:

> One of the things ... that I love about Islam is that there is no racism in Islam. ... Allah made the beauty in all the races ... I am a black man and I am proud to be what I am ... If Allah is pleased to make me a black man, with kinky hair and a broad nose and thick lips, I'm happy to be that. And by the same token whatever you are, your red hair, your blonde hair, your white skin ... whatever it is, you should be happy because God created you that way. ... This is the beauty of Islam, and there's no racism in Islam.[35]

'It's a nice idea to say,' Daoud told me. 'But in reality it's never the case, and you only realise that if you're the person who is on the receiving end.' To Daoud, that didn't just mean the overt racist abuse he had faced as a teenager in madrassa, but also subtle, everyday kinds of discrimination and rejection, from 'when you're applying to committee positions at a South Asian- or Arab-dominated *masjid*', to trying to get married. Daoud told me that widespread anti-black prejudice in Muslim communities meant that it was hard for many black Muslims to find marriage partners. 'A lot of the time the parents of South Asian sisters will disapprove of their children marrying black people, even if they are of the same religion, and even if they are pious and believing. So many black brothers I know have experienced this racism from within the community, all while being told that such racism doesn't exist.'

As expected, the internet isn't immune from this kind of racism. In fact, Daoud added, 'in online spaces, anti-black prejudice can be amplified and vocalised in ways that you can't do offline'. Daoud isn't as active online as he used to be, but remembers that when he was once a member of large Muslim discussion groups on Facebook, he had received racially charged messages from strangers accusing him of practising Islam incorrectly. The accounts would usually be registered under *kunyas*—pseud- onyms—and their profile pictures would be Arabic calligraphy. 'I had a picture of myself on my Facebook account where I was playing a djembe'—a West African drum—'while wearing a *thawb* and a skullcap,' Daoud said. 'There was a guy who kept messaging me to say that I should take my profile picture down, that playing instruments was *haram* and not from Islam ... It was so weird! Like, my family have been playing music for genera- tions and it was very much part of my culture and my faith. And then, all of a sudden, this guy, who I don't know, is telling me about how to practise Islam!'

Omar's story was only one of many that I heard from black British Muslims about their mistreatment by other Muslims online.

One black Muslim told me that her South Asian counterparts wouldn't see her as Muslim. 'They wouldn't take my religiosity seriously compared to other Pakistanis or Bengalis,' she said. 'My religion—my Muslimness—is considered to be a quirk, rather than a part of my identity. I had Muslims who were surprised I would fast in Ramadan, even though I've done it my entire life, just because they had never encountered black Muslims before.'

Others said they felt under-represented in online Muslim groups. One of my interviewees said he felt 'outnumbered by Desi [South Asian] Muslims, who would dominate the group conversations with threads about traditional *shaadis* [weddings], or with Urdu or Bengali lectures from YouTube that would get so much more engagement compared to anything black Muslims posted.'

* * *

While these anecdotes hinted at hidden forms of anti-blackness, I was told that these latent sentiments would rise to the surface whenever race was placed at the forefront of a conversation. In early 2017, this was illustrated when Hamza Yusuf, a respected white American Muslim scholar, argued that Muslims living in the West would be ill advised to work with movements like Black Lives Matter, an organisation whose mission is to build local power and intervene when violence is inflicted on black communities by the state and vigilantes. Yusuf said in a lecture: 'We have between 15,000 and 18,000 homicides per year. Fifty percent are black-on-black crime, literally. ... There are twice as many whites that have been shot by police, but nobody ever shows those videos.' He went on to say, 'It's the assumption that the police are racist. It's not always the case ... Any police now that shoots a black is immediately considered a racist.'[36]

Yusuf's comments, especially because of his reputation as a 'celebrity sheikh', drew condemnation and outrage as the video clips spread across Facebook, Twitter and YouTube. They also sparked a global conversation about the visibility of black people in mainstream Muslim communities, both in the United States as well as in the United Kingdom.

'So few South Asian Muslims understand what black Muslim history is, beyond Malcolm X quotes they've recognised,' wrote Abdullah Saani, a London-based black Muslim, shortly after Yusuf's comments. In a post in the Facebook private group 'UK Muslims',[37] Saani continued: 'Until there is a proper effort by Desi Muslims to learn about black history, include it in their mosque curriculums, and to bring black Muslims INTO their discussion groups, there will always be that level of ignorance.'

Other black Muslims were far more blunt in their statements.

'These comments show how so many of our supposedly "united" Muslim community will rally behind things that white reverts [like Yusuf] will say, even if they are offensive toward black communities,' said Bristol-based Shereen Ajileye in the Facebook group 'Muslim Changemakers'.[38] 'No wonder why so many black Muslims feel so alienated ... why so many of them lose their Islam.'

* * *

For many young black Muslims, creating their own spaces online has become increasingly important. In October 2017, during Black History Month, the poet Mohamed Mohamed was part of a team that produced an online web series called *Black and Muslim in Britain*. Speaking to BuzzFeed, Mohamed said that he had noticed an absence of Black History Month programmes in Muslim spaces at university, and wanted to rectify it.[39] The series featured black British Muslims, like historian Habeeb Akande and rapper Tanya Muneera Williams, talking about a range of topics, from finding love to who their black role models are. In one video, educator Amira Marius said: 'People don't recognise Islam as a "black" religion a lot of the times because they don't have that knowledge and that understanding ... so they see it as an adopted religion.'[40]

Black Muslims have also been using Twitter to assert their religious identity, far from the blueprints set by their Arab and South Asian counterparts. For example, in June 2016, black Muslims across the UK used the hashtag #BlackOutEid, alongside images of themselves on Eid day, often wearing clothing associated with their cultural traditions, to challenge mainstream media coverage of annual Eid-ul-Fitr celebrations, which mostly tend to focus on large gatherings of South Asian men at Eid prayers.[41]

Aamina Mohamed, who started the hashtag, told BuzzFeed: 'I created #BlackOutEid after thinking of how much I admire the holiday, and how it felt, and how vibrantly my people's celebration looked. And I wondered how this looked throughout the black diaspora.'[42]

'I was always frustrated that black Muslim communities would be ignored by the media,' said Sulayman al-Bakr, a twenty-two-year-old Muslim whose picture of himself wearing a traditional *thawb* and *taqiya*, embroidered in Sudan, was retweeted over 300 times. 'Obviously I put out the picture of myself because I looked good—and it's not that often it happens,' he laughed, 'but at the same time, it was the first time that I actually felt part of Eid celebrations, you know? Like, after feeling excluded by the wider Muslim community for so long, Black Twitter made me feel Muslim again.'

Black Muslims are asserting themselves online in artistic ways too. Najwa Umran, the creator of the 'Female Muslim Creatives' network on Instagram, started the hashtag campaign #Black MuslimahExcellence, in retaliation against colourism in the modest fashion industry.[43] The young British Somali photographer Hassan Gazali has built an Instagram following of nearly 15,000 people, by documenting his everyday life in London, as well as photographing up-and-coming artists who are set to define the city's next generation.[44] Being at the forefront of this cultural shift hasn't gone unnoticed—London-based photographer Mohamed Abdulle, also British Somali, has created work for some of the world's biggest brands and musicians, including Apple Music, Nike and grime artist Stormzy.[45]

While these creative projects don't necessarily draw directly from Islam and Muslim identity, online engagement with them, especially from other black Muslims, often does. It's not uncommon to find comments like 'MASHALLAH you are stunning!' and 'Keep representing us Hijabi women!' underneath photos on Instagram of Muslim models like Ramla Jamac.[46] Podcasts from the Baraka Boys—a collective of black Muslim musicians and spoken word poets, who produce shows about the cultural experiences of Muslims living in the UK—are frequently shared across 'Black Twitter', with statements like 'Finally, an interesting discussion about anti-blackness in the Muslim community'.[47]

* * *

'There's definitely been progress when it comes to black voices being heard in Muslim circles,' said Daoud. 'But there is still a long way to go'—especially, he added, at a time when 'identity politics' on the internet is rife and 'there's less willingness to listen to views that make you uncomfortable'.

Daoud was heartened by cases that showed that some South Asian Muslims were becoming more aware of their dominance in Islamic conversations. In 2018, he saw many of his South Asian Muslim friends share a Twitter thread by Etaf Kawaldeh, a twenty-year-old student, about black Muslim figures in history, such as the Sudanese writer Fatima Ahmed Ibrahim, or Princess Nana Asma'u, the daughter of the founder of the Sokoto Caliphate.[48]

Daoud had also seen more South Asians calling out anti-blackness online, openly supporting movements like Black Lives

Matter, and becoming more aware of the effects of colourism, as well as of their own social privileges compared to black people.

Despite this progress, Daoud believed that there needed to be a 'generational shift' for things to really change. 'That means that South Asian Muslims, Arab Muslims, they need to interrogate the anti-blackness of their histories and the prejudices that have led us to have such huge inequalities in our wider British Muslim community.'

'It's like with any form of racism,' he concluded. 'Unless you're willing to ask how you've been complicit, or how your family has been complicit, nothing will change. We'll always end up going back to the story of Bilal.'

CONCLUSION

I never found out what happened to Abu Antaar.

It has been five years since our first conversation, during which time the caliphate that enticed him on the internet, for which he was willing to give up his comfortable life, his family and his friends, has entered its death throes.[1] At the time of writing, ISIS is being flushed out of its last territorial stronghold, having lost more than 99 per cent of the estimated 88,000 sq km it once controlled across Iraq and Syria.[2] Some 900 Britons like Abu Antaar left the UK to join ISIS's ranks.[3] A large number of foreign fighters from the West were either killed in combat, or captured by Kurdish military forces. Many now await their fate as European governments decide whether they should face trial, be placed in de-radicalisation programmes, or have their citizenship revoked entirely.

In the course of writing this book, a question I often returned to was whether Abu Antaar was a product of the modern internet, or if his move to radical militant Islamism had simply been accelerated by it. I speculated as to what he might have been like before coming across ISIS material on social media. Perhaps, like me, he was a lukewarm believer, someone who identified himself as a Muslim, but whose practice of the faith sometimes fluctuated under the weight of personal struggles. Perhaps, in rejecting his parents' version of Islam, he had gone through a phase of non-belief, before finding online communities that introduced him to conservative, literalist interpretations of the religion.

Or I could be entirely wrong. Maybe Abu Antaar had identified with violent, militant Salafism for longer than anyone in his life had known, and was always waiting for a group like ISIS to offer him the opportunity to fulfil what he'd always believed was his religious duty. Whatever the case, because I only got to know Abu Antaar online, I was aware that I would never know the whole truth.

For Abu Antaar, the vastness of the internet, and the anonymity it offered, allowed him to create his own backstory—of a disenchanted, 'cultural' Muslim who had discarded all the so-called innovations and misinterpretations of Islam to pursue a true, authentic version of the faith. Such a neat, concise narrative could then be used to convince others, like me, to join him. At the same time, the internet was also a tool he used to define himself against others, whether that was by sending me links to negative articles about ISIS as 'proof' that journalists like me were *kuffar* engaged in a holy war against him, or by sharing something as simple as a compilation video of goals from football matches that he'd found on YouTube—the kind of online content that distinguished him from other foreign fighters as uniquely British, and that signalled that there were parts of his old life that were still intrinsic to his identity.

* * *

I might never find out the truth about Abu Antaar. But as I wrote this book, one thing that did stand out was how common his online journey was, and how nearly every young Muslim I interviewed and spent time with had gone through a similar process in trying to determine their religious identity on the internet, even if it led them to very different places. The dominance of social media as the site of conversations and interactions in modern life inevitably means that it will impact the most intimate parts of our lived experiences. It is true that for some Muslims, social media represents a threat to traditional forms of authority, such as classically trained scholars and imams in local mosques. But for others, access to the internet and online communities offers, for the first time, the ability to form communities and safe spaces where they can have difficult, challenging conversations in a way that wouldn't be possible in traditional madrassas and places of worship. I met Muslims who had formed their own prayer spaces outside of their mosque, created inclusive online environments for LGBTQ Muslims living outside of the UK's major cities, and set up support networks for Muslim women who had been subject to domestic abuse. All these groups had the same origin story: Muslims who felt disenfranchised, unrepresented or restricted by traditional Islamic structures of authority were using social media to express their grievances, collectively attempting to use the resources available to them to tackle problems they felt their communities were either too slow to address, or unwilling to acknowledge at all.

Social media has also allowed Muslims living in the UK to express themselves as individuals, in a way that traditional Islamic environments simply cannot allow them to do. By their nature, mosques and Islamic community centres function in hierarchical structures, in which an imam serves his congregation, and committees make decisions on behalf of the community in the institution's day-to-day running. A complaint I often heard during my interviews was that these committees didn't 'represent me', and that because most were 'run by men in the past generation', the priorities of many mosques around the UK weren't reflective of the experiences of most young Muslims.

It makes sense, then, that social media platforms like Instagram are so popular among Muslim influencers, who can use the aesthetic-driven platform to express their Islam to their millennial and 'Gen-Z' fanbase. Sometimes, that can be articulated through make-up and hijab tutorials, presenting the idea that Muslims can indulge an interest in fashion while remaining true to their faith. But it can also be represented by Muslim influencers like Imran Ibn Mansur, known online as 'Dawah Man', who uses Instagram and YouTube to advocate for a Salafi version of Islam to his young audience, most of whom are in their teens and early twenties.

In many cases, while social media has allowed Muslims to meet and interact more of their co-religionists than ever before, it has also changed the way in which influence can be exerted. Those who wish to be influencers in Muslim communities online have to be conscious of how they present themselves on social media, which can result in critiques from strangers about how they dress, whom they spend time with offline, and how 'authentic' their political and religious views are. All online influencers face pressures from advertisers, brands and audiences to cultivate online authenticity. Muslim influencers face all of this, plus the added pressure of audience scepticism in how 'true' their belief in Islam is. Any sign of struggles or fluctuations in belief can be met with accusations of appropriating Islam to further their 'personal brand'. This was the experience of British Egyptian fashion blogger Dina Tokio, whose announcement in 2018 that she had decided to stop wearing hijab was met with a barrage of hateful comments, some of which she read out in a YouTube video.[4]

* * *

From the beginning, this book set out to argue that understanding internet culture is essential for understanding the lives of Muslims living in Britain today. While the stories contained in this volume shed light on how social media has disrupted traditional manifestations of religious authority and community, the fast pace of technological development inevitably means that there are aspects of online culture that I was unable to explore, but which are likely to further impact British Muslim experiences. One of these advances is in virtual reality, which the Denmark-based company VR Karbala is using to produce simulations that will allow users to 'travel back in time and experience the tragedy of Karbala', the battle at which the Shi'a Imam Hussein, the Prophet's grandson, was killed.[5] Such a technology could add another dimension to how Shi'a Muslims mourn the death of Hussein during the holy month of Muharram.

One new technology to have become popular in some Muslim spaces is cryptocurrency. In 2018, Sheikh Haitham al-Haddad, a well-known Sunni scholar, suggested that Muslim communities start looking at alternative digital currencies as a means of conducting 'halal' transactions and creating Sharia-compliant banking structures in the West.[6] Al-Haddad's speech was taken to heart by Masjid Ramadan in Dalston, East London, which in May 2018 became the first mosque in the UK to accept donations in Bitcoin and Ethereum when collecting *zakat*.[7]

Whether cryptocurrency really takes off among British Muslims will be dependent on how successful it becomes generally. But what is clear is that Muslim communities are far from hesitant when it comes to embracing new technology, and in most cases welcome its incorporation into their religious lives. Hundreds of Islamic apps exist across Apple and Android mobile platforms, ranging from Qur'an study programmes, to compasses to determine the direction of Mecca, to daily Islamic reminders. And, with technological barriers to entry lowering, more young Muslims are making their own content to express their beliefs, their identity, and their experiences of living in modern Britain.

One of the most popular mediums for this has been podcasts. In the course of writing this book, I frequently listened to

Islamic podcasts like *One Foot In The Sink*, *Group Chat Podcast*, *Mind Heist* and *Really & Truly*—all of which are independently hosted and produced by young Muslims, who take on issues ranging from sexual health to politics to drama on 'Muslim Twitter', in ways that are informal, unthreatening and, ultimately, relatable. I was unsure whether podcasting would be an effective medium in an online world where so many conversations about faith seem to focus on its visible manifestations. But the relative ease by which a podcast can be produced compared to a YouTube video means that it is likely we will see more youth-facing Muslim podcasts emerging on the internet soon.

* * *

None of this is to suggest that traditional Islamic authorities, structures and community spaces will be undermined or replaced by social media platforms. None of the Muslims I spoke to suggested that the internet was an adequate replacement for the mosque, or stated that their preference for listening to particular Islamic lectures online meant that there was no need for a local imam. In some cases, exposure to the internet even helped Muslims, who had once felt alienated in their communities, to feel more comfortable attending prayers and sermons at their mosque. This is why groups like Imams Online, rather than being hesitant and worried about social media, believe that the internet has to play a key role in how mosques are run, and offer training to imams in how to use social media in conjunction with their traditional duties. More mosques across the UK are setting up YouTube channels and Facebook pages to stream lectures and events to worshippers, while imams in the UK are being encouraged to follow the examples set by preachers around the world like Mufti Menk and Omar Suleiman, classically trained imams who have successfully been able to incorporate social media into their preaching and thereby reach hundreds of thousands of people.

CONCLUSION

What the internet in its current form does offer to young Muslims, then, is choice. With every individual I interviewed and every group I spent time with, the common thread was that the internet allowed them to navigate and negotiate their faith on their own terms. Online, some could present themselves as being more devout than they were, in the hope that spending more time with other 'devout' Muslims would make their faith stronger. In other cases, the internet could provide a safe, non-judgemental space for Muslims whose beliefs deviated from those of their families and communities. On social media, they could be recognised as Muslims while also belonging to minority communities. Private Facebook groups and encrypted chat networks meant that Muslims who felt pressure to behave conservatively in real-life settings could make risqué jokes and indulge in dark humour without their faith being interrogated.

Indeed, for many Muslims the internet provides safe and supportive environments where they can grapple with the complexities of Islam and their relationship with it. For ex-Muslims, that might mean access to support networks of people who understand the emotional difficulties of leaving a faith like Islam and who can provide both moral and practical support. For others, it can mean finding refuge in groups that, for example, actively ban sectarianism on their platforms, or discovering communities of like-minded people in groups like 'British Muslims for Secular Democracy', an organisation that aims to 'encourage the secular Muslim voice'.[8]

One thing I hope this book makes clear, however, is that the identities of British Muslims are vastly complex, which makes it important to resist simple categories. Serious study of how internet culture has shaped the British Muslim experience will ultimately show that compartmentalising Muslims—by political outlook or by sect—is unhelpful in terms of analysis and in policymaking. It has been said before that Muslims are not a monolith, that 'Islamic identity' means something different for every Muslim, and that to understand what Muslims feel is their place in Britain today, we must depart from the idea that certain Muslims can speak on behalf of their entire communities. Online groups like those described in this volume show how complicated that understanding of place and identity can be. At the same time, the stories in this book represent only a speck of the true diversity that exists among British Muslims. Future generations of British-born Muslims will use social media to express their faith in different ways, perhaps even abandoning it in favour of more advanced and secure forms of communication unbeknown to us. They will be at the forefront of defining what it means to be a Muslim living in Britain.

It is worth following them.

NOTES

INTRODUCTION

1. Robert Mendick, Robert Verkaik and Tim Ross, *The Telegraph*, 'Muslim MP: 2,000 Britons fighting for Islamic State', 23 November 2014, https://www.telegraph.co.uk/news/worldnews/islamic-state/11248114/Muslim-MP-2000-Britons-fighting-for-Islamic-State.html, last accessed 22 February 2019.

2. Madeline Grant and Damien Sharkov, *Newsweek*, '"Twice as Many" British Muslims Fighting for ISIS Than in UK Armed Forces', 20 August 2014, https://www.newsweek.com/twice-many-british-muslims-fighting-isis-armed-forces-265865, last accessed 22 February 2019; Zeeshan Hashmi, *The Telegraph*, 'Why more British Muslims are fighting for ISIL than the Army', 28 February 2015, https://www.telegraph.co.uk/news/worldnews/islamic-state/11439401/Why-more-British-Muslims-are-fighting-for-ISIL-than-the-Army.html, last accessed 22 February 2019.

3. Office for National Statistics, 'Religion in England and Wales 2011', 11 December 2012, https://www.ons.gov.uk/peoplepopulationandcommunity/culturalidentity/religion/articles/religioninenglandandwales2011/2012–12–11, last accessed 22 February 2019.

4. The Muslim Council of Britain, 'British Muslims in Numbers', January 2015, pp. 12, 27, https://www.mcb.org.uk/wp-content/uploads/2015/02/MCBCensusReport_2015.pdf, last accessed 22 February 2019.

5. Sirin Kale, *The Guardian*, 'Logged off: meet the teens who refuse to use social media', 29 August 2018, https://www.theguardian.com/

society/2018/aug/29/teens-desert-social-media, last accessed 22 February 2019.

6. Saleem Kassim, Mic, 'Twitter Revolution: How the Arab Spring Was Helped By Social Media', 3 July 2012, https://mic.com/articles/10642/twitter-revolution-how-the-arab-spring-was-helped-by-social-media, last accessed 22 February 2019.

7. Angela Giuffrida, Michael Safi and Ammar Kalia, *The Guardian*, 'The populist social media playbook: the battle for Facebook, Twitter and Instagram', 17 December 2018, https://www.theguardian.com/world/2018/dec/17/populist-social-media-playbook-who-is-best-facebook-twitter-instagram-matteo-salvini-narendra-modi, last accessed 22 February 2019.

8. Monique Judge, *The Root*, 'Twitter Has a Serious Harassment and Abuse Problem but Doesn't Seem to Want to Cure It', 30 October 2017, https://www.theroot.com/twitter-has-a-serious-harassment-and-abuse-problem-but-1819979725, last accessed 22 February 2019; Alex Hern, *The Guardian*, 'MPs question Google, Facebook and Twitter on problematic content', 16 October 2018, https://www.theguardian.com/politics/2018/oct/16/mps-grill-facebook-google-twitter-problematic-content-commons, last accessed 22 February 2019.

9. Paul Mozur, *The New York Times*, 'A Genocide Incited on Facebook, With Posts From Myanmar's Military', 15 October 2018, https://www.nytimes.com/2018/10/15/technology/myanmar-facebook-genocide.html, last accessed 22 February 2019.

10. BBC News, 'India WhatsApp "child kidnap" rumours claim two more victims', 11 June 2018, https://www.bbc.co.uk/news/world-asia-india-44435127, last accessed 22 February 2019.

11. NPR, 'The Reason Your Feed Became An Echo Chamber—And What To Do About It', 24 July 2016, https://www.npr.org/sections/alltech-considered/2016/07/24/486941582/the-reason-your-feed-became-an-echo-chamber-and-what-to-do-about-it, last accessed 22 February 2019; Pablo Barberá, John T. Jost, Jonathan Nagler, Joshua A. Tucker, and Richard Bonneau, 'Tweeting From Left to Right: Is Online Political Communication More Than an Echo Chamber?', *Psychological Science*, 26 (10): 1531–42, 2015, http://citeseerx.ist.psu.edu/viewdoc/downloa

d?doi=10.1.1.715.7520&rep=rep1&type=pdf, last accessed 22 February 2019.

12. Eric Urban, 'Identity politics, social media and the 2016 presidential election', MA thesis, Rutgers University, 2018.

13. Gary Bunt, *Hashtag Islam How Cyber-Islamic Environments Are Transforming Religious Authority*, Chapel Hill, NC: University of North Carolina Press, 2018.

1. PREACHERS AND MOSQUES

1. The Muslim 500, 'Nouman Ali Khan', https://www.themuslim500.com/profiles/nouman-ali-khan, last accessed 22 February 2019.

2. faith & knowledge, YouTube, 'Patience—Beautiful Lecture—All need it today—Hamza Yusuf', 18 April 2017, https://www.youtube.com/watch?v=2wp3qA7FoJY, last accessed 22 February 2019.

3. Gary Vaynerchuk Fan Page, YouTube, 'How To Escape The RAT RACE—Gary Vaynerchuk Motivation | Part 2', 3 December 2018, https://www.youtube.com/watch?v=QQphKaNnzzc, last accessed 22 February 2019.

4. Paula Dear, BBC News, 'Crowds flock to new Muslim centre', 12 June 2004, http://news.bbc.co.uk/2/hi/uk_news/3799353.stm, last accessed 22 February 2019.

5. Lela Mosemghvdlishvili and Jeroen Jansz, 'Framing and praising Allah on YouTube: Exploring user-created videos about Islam and the motivations for producing them', *New Media & Society*, 15 (4): 482–500, 2012.

6. *Ibid.*

7. House of Commons Home Affairs Committee, 'Radicalisation: the counter-narrative and identifying the tipping point, Eighth Report of Session 2016–17', 25 August 2016, https://publications.parliament.uk/pa/cm201617/cmselect/cmhaff/135/135.pdf, last accessed 22 February 2019.

8. House of Commons Home Affairs Committee, 'Hate crime: abuse, hate and extremism online, Fourteenth Report of Session 2016–17', 1 May 2017, https://publications.parliament.uk/pa/cm201617/cmselect/cmhaff/609/609.pdf, last accessed 22 February 2019; Lizzie Dearden, *The*

Independent, 'Social media companies accused of "radicalising and grooming" users with algorithms', 19 December 2017, https://www.independent.co.uk/news/uk/home-news/terror-manuals-online-facebook-google-twitter-youtube-radicalising-grooming-isis-al-qaeda-a8119336.html, last accessed 22 February 2019.

9. Mosemghvdlishvili and Jansz, 'Framing and praising Allah on YouTube'.

10. EpicIslamicLectures, YouTube, https://www.youtube.com/user/EpicIslamicLectures, last accessed 22 February 2019.

11. Mufti Abu Layth al-Maliki, Facebook, https://www.facebook.com/MuftiALMaliki, last accessed 22 February 2019.

12. Ummah.com, https://www.ummah.com/forum/forum/islam/general-islamic-topics/12550393-what-do-you-guys-think-of-this-guy-that-calls-himself-mufti-abu-layth, last accessed 22 February 2019.

13. The Polemicist, YouTube, 'Masturbation Is Not Haraam—The Salaf Encouraged It—Mufti Abu Layth', 1 May 2018, https://www.youtube.com/watch?v=7d49s02sf8A, last accessed 22 February 2019.

14. Abu Abdul Aziz, Instagram, https://www.instagram.com/abuabdulazizahmed, last accessed 22 February 2019.

15. Abu Safiyyah Mohammed Osman, Instagram, https://www.instagram.com/abu_safiyyah_mohammed, last accessed 22 February 2019.

16. SQ, Instagram, https://www.instagram.com/wayoflifesq, last accessed 22 February 2019.

17. Imams Online, http://imamsonline.com, last accessed 22 February 2019.

18. BBC News, 'UK imams condemn Isis in online video', 11 July 2014, https://www.bbc.com/news/av/uk-28273888/uk-imams-condemn-isis-in-online-video, last accessed 22 February 2019.

19. Al Kalimah, YouTube, 'Outside Shisha Café's On Eid [Emotional] || Da'wah Man' https://www.youtube.com/watch?v=PKN_Ed5GA9Y, last accessed 22 February 2019.

20. Amir Webb, The Muslim Vibe, 'Dawah Man and the dangers of aggressive street dawah', 4 November 2018, https://themuslimvibe.com/featured/dawah-man-and-the-dangers-of-aggressive-street-dawah, last accessed 22 February 2019.

21. Naseeha Sessions, YouTube, 'The TRUTH about the MAWLID!!! ||

Naseeha Sessions', 26 December 2015, https://www.youtube.com/watch?v=8tHdrV78m4Y, last accessed 22 February 2019.

22. almadina786, YouTube, 'Celebrating Mawlid un Nabi from Quraan and Hadith By Imam Muhammed Asim Hussain', 31 January 2012, https://www.youtube.com/watch?v=r7KHATlhpa0, last accessed 22 February 2019.

23. Speakers' Corner Trust, 'A Brief History of London's Speakers' Corner', http://www.speakerscornertrust.org/library/about-free-speech/a-brief-history-of-londons-speakers-corner, last accessed 22 February 2019.

24. Phil Coomes, BBC News, 'Speakers' Corner: The home of free speech', 15 May 2015, https://www.bbc.co.uk/news/in-pictures-32703071, last accessed 22 February 2019.

25. SCDawah Channel, YouTube, 'Free Gift! Shamsi Vs Christian | Speakers Corner | Hyde Park', 15 April 2018, https://www.youtube.com/watch?v=KdOHNIFMLts, last accessed 22 February 2019.

26. SCDawah Channel, YouTube, 'P1—Feminism & Patriarchy Muhammad Hijab & Female Visitor | Speakers Corner | Hyde Park', 13 May 2018, https://www.youtube.com/watch?v=RT4KkDXZpZs, last accessed 22 February 2019.

27. Ali Dawah, YouTube, 'MUSLIM MURDER EXPERIMENT!!!', 25 June 2014, https://www.youtube.com/watch?v=PO25TJYvA4Q, last accessed 22 February 2019.

28. Shireen, Patheos.com, 'Privilege and Prayer Spaces: An Interview with Hind Makki of Side Entrance', 29 August 2013, https://www.patheos.com/blogs/mmw/2013/08/privilege-and-prayer-spaces-an-interview-with-hind-makki-of-side-entrance, last accessed 22 February 2019.

29. 'Muslimahs UK' no longer exists but has become part of a larger group called 'United Muslims': United Muslims, Facebook, https://www.facebook.com/groups/749169628534460, last accessed 22 February 2019.

30. Dr Abdullah Rahim, Al-Mawrid.org, 'Permissibility Of Eating Chicken From Non-Halal Restaurants', 23 January 2015, http://www.al-mawrid.org/index.php/questions/view/permissibility-of-eating-chicken-from-non-halal-restaurants, last accessed 22 February 2019.

31. Gary Bunt, *Hashtag Islam How Cyber-Islamic Environments Are Transforming Religious Authority*, Chapel Hill, NC: University of North Carolina Press, 2018, pp. 83–5.

32. TheProphetsPath, YouTube, 'Sheikh Google[HD] | Mufti Menk', 20 October 2013, https://www.youtube.com/watch?v=-mgweBnZil8, last accessed 22 February 2019.

33. Scholarly Subtitles, YouTube, 'But They Know Who Google Is by Shaykh 'Abdurrazzāq ibn 'Abdulmuhsin al-Badr', 27 February 2017, https://www.youtube.com/watch?v=VcUunDJ5w80, last accessed 22 February 2019.

34. Yahya Birt, 'Sheikh Google vs Wiki Islam', 4 June 2008, https://yahy-abirt1.wordpress.com/2008/06/04/sheikh-google-vs-wiki-islam, last accessed 22 February 2019.

35. Assembly of Muslim Jurists of America, 'Fatwa Bank', http://www.amjaonline.org/en/fatwa-corner/fatwa-bank, last accessed 22 February 2019.

36. Office for National Statistics, 'Internet access—households and individuals, Great Britain: 2018', 7 August 2018, https://www.ons.gov.uk/peoplepopulationandcommunity/householdcharacteristics/homeinternetandsocialmediausage/bulletins/internetaccesshouseholdsandindividuals/2018, last accessed 22 February 2019.

2. SEX AND DATING

1. Number collected in an author interview with muzmatch.

2. Lydia Green, BBC News, 'Why millions of Muslims are signing up for online dating', 10 December 2014, https://www.bbc.com/news/magazine-30397272, last accessed 22 February 2019.

3. The Muslim Council of Britain, 'British Muslims in Numbers', January 2015, https://www.mcb.org.uk/wp-content/uploads/2015/02/MCBCensusReport_2015.pdf, last accessed 22 February 2019.

4. Statista, 'Share of individuals who are current users of Tinder or used the app in the past in the United Kingdom (UK) in June 2017, by age group*', https://www.statista.com/statistics/720850/tinder-current-and-former-usage-in-the-united-kingdom-uk-by-age-group, last accessed 22 February 2019.

5. Diaspora Ukhti, YouTube, 'Black, Muslim and Struggling to Get Married', 13 September 2017, https://www.youtube.com/watch?v= EVuEnvyupZY, last accessed 22 February 2019.

6. Cheryl V. Jackson, *Chicago Tribune*, 'Why dating site OKCupid performed secret experiments on its users', 22 April 2015, https://www. chicagotribune.com/bluesky/originals/chi-christian-rudder-okcupid-bsi-20150422-story.html, last accessed 22 February 2019.

7. Jessica Strubela and Trent A. Petrie, 'Love me Tinder: Body image and psychosocial functioning among men and women', *Body Image*, 21: 34–8, June 2017, http://www.sciencedirect.com/science/article/pii/ S1740144516303254, last accessed 22 February 2019.

8. Laila Alawa, Mic, 'Here's What It's Like to Use Dating Apps As a Muslim American Woman', 7 January 2016, https://mic.com/articles/131922/here-s-what-it-s-like-to-use-dating-apps-as-a-muslim-american-woman, last accessed 22 February 2019.

9. Bintou Waiga, YouTube, 'We met on MuzMatch but He Won't Marry Me | Unapologetic Letters 3 | Bintou Waiga', 7 January 2018, https:// www.youtube.com/watch?v=eM_lKE1_ffQ, last accessed 22 February 2019.

10. Reddit, https://www.reddit.com/r/MuslimNoFap, last accessed 22 February 2019.

11. Purify Your Gaze, https://purifyyourgaze.com, last accessed 22 February 2019.

12. Mobeen Azhar, *The Independent*, 'The Muslim Sex Doctor: How Imam Alyas Karmani Uses Religious Texts to Counsel a Community "In Sexual Denial"', 9 November 2015, https://www.independent.co.uk/ life-style/love-sex/the-muslim-sex-doctor-how-imam-alyas-karmani-uses-religious-texts-to-counsel-a-community-in-sexual-a6726571.html, last accessed 22 February 2019.

13. Ronan Farrow, *The New Yorker*, 'From Aggressive Overtures to Sexual Assault: Harvey Weinstein's Accusers Tell Their Stories', 23 October 2017, https://www.newyorker.com/news/news-desk/from-aggressive-overtures-to-sexual-assault-harvey-weinsteins-accusers-tell-their-stories, last accessed 22 February 2019.

14. Aisha Gani, BuzzFeed, 'Meet The Black Woman Who Started The

"Me Too" Campaign Against Sexual Assault A Decade Ago', 19 October 2017, https://www.buzzfeed.com/aishagani/people-are-pointing-out-a-black-woman-started-the-me-too, last accessed 22 February 2019.

15. Nadja Sayej, *The Guardian*, 'Alyssa Milano on the #MeToo movement: "We're not going to stand for it any more"', 1 December 2017, https://www.theguardian.com/culture/2017/dec/01/alyssa-milano-mee-too-sexual-harassment-abuse, last accessed 22 February 2019.

16. Faranak Amidi, BBC News, '100 Women: Muslim women rally round #MosqueMeToo', 9 February 2018, https://www.bbc.com/news/world-43006952, last accessed 22 February 2019.

17. Mona Eltahawy, Twitter, 6 February 2018, https://twitter.com/monael-tahawy/status/960701491328712706?ref_src=twcamp%255Eshare%257Ctwsrc%255Eios%257Ctwgr%255Eother, last accessed 22 February 2019.

18. Mona Eltahawy, *The Washington Post*, '#MosqueMeToo: What happened when I was sexually assaulted during the hajj', 15 February 2018, https://www.washingtonpost.com/news/global-opinions/wp/2018/02/15/mosquemetoo-what-happened-when-i-was-sexually-assaulted-during-the-hajj, last accessed 22 February 2019.

19. *Ibid.*

20. Megan Garber, *The Atlantic*, 'Is #MeToo Too Big?', 4 July 2018, https://www.theatlantic.com/entertainment/archive/2018/07/is-metoo-too-big/564275, last accessed 22 February 2019.

21. Yasir Qadhi, YouTube, 'The #MeToo Movement & Sexual Crimes from an Islamic Perspective—Shaykh Dr. Yasir Qadhi', 3 October 2018, https://www.youtube.com/watch?v=8QX43QXDqlU, last accessed 22 February 2019.

22. Let the Quran Speak, YouTube, '#MeToo | #MosqueMeToo', 19 March 2018, https://www.youtube.com/watch?v=o0Shnl6fIII, last accessed 22 February 2019.

23. Sara Roncero-Menendez, Mashable, 'The 7 Best Uses for Tumblr', 9 December 2013, https://mashable.com/2013/12/09/tumblr-uses, last accessed 22 February 2019.

24. Elspeth Reeve, *The New Republic*, 'The Secret Life of Tumblr Teens', 17 February 2016, https://newrepublic.com/article/129002/secret-lives-tumblr-teens, last accessed 22 February 2019.

25. Tumblr, https://www.tumblr.com/tagged/why-you-lying-tumblr, last accessed 22 February 2019.

26. Caitlin Dewey, *The Washington Post*, '2015 is the year that Tumblr became the front page of the internet', 23 December 2015, https://www.washingtonpost.com/news/the-intersect/wp/2015/03/11/move-over-reddit-tumblr-is-the-new-front-page-of-the-internet, last accessed 22 February 2019.

27. Reeve, 'The Secret Life of Tumblr Teens'.

3. ISLAMOPHOBIA AND THE ALT-RIGHT

1. The Runnymede Trust, 'Islamophobia: A challenge for us all', 1997, https://www.runnymedetrust.org/companies/17/74/Islamophobia-A-Challenge-for-Us-All.html, last accessed 22 February 2019.

2. Chris Allen, 'The "first" decade of Islamophobia: 10 years of the Runnymede Trust report "Islamophobia: a challenge for us all"', 2007, http://www.islamiccouncilwa.com.au/wp-content/uploads/2014/05/Decade_of_Islamophobia.pdf, last accessed 22 February 2019.

3. The Runnymede Trust, 'Islamophobia: Still a challenge for us all', 2017, https://www.runnymedetrust.org/uploads/Islamophobia%20Report%202018%20FINAL.pdf, last accessed 22 February 2019.

4. Aina Khan, Al Jazeera, 'How has Islamophobia changed over the past 20 years?', 16 November 2017, https://www.aljazeera.com/news/2017/11/islamophobia-changed-20-years-171116120107753.html, last accessed 22 February 2019.

5. Mattias Ekman, 'Online Islamophobia and the politics of fear: manufacturing the green scare', *Ethnic and Racial Studies*, 38 (11): 1986–2002, https://www.tandfonline.com/doi/abs/10.1080/01419870.2015.1021264, last accessed 22 February 2019.

6. *Ibid*.

7. Sarah Marsh, *The Guardian*, 'Record number of anti-Muslim attacks reported in UK last year', 20 July 2018, https://www.theguardian.com/uk-news/2018/jul/20/record-number-anti-muslim-attacks-reported-uk-2017, last accessed 22 February 2019.

8. Tell MAMA, 'Beyond the Incident: Outcomes for Victims of Anti-Muslim Prejudice', 23 July 2018, https://tellmamauk.org/wp-content/

uploads/2018/07/Tell-MAMA-Report-2017.pdf, last accessed 22 February 2019.

9. Louis Emanuel, *The Times*, 'Heavy police presence in London as Football Lads Alliance and EDL march', 24 June 2017, https://www.thetimes.co.uk/article/heavy-police-presence-in-the-capital-as-football-lads-alliance-and-edl-march-xtcprkrw7, last accessed 22 February 2019.

10. Elle Hunt and David Pegg, *The Guardian*, 'Woman photographed in hijab on Westminster Bridge responds to online abuse', 24 March 2017, https://www.theguardian.com/uk-news/2017/mar/24/woman-hijab-westminster-bridge-attack-victim-photo-misappropriated, last accessed 22 February 2019.

11. Nicola Woolcock, *The Times*, 'Islamic school can segregate boys and girls', 9 November 2016, https://www.thetimes.co.uk/article/islamist-school-can-segregate-boys-and-girls-zk8ztfqd0, last accessed 22 February 2019; Steve Hawkes, *The Sun*, 'SECRET I.S. SAFE Half of British Muslims would not go to cops if they knew someone with ISIS links', 1 December 2016, https://www.thesun.co.uk/news/2308529/half-british-muslims-would-not-report-is-supporters, last accessed 22 February 2019; Dominic Ponsford, *Press Gazette*, 'Dossier of 20 inaccurate UK news stories about Muslims revealed, warning false coverage fuels the far right', 19 January 2017, https://www.pressgazette.co.uk/dossier-of-20-inaccurate-uk-news-stories-about-muslims-revealed-with-warning-coverage-fuels-the-far-right, last accessed 22 February 2019.

12. Katy Sian, Ian Law, S. Sayyid, 'The Media and Muslims in the UK', Leeds: Centre for Ethnicity and Racism Studies, University of Leeds, 2012, pp. 264–5, https://www.ces.uc.pt/projectos/tolerace/media/Working%20paper%205/The%20Media%20and%20Muslims%20in%20the%20UK.pdf, last accessed 22 February 2019.

13. Andrew Norfolk, *The Times*, 'Christian child forced into Muslim foster care', 28 August 2017, https://www.thetimes.co.uk/article/christian-child-forced-into-muslim-foster-care-by-tower-hamlets-council-3gcp6l8cs, last accessed 22 February 2019.

14. Freddy Mayhew, *Press Gazette*, 'Times uses front page for IPSO rul-

ing that paper's article "distorted" facts on Christian girl in Muslim foster care', 25 April 2018, https://www.pressgazette.co.uk/times-uses-front-page-for-ipso-ruling-that-papers-article-distorted-facts-on-christian-girl-in-muslim-foster-care, last accessed 22 February 2019.

15. Jamie Doward, *The Observer*, 'Furore about child's Muslim foster carer "a threat to service"', 2 September 2017, https://www.theguardian.com/society/2017/sep/02/furore-childs-muslim-foster-carer-threat-service, last accessed 22 February 2019; Samanth Subramanian, *The Guardian*, 'One man's (very polite) fight against media Islamophobia', 18 October 2018, https://www.theguardian.com/news/2018/oct/18/miqdaad-versi-very-polite-fight-against-british-media-islamophobia, last accessed 22 February 2019.

16. Oscar Williams, *The Guardian*, 'British journalism is 94% white and 55% male, survey reveals', 24 March 2016, https://www.theguardian.com/media-network/2016/mar/24/british-journalism-diversity-white-female-male-survey, last accessed 22 February 2019.

17. Olfa, 5Pillars, 'Birmingham's Green Lane Mosque opens its doors to homeless amid cold weather', 13 February 2019, https://5pillarsuk.com/2019/02/13/birminghams-green-lane-mosque-opens-its-doors-to-homeless-amid-cold-weather, last accessed 22 February 2019.

18. Sara Khan with Tony McMahon, *The Battle for British Islam: Reclaiming Muslim Identity from Extremism*, London: Saqi Books, 2016, pp. 72–3.

19. Dilly uses the word 'normative' to mean conservative. 'Normative' can range from Muslims who dress conservatively, to those who believe that gay relationships are incompatible with Islam.

20. 5Pillars, Facebook, https://www.facebook.com/5pillarsuk, last accessed 22 February 2019.

21. The Muslim Vibe, https://themuslimvibe.com/about, last accessed 22 February 2019.

22. Shaheen Merali, The Muslim Vibe, 'Why It's Important To Let Our Children Express Their Emotions And Cry: A Parenting By Connection Perspective', 21 March 2018, https://themuslimvibe.com/muslim-life-style-matters/parents/why-its-important-to-let-our-children-express-their-emotions-and-cry, last accessed 22 February 2019.

23. Your Vibe, The Muslim Vibe, '3 quick personal audits to ensure your

finances are halal', 27 June 2018, https://themuslimvibe.com/muslim-lifestyle-matters/money/three-quick-personal-audits-to-ensure-your-finances-are-halal, last accessed 22 February 2019.

24. Muslim Travel Girl, The Muslim Vibe, '7 Cool Destinations Perfect For Halal Holidays In Europe', 8 December 2018, https://themuslimvibe.com/western-muslim-culture/7-cool-destinations-perfect-for-halal-holidays-in-europe, last accessed 22 February 2019.

25. The Muslim Vibe, https://themuslimvibe.com/about, last accessed 22 February 2019.

26. The Muslim Vibe, https://themuslimvibe.com/topic/what-is-shia-islam, last accessed 22 February 2019.

27. Nouri Sardar, The Muslim Vibe, '10 lessons from the day of Ashura', 30 September 2017, https://themuslimvibe.com/faith-islam/10-lessons-from-the-day-of-ashura, last accessed 22 February 2019.

28. Your Vibe, The Muslim Vibe, 'Dear Shia Muslims, Hussain ibn Ali is my Imam too', 1 October 2017, https://themuslimvibe.com/featured/dear-shia-muslims-hussain-ibn-ali-is-my-imam-too, last accessed 22 February 2019.

29. Amaliah, https://www.amaliah.com/about, last accessed 22 February 2019.

30. Eman Yusuf, Amaliah, 'Beekeeping: My Interest in Nature Brought Me Closer to Allah', 15 January 2019, https://www.amaliah.com/post/41253/bee-keeping-helping-better-muslim-surah-an-nahl-animals-and-insects-in-the-quran, last accessed 22 February 2019; Hanna Johara Dokal, Amaliah, 'How the Quran and Sunnah Taught Me to Go Vegan', 2 April 2018, https://www.amaliah.com/post/43464/quran-sunnah-taught-go-vegan, last accessed 22 February 2019; Wardah Abbas, Amaliah, 'A Woman's Right to Orgasm: Feminism in the Bedroom & Sexual Liberation Through Islam Not Despite It', 9 October 2018, https://www.amaliah.com/post/51477/womans-right-orgasm-feminism-bedroom-muslim-womans-right-to-sex-marriage-what-does-islam-say-about-sex, last accessed 22 February 2019.

31. Israa Abid, Amaliah, 'Do You Know the Plight of the Uyghur Muslims in China?', 7 September 2018, https://www.amaliah.com/post/35613/know-plight-chinese-uyghur-muslims, last accessed 22 February 2019;

Ryssa Choudhury, Amaliah, 'Reflections From a Day Spent in a Rohingya Refugee Camp: Part 2', 5 February 2018, https://www.amaliah.com/post/40259/outside-looking-reflections-day-spent-rohingya-refugee-camp-part-2–2, last accessed 22 February 2019.

32. Centre for the Analysis of Social Media, Demos, 'Islamophobia on Twitter: March to July 2016', 2016, https://demosuk.wpengine.com/wp-content/uploads/2016/08/Islamophobia-on-Twitter_-March–to–July–2016-.pdf, last accessed 22 February 2019.

33. Bertie Vidgen and Taha Yasseri, The Conversation, 'How we built a tool that detects the strength of Islamophobic hate speech on Twitter', 2 January 2019, https://theconversation.com/how-we-built-a-tool-that-detects-the-strength-of-islamophobic-hate-speech-on-twitter-102536, last accessed 22 February 2019.

34. Michael Newberg, CNBC, 'As many as 48 million Twitter accounts aren't people, says study', 10 March 2017, https://www.cnbc.com/2017/03/10/nearly-48-million-twitter-accounts-could-be-bots-says-study.html, last accessed 22 February 2019.

35. Mark Townsend, The Observer, 'Anti-Muslim online surges driven by fake accounts', 26 November 2017, https://www.theguardian.com/media/2017/nov/26/anti-muslim-online-bots-fake-acounts, last accessed 22 February 2019.

36. Zeynep Tufekci, The New York Times, 'YouTube, the Great Radicalizer', 10 March 2018, https://www.nytimes.com/2018/03/10/opinion/sunday/youtube-politics-radical.html, last accessed 22 February 2019.

37. Jack Nicas, The Wall Street Journal, 'How YouTube Drives People to the Internet's Darkest Corners', 7 February 2018, https://www.wsj.com/articles/how-youtube-drives-viewers-to-the-internets-darkest-corners-1518020478, last accessed 22 February 2019.

38. Elizabeth Weise, USA Today, 'Anti-extremist crackdown on YouTube, Facebook, Twitter only solves part of the problem', 2 November 2017, https://www.usatoday.com/story/tech/news/2017/11/01/anti-extremist-crackdown-youtube-facebook-twitter-only-solves-part-problem/823111001, last accessed 22 February 2019.

39. IntelligenceSquared Debates, YouTube, 'Islam is a Religion of Peace', 20 July 2011, https://www.youtube.com/watch?v=rh34Xsq7D_A, last accessed 22 February 2019.

40. Channel 4 News, YouTube, 'Jordan Peterson debate on the gender pay gap, campus protests and postmodernism', 16 January 2018, https://www.youtube.com/watch?v=aMcjxSThD54, last accessed 22 February 2019.

41. Katrina Flemming, YouTube, 'Jordan Peterson Swarmed by Narcissistic SJW Ideologues after UofT Rally', 12 October 2016, https://www.youtube.com/watch?v=O-nvNAcvUPE, last accessed 22 February 2019.

42. Jordan B Peterson, YouTube, https://www.youtube.com/user/JordanPetersonVideos, last accessed 22 February 2019.

43. Reddit, https://www.reddit.com/r/JordanPeterson/search?q=Islam&restrict_sr=1, last accessed 22 February 2019.

44. Reddit, https://www.reddit.com/r/JordanPeterson/comments/8i10a6/islam_and_why_perhaps_mohamed_couldnt_be_other, last accessed 22 February 2019.

45. Acts17Apologetics, YouTube, 'Jordan Peterson Destroys Islam in 15 Seconds', 29 January 2018, https://www.youtube.com/watch?v=qrLoFzKhE-o, last accessed 22 February 2019.

46. Diana Tourjée, Broadly, 'Trans Student Harassed by Milo Yiannopoulos Speaks Out', 3 January 2017, https://broadly.vice.com/en_us/article/vb4e44/trans-student-harassed-by-milo-yiannopoulos-speaks-out, last accessed 22 February 2019.

47. POTUS Putin, YouTube, 'Milo Yiannopoulous Bullies Transgender Student on Stage in the Name of Free Speech', 17 December 2016, https://www.youtube.com/watch?v=h2oV1QKUMdM, last accessed 22 February 2019.

48. Hussein Kesvani, MEL Magazine, 'The Small, Growing World of Muslim MRAs', https://melmagazine.com/en-us/story/the-small-growing-world-of-muslim-mras, last accessed 22 February 2019.

49. Reddit, https://www.reddit.com/r/MGTOW, last accessed 22 February 2019.

50. Mack Lamoureux, Vice, 'This Group of Straight Men Is Swearing Off Women', https://www.vice.com/en_us/article/7bdwyx/inside-the-global-collective-of-straight-male-separatists, last accessed 22 February 2019.

51. Reddit, https://www.reddit.com/r/MGTOW/comments/8bpsad/what_

will_happen_when_the_sex_robots_arrive, last accessed 22 February 2019; Reddit, https://www.reddit.com/r/MGTOW/comments/7n98kg/women_fake_iterally_everything_dont_get_bothered, last accessed 22 February 2019.

52. Dylan Love, *Business Insider*, 'Inside Red Pill, The Weird New Cult For Men Who Don't Understand Women', 15 September 2013, https://www.businessinsider.com/the-red-pill-reddit-2013–8, last accessed 22 February 2019.

53. Becoming the Alpha Muslim, https://becomingthealphamuslim.com, last accessed 22 February 2019.

54. tareq, Twitter, 1 August 2018, https://twitter.com/ibnabitareq/status/1024526961354399745, last accessed 22 February 2019.

4. INFLUENCERS, GAMERS AND TROLLS

1. Pete Kowalczyk, CNN, 'Somalia's diaspora poets step into the mainstream', 25 February 2017, https://edition.cnn.com/2017/02/22/africa/somalia-diaspora-poets-step-into-mainstream/index.html, last accessed 22 February 2019.

2. Ihmisoikeusliitto, YouTube, 'The Finnish League for Human Rights presents: "Woman" by Farah Gabdon', 22 May 2017, https://www.youtube.com/watch?v=mhpjiGwnm-0, last accessed 22 February 2019.

3. Farah Gabdon, YouTube, 'This Poem Is All Woman—Farah Gabdon', 11 January 2014, https://www.youtube.com/watch?v=iSwa5prn4mY, last accessed 22 February 2019.

4. E. Ce Miller, *Bustle*, 'Are "InstaPoets" Destroying The Art Form Or Reviving It? A Defense Of Social Media Poetry', 21 March 2018, https://www.bustle.com/p/are-instapoets-destroying-the-art-form-reviving-it-a-defense-of-social-media-poetry-8530426, last accessed 22 February 2019.

5. Lavanya Ramanathan, *The Washington Post*, 'From Instapoets to the bards of YouTube, poetry is going viral. And some poets hate that.', 6 May 2018, https://www.washingtonpost.com/lifestyle/style/from-instapoets-to-the-bards-of-youtube-poetry-is-going-viral-and-some-poets-hate-that/2018/05/06/ea4240fa-4329–11e8–8569–26fda6b404c7_story.html, last accessed 22 February 2019.

6. Roundhouse, YouTube, 'The Last Word Festival 2017—Poetry Slam Final—Suhaiymah Manzoor-Khan', 20 June 2017, https://www.youtube.com/watch?v=G9Sz2BQdMF8, last accessed 22 February 2019.

7. Suhaiymah Manzoor Khan, *This Is Not a Humanising Poem*, reproduced with the poet's permission.

8. Marwa Abdulhai, #MuslimGirl, 'Meet the Muslim Slam Poet Who Shook the World With This Viral Piece', 2017, http://muslimgirl.com/43782/meet-muslim-slam-poet-shook-world-viral-piece, last accessed 22 February 2019.

9. Muslim Poets UK, http://www.mohamedwrites.com/muslim-poets-uk, last accessed 22 February 2019.

10. Joshua Fruhlinger, 'You won't find the new pop stars in movies. You'll find them on Twitch.', 9 June 2018, https://www.digitaltrends.com/gaming/the-popularity-of-twitch-youtube-gaming-other-streaming-sites-on-the-rise, last accessed 22 February 2019.

11. Esports Earnings, https://www.esportsearnings.com/players/1176-destiny-steven-bonnell/results-by-year, last accessed 22 February 2019.

12. Esports Earnings, https://www.esportsearnings.com/players, last accessed 22 February 2019.

13. Stefanie Fogel, *Variety*, 'Discord Turns Three, Hits 130 Million User Milestone', 15 May 2008, https://variety.com/2018/gaming/news/discord-turns-three-1202810983, last accessed 22 February 2019.

14. May Bulman, *The Independent*, 'Brexit vote sees highest spike in religious and racial hate crimes ever recorded', 7 July 2017, https://www.independent.co.uk/news/uk/home-news/racist-hate-crimes-surge-to-record-high-after-brexit-vote-new-figures-reveal-a7829551.html, last accessed 22 February 2019.

15. Joe Heim, *The Washington Post*, 'Recounting a day of rage, hate, violence and death', 14 August 2017, https://www.washingtonpost.com/graphics/2017/local/charlottesville-timeline, last accessed 22 February 2019.

16. Matt Weinberger, *Business Insider*, 'A popular chat app just shut down a major online hangout for the alt-right after Charlottesville', 14 August 2017, https://www.businessinsider.com/discord-nazi-white-supremacist-alt-right-ban-2017-8, last accessed 22 February 2019; Kevin Roose,

The New York Times, 'This Was the Alt-Right's Favorite Chat App. Then Came Charlottesville.', 15 August 2017, https://www.nytimes.com/2017/08/15/technology/discord-chat-app-alt-right.html, last accessed 22 February 2019.

17. Faisal, YouTube, 'GOT INTO AN ALTERCATION AT THE GYM', 25 August 2017, https://www.youtube.com/watch?v=4qqrY-QCgZg, last accessed 22 February 2019.

18. Faisal, YouTube, 'WE MADE IT TO DUBAI', 21 September 2017, https://www.youtube.com/watch?v=SuNXztlrjiE, last accessed 22 February 2019.

19. Faisal, YouTube, 'Q&A with FAISAL!!', 9 February 2016, https://www.youtube.com/watch?v=D0SIfg-WVsk, last accessed 22 February 2019.

20. Ben Gilbert, *Business Insider*, 'YouTube now has over 1.8 billion users every month, within spitting distance of Facebook's 2 billion', 4 May 2018, https://www.businessinsider.com/youtube-user-statistics-2018-5, last accessed 22 February 2019.

21. MerchDope, '37 Mind Blowing YouTube Facts, Figures and Statistics—2019', 5 January 2019, https://merchdope.com/youtube-stats, last accessed 22 February 2019.

22. Stuart Dredge, *The Guardian*, 'Why are YouTube stars so popular?', 3 February 2016, https://www.theguardian.com/technology/2016/feb/03/why-youtube-stars-popular-zoella, last accessed 22 February 2019.

23. Donald Horton and R. Richard Wohl, 'Mass Communication and Para-Social Interaction: Observations on Intimacy at a Distance', *Psychiatry: Interpersonal and Biological Processes*, 19 (3): 251–66, 1956.

24. Megan Farokhmanesh, The Verge, 'YouTubers Are Not Your Friends', 17 September 2018, https://www.theverge.com/2018/9/17/17832948/youtube-youtubers-influencer-creator-fans-subscribers-friends-celebrities, last accessed 22 February 2019.

25. Faisal, YouTube, 'LET'S TALK ABOUT HARAM RELATIONSHIPS', 19 January 2018, https://www.youtube.com/watch?v=l_oH6rkzdi4, last accessed 22 February 2019.

26. Bahath, 'BEHIND THE BRAND | FAISAL CHOUDHRY | IZAHA LONDON', 19 September 2016, http://www.bahath.co/behind-the-brand-izaha/faisal-choudhry, last accessed 22 February 2019.

27. Yarimi, YouTube, https://www.youtube.com/channel/UC9qkYLMwp9 DzZU6dEIR15WQ/videos, last accessed 22 February 2019.

28. Diya Eddine, YouTube, https://www.youtube.com/channel/UCS3t VVcM4qGphtS6GjmryvA/videos, last accessed 22 February 2019.

29. George Caspar, *Shame and Internet Trolling: A Personal Exploration of the Mindset Behind this Modern Behavior*, BookBaby, pp. 31–2.

30. Helen Warrell, Madhumita Murgia and David Bond, *Financial Times*, 'Online trolls face prosecution under UK legal guidelines', 10 October 2016, https://www.ft.com/content/a8fa7ae8–8ecd-11e6–8df8-d3778b 55a923, last accessed 22 February 2019.

31. Hina Tai, *HuffPost*, 'Meet the "Jannah Minded Teen" Behind the Viral Muslim Memes Facebook Group', 2 June 2017, https://www.huffing-tonpost.com/entry/meet-the-jannah-minded-teen-behind-the-viral-muslim_us_59318963e4b062a6ac0acf1c, last accessed 22 February 2019.

32. Rahat Ahmed, *Wired*, 'The Uncanny World of Muslim Memes', 16 May 2016, https://www.wired.com/2016/05/the-uncanny-world-of-muslim-memes, last accessed 22 February 2019.

5. EXTREMISM, COUNTER-EXTREMISM

1. Josh Halliday and Vikram Dodd, *The Guardian*, 'Theresa May refuses to be drawn on Isis runaways' right to return to UK', 13 May 2015, https://www.theguardian.com/uk-news/2015/may/13/theresa-may-refuses-to-be-drawn-on-isis-runaways-right-to-return-to-uk,   last accessed 22 February 2019.

2. Ahmad Shehabat and Teodor Mitew, 'Black-boxing the Black Flag: Anonymous Sharing Platforms and ISIS Content Distribution Tactics', *Perspectives on Terrorism*, 12 (1): 81–99, February 2018, https://www. jstor.org/stable/26343748, last accessed 22 February 2019.

3. Lizzie Dearden, *The Independent*, 'Isis' British brides: What we know about the girls and women still in Syria after the death of Kadiza Sultana', 12 August 2016, https://www.independent.co.uk/news/uk/home-news/ isis-british-brides-kadiza-sultana-girls-women-syria-married-death-killed-aqsa-mahmood-islamic-state-a7187751.html,   last   accessed 22 February 2019.

4. Jessica Stern and JM Berger, *The Guardian*, 'Thugs wanted—bring your

own boots: how Isis attracts foreign fighters to its twisted utopia', 9 March 2015, https://www.theguardian.com/world/2015/mar/09/how-isis-attracts-foreign-fighters-the-state-of-terror-book, last accessed 22 February 2019.

5. Emine Saner, *The Guardian*, 'How the 'Pompey Lads' fell into the hands of Isis', 27 July 2015, https://www.theguardian.com/world/2015/jul/27/pompey-lads-isis-deluded-british-recruits-died-syria,   last accessed 22 February 2019.

6. Commons Select Committee, 'Internet giants "consciously failing" to tackle extremism on the web', 25 August 2016, https://www.parliament.uk/business/committees/committees-a-z/commons-select/home-affairs-committee/news-parliament-2015/radicalisation-report-published-16–17, last accessed 22 February 2019.

7. Channel 4 News, 'Unmasked: the man behind top Islamic State Twitter account', 11 December 2014, https://www.channel4.com/news/unmasked-the-man-behind-top-islamic-state-twitter-account-shami-witness-mehdi, last accessed 22 February 2019.

8. Clara Pellerin, 'Communicating Terror: An Analysis of ISIS Communication Strategy', 2016, https://www.sciencespo.fr/kuwait-program/wp-content/uploads/2018/05/KSP_Paper_Award_Spring_2016_PELLERIN_Clara.pdf, last accessed 22 February 2019.

9. Channel 4 News, 'ISIS propagandist ShamiWitness: Man charged in India', 1 June 2015, https://www.channel4.com/news/isis-shami-witness-medhi-masroor-biswas-charged, last accessed 22 February 2019.

10. Kieran Corcoran, *Business Insider*, 'UK threatens to tax "ruthless profiteers" Facebook and Google if they don't do more to combat extremism', 31 December 2017, https://www.businessinsider.com/uk-minister-threatens-to-tax-facebook-google-over-online-extremism-2017–12, last accessed 22 February 2019.

11. BBC News, 'Social media: How can governments regulate it?', 7 February 2019, https://www.bbc.co.uk/news/technology-47135058, last accessed 22 February 2019.

12. BBC News, 'Reality Check: What is the Prevent strategy?', 4 June 2017, https://www.bbc.co.uk/news/election-2017–40151991, last accessed 22 February 2019.

13. Ben Quinn, *The Guardian*, 'Nursery "raised fears of radicalisation over boy's cucumber drawing"', 11 March 2016, https://www.theguardian.com/uk-news/2016/mar/11/nursery-radicalisation-fears-boys-cucumber-drawing-cooker-bomb, last accessed 22 February 2019; Jamie Grierson, *The Guardian*, '"My son was terrified": how Prevent alienates UK Muslims', 27 January 2019, https://www.theguardian.com/uk-news/2019/jan/27/prevent-muslim-community-discrimination, last accessed 22 February 2019.

14. Chris Graham, 'What is the anti-terror Prevent programme and why is it controversial?', *The Telegraph*, 26 May 2017, https://www.telegraph.co.uk/news/0/anti-terror-prevent-programme-controversial, last accessed 22 February 2019.

15. Economic and Social Research Council, 'Prevent: UK's Counter Terrorism Strategy', https://esrc.ukri.org/public-engagement/social-science-for-schools/resources/prevent-the-uk-s-counter-terrorism-strategy, last accessed 22 February 2019.

16. Jamie Bartlett, *Radicals: Outsiders Changing the World*, London: Penguin Random House, 2017.

17. Anne Lynn Dudenhoefer, 'Resisting Radicalisation: A Critical Analysis of the UK Prevent Duty', *Journal for Deradicalization*, 14, 2018.

18. The Home Office, '*Prevent* Strategy', June 2011, https://assets.publishing.service.gov.uk/government/uploads/system/uploads/attachment_data/file/97976/prevent-strategy-review.pdf, last accessed 22 February 2019.

19. UK Government, 'The Prevent Strategy: A Guide for Local Partners in England', 2008, http://www.tedcantle.co.uk/publications/039%20CLG%20Prevent%20Guide%20guide%20for%20local%20partners%202008.pdf, last accessed 22 February 2019.

20. RAND corporation, 'Radicalisation in the digital era', 2013, https://www.rand.org/pubs/research_reports/RR453.html, last accessed 22 February 2019.

21. The Home Office, 'Counter-Extremism Strategy', October 2015, p. 7, https://assets.publishing.service.gov.uk/government/uploads/system/uploads/attachment_data/file/470088/51859_Cm9148_Accessible.pdf, last accessed 22 February 2019.

22. *The Telegraph*, 'Prevent scheme: hundreds of children referred for Far-Right extremism', 27 March 2018, https://www.telegraph.co.uk/news/2018/03/27/prevent-scheme-hundreds-children-reffered-far-right-extremism, last accessed 22 February 2019.

23. Ian Cobain, Alice Ross, Rob Evans and Mona Mahmood, *The Guardian*, 'Inside Ricu, the shadowy propaganda unit inspired by the cold war', 2 May 2016, https://www.theguardian.com/politics/2016/may/02/inside-ricu-the-shadowy-propaganda-unit-inspired-by-the-cold-war, last accessed 22 February 2019.

24. *Ibid.*

25. Fahid Qurashi, 'The Prevent strategy and the UK "war on terror": embedding infrastructures of surveillance in Muslim communities', *Palgrave Communications*, 4 (17), 2018, https://www.nature.com/articles/s41599-017-0061-9, last accessed 22 February 2019.

26. Bartlett, *Radicals*, p. 132.

27. Independent Voices, *The Independent*, 'PREVENT will have a chilling effect on open debate, free speech and political dissent', 10 July 2015, https://www.independent.co.uk/voices/letters/prevent-will-have-a-chilling-effect-on-open-debate-free-speech-and-political-dissent-10381491.html, last accessed 22 February 2019.

28. Sara Khan with Tony McMahon, *The Battle for British Islam: Reclaiming Muslim Identity from Extremism*, London: Saqi Books, 2016, p. 94.

29. *Ibid.*, p. 96.

30. UK Parliament, 'Counter-terrorism: Written question—51248', 29 November 2016, https://www.parliament.uk/business/publications/written-questions-answers-statements/written-question/Commons/2016-10-31/51248, last accessed 22 February 2019.

31. Jenny Jones, *The Guardian*, 'Prevent and political judgments by police', 14 February 2019, https://www.theguardian.com/uk-news/2019/feb/14/prevent-and-political-judgments-by-police, last accessed 22 February 2019.

32. George Parker, *Financial Times*, 'Theresa May warns tech companies: "no safe space" for extremists', 4 June 2017, https://www.ft.com/content/0ae646c6-4911-11e7-a3f4-c742b9791d43, last accessed 22 February 2019.

33. Andrew Sparrow, *The Guardian*, 'WhatsApp must be accessible to authorities, says Amber Rudd', 26 March 2017, https://www.theguardian.com/technology/2017/mar/26/intelligence-services-access-whatsapp-amber-rudd-westminster-attack-encrypted-messaging; https://www.bbc.co.uk/news/uk-41479620, last accessed 22 February 2019.

34. Michael Holden, Reuters, 'Britain is facing serious far-right terrorism threat, says top UK officer', 26 February 2018, https://uk.reuters.com/article/uk-britain-security/britain-is-facing-serious-far-right-terrorism-threat-says-top-uk-officer-idUKKCN1GA2K9, last accessed 22 February 2019.

35. Imran Awan, Al Jazeera, 'Why UK's "Prevent" programme doesn't work', https://www.aljazeera.com/indepth/opinion/uk-prevent-programme-doesn-work-180411114522226.html, last accessed 22 February 2019.

36. Bartlett, *Radicals*, p. 144.

37. David Cameron, *The Times*, 'We won't let women be second class citizens', 18 January 2016, https://www.thetimes.co.uk/article/we-wont-let-women-be-second-class-citizens-brh07l6jttb, last accessed 22 February 2019.

38. Laura Hughes, *The Telegraph*, 'David Cameron: More Muslim women should "learn English" to help tackle extremism', 17 January 2016, https://www.telegraph.co.uk/news/uknews/terrorism-in-the-uk/12104556/David-Cameron-More-Muslim-women-should-learn-English-to-help-tackle-extremism.html, last accessed 22 February 2019.

39. *Ibid.*

40. Zahra al-Alawi, Twitter, 24 January 2016, https://twitter.com/ZahraAlawi/status/691358456406790153, last accessed 22 February 2019.

41. Zahra Khimji, Twitter, 24 January 2016, https://twitter.com/zahrakhimji/status/691335436141207557, last accessed 22 February 2019.

42. Hussein Kesvani, BuzzFeed, 'Muslim Women Use The #Traditionally Submissive Hashtag To Challenge David Cameron', https://www.buzzfeed.com/husseinkesvani/muslim-women-hashtag-traditionally-submissive, last accessed 20 February 2019.

43. Tell MAMA, 'Beyond the Incident: Outcomes for Victims of Anti-Muslim Prejudice', 23 July 2018, https://tellmamauk.org/wp-content/uploads/2018/07/EXECUTIVE-SUMMARY.pdf, last accessed 22 February 2019.

44. Alan Cowell and Stephen Castle, 'Muslim Minister Quits British Government to Protest Gaza Policies', *The New York Times*, 5 August 2014, https://www.nytimes.com/2014/08/06/world/europe/muslim-minister-quits-british-government-to-protest-gaza-policies.html, last accessed 22 February 2019.

45. Sarah Ann Harris, *HuffPost*, 'Muslim Leaders Warn David Cameron Educating Women Is Not The Same As Tackling Radicalisation', 18 January 2016, https://www.huffingtonpost.co.uk/2016/01/18/english-lessons-muslim-women-radicalisation_n_9008418.html, last accessed 22 February 2019.

46. Citizens Commission on Islam, Participation and Public Life, 'The Missing Muslims: Unlocking British Muslim Potential for the Benefit of All', 2017, https://www.citizensuk.org/missing_muslims, last accessed 22 February 2019.

47. MEND, 'Jeremy Corbyn launches Islamophobia Awareness Month 2017 in Parliament with MEND', 3 November 2017, https://mend.org.uk/news/jeremy-corbyn-launches-islamophobia-awareness-month-2017-parliament-mend, last accessed 22 February 2019.

48. Miqdaad Versi, *The Guardian*, 'It isn't just young people who have turned to Labour. Muslims have too', 12 June 2017, https://www.theguardian.com/commentisfree/2017/jun/12/muslims-turned-to-labour-rejected-tory-party, last accessed 22 February 2019.

49. Boris Johnson, *The Telegraph*, 'Denmark has got it wrong. Yes, the burka is oppressive and ridiculous—but that's still no reason to ban it', 5 August 2018, https://www.telegraph.co.uk/news/2018/08/05/denmark-has-got-wrong-yes-burka-oppressive-ridiculous-still, last accessed 22 February 2019.

50. Dan Sabbagh, *The Guardian*, 'Sayeeda Warsi calls for inquiry into Islamophobia within Tory party', 4 July 2018, https://www.theguardian.com/politics/2018/jul/04/sayeeda-warsi-calls-for-inquiry-into-islamophobia-within-tory-party, last accessed 22 February 2019.

51. Hashim Bhatti, *The Guardian*, 'I'm a Tory councillor. Islamophobia in my party goes beyond Boris Johnson', 7 August 2018, https://www.theguardian.com/commentisfree/2018/aug/07/conservative-party-inquiry-islamophobia-boris-johnson, last accessed 22 February 2019.

52. Versi, 'It isn't just young people'.

6. SPACES FOR MINORITIES

1. BBC News, 'Asad Shah killing: "Disrespecting Islam" murderer jailed', 9 August 2016, https://www.bbc.com/news/uk-scotland-glasgow-west-37021385, last accessed 22 February 2019.

2. Sajid Iqbal and Calum McKay, BBC News, 'Asad Shah murder: Killer Tanveer Ahmed releases prison message', 31 January 2017, https://www.bbc.com/news/uk-scotland-38815366, last accessed 22 February 2019.

3. Matt Payton, *The Independent*, 'Asad Shah murder: Facebook page celebrates killing of the popular Muslim shopkeeper', 30 March 2016, https://www.independent.co.uk/news/uk/crime/asad-shah-murder-facebook-page-celebrates-the-death-of-the-popular-muslim-shopkeeper-a6959431.html, last accessed 22 February 2019.

4. Hussein Kesvani, *The Spectator*, 'Sectarianism is on the rise in Britain—as any Ahmadiyya Muslim can tell you', 18 April 2016, https://blogs.spectator.co.uk/2016/04/sectarianism-is-on-the-rise-in-britain-as-any-ahmadiyya-muslim-can-tell-you, last accessed 22 February 2019.

5. Secunder Kermani, BBC News, 'Why was shopkeeper Asad Shah murdered?', 7 July 2016, https://www.bbc.co.uk/news/uk-scotland-3673
2596, last accessed 22 February 2019.

6. BrailveeOnline, YouTube, 'Asad Shah (Ahmadi) False Claims of Prophecy which instigated Tanveer Ahmed', 11 April 2016, https://www.youtube.com/watch?v=KiWThVyQg_Y, last accessed 22 February 2019.

7. Ali Usman Qasmi, *The Ahmadis and the Politics of Religious Exclusion in Pakistan*, London: Anthem Press, 2014.

8. Tahir Nasser, *The Guardian*, 'The Muslim Council of Britain is failing Ahmadis like Asad Shah', 25 April 2016, https://www.theguardian.com/commentisfree/2016/apr/25/muslim-council-of-britain-ahmadi-asad-shah, last accessed 22 February 2019.

9. The Royal British Legion, https://www.britishlegion.org.uk/community/

stories/remembrance/meet-our-poppy-appeal-collectors, last accessed 22 February 2019.

10. *Dawn*, 'The day Salman Taseer fell silent', 4 January 2011, https://www.dawn.com/news/1230498, last accessed 22 February 2019.

11. BBC News, 'Salman Taseer murder: Pakistan hangs Mumtaz Qadri', 29 February 2016, https://www.bbc.com/news/world-asia-35684452, last accessed 22 February 2019.

12. *Pakistan Today*, 'For Sharif son-in-law Safdar, Mumtaz Qadri remains a hero', 9 November 2018, https://www.pakistantoday.com.pk/2018/01/18/for-sharif-son-in-law-safdar-mumtaz-qadri-remains-a-hero, last accessed 22 February 2019.

13. BBC News, 'Mumtaz Qadri admits killing Governor Salman Taseer', 10 January 2011, https://www.bbc.com/news/world-south-asia-1214 9607, last accessed 22 February 2019.

14. Euan McLelland, *Daily Mail*, 'Pictured: Taxi driver who admits killing fellow Muslim shopkeeper because "he disrespected Islam by claiming he was a prophet"', 7 April 2016, https://www.dailymail.co.uk/news/article-3527759/Pictured-Taxi-driver-admits-killing-fellow-Muslim-shopkeeper-disrespected-Islam-claiming-prophet.html, last accessed 22 February 2019.

15. Vanguard, 'Ahmadiyya set to preach Islam on social media', 23 March 2018, https://www.vanguardngr.com/2018/03/ahmadiyya-set-preach-islam-social-media, last accessed 22 February 2019.

16. Shahid Badruddin, *The Muslim Times*, 'Must Read: Jama'at-e-Ahmadiyya Muslimah On the World Wide Web', 12 March 2013, https://themuslimtimes.info/2013/03/12/jamaat-e-ahmadiyya-muslimah-on-the-world-wide-web, last accessed 22 February 2019.

17. Ahmadiyya Muslim Community UK, http://www.loveforallhatredfornone.org/Press, last accessed 22 February 2019.

18. BBC News, 'Ahmadiyya Muslims launch peace campaign in Glasgow', 18 April 2016, https://www.bbc.com/news/uk-scotland-glasgow-west-36072051, last accessed 22 February 2019.

19. I Stand with Ahmadis, Twitter, 4 December 2015, https://twitter.com/istandwahmadis/status/672634331978969088, last accessed 22 February 2019.

20. Felix Tamsut, DW, '#IstandWithAhmadis: Pakistanis show support for religious minority on social media', 12 February 2015, https://www.dw.com/en/istandwithahmadis-pakistanis-show-support-for-religious-minority-on-social-media/a-18889718, last accessed 22 February 2019.

21. Simon Hooper, CNN, 'The rise of the "New Atheists"', 9 November 2006, http://edition.cnn.com/2006/WORLD/europe/11/08/atheism.feature/index.html, last accessed 22 February 2019.

22. Christopher Hitchens, *The Boston Globe*, 'It's a good time for war', 8 September 2002, http://archive.boston.com/news/packages/sept11/anniversary/globe_stories/090802_hitchens_entire.htm, last accessed 22 February 2019; Sarah Knapton, *The Telegraph*, 'Richard Dawkins: religious education is crucial for British schoolchildren', 11 June 2017, https://www.telegraph.co.uk/science/2017/06/11/richard-dawkins-religious-education-crucial-british-schoolchildren, last accessed 22 February 2019.

23. Council of Ex-Muslims of Britain, https://www.ex-muslim.org.uk, last accessed 22 February 2019.

24. Mufassil Islam, Facebook, https://www.facebook.com/Mufassil-Islam-1630314843871729, last accessed 22 February 2019.

25. 5Pillars, 'VIDEO: Mufassil Islam—I have left Islam', 15 April 2016, https://5pillarsuk.com/video/video-mufassil-islam-i-have-left-islam, last accessed 22 February 2019.

26. Harriet Agerholm, *The Independent*, 'Women "bearing brunt" of rising Islamophobic attacks in the UK', 3 November 2017, https://www.independent.co.uk/news/uk/home-news/uk-islamophobia-attacks-women-bearing-brunt-hate-crimes-a8036581.html, last accessed 22 February 2019.

27. Reddit, https://www.reddit.com/r/exmuslim, last accessed 22 February 2019.

28. Sahih Muslim 1887, Book 33, Hadith 181, https://sunnah.com/muslim/33/181, last accessed 22 February 2019.

29. Hussein Kesvani, BuzzFeed, 'Meet The Gay Muslims Living In Straight Marriages', 18 April 2015, https://www.buzzfeed.com/husseinkesvani/gay-muslims-in-straight-marriages, last accessed 22 February 2019.

30. Imaan, https://imaanlondon.wordpress.com, last accessed 22 February 2019.

31. Hidayah, https://www.hidayahlgbt.co.uk, last accessed 22 February 2019.

32. LQM, Meetup, https://www.meetup.com/queermuslims, last accessed 22 February 2019.

33. Muhammad Abdul-Rauf, *Bilāl Ibn Rabāh: A Leading Companion of The Prophet Muhammad (SAW)*, Indianapolis, IN: American Trust Publications, 1977, p. 5.

34. The Daily Reminder, YouTube, 'How Islam Killed Racism—The Story Of Bilal[HD] | by Shaykh Zahir Mahmood | TDR Production |', 14 December 2014, https://www.youtube.com/watch?v=TyL0abQT5xs, last accessed 22 February 2019.

35. Islam On Demand, YouTube, 'Is There Racism in Islam?—Siraj Wahhaj', 16 January 2014, https://www.youtube.com/watch?v=BZfh53u WhyY, last accessed 22 February 2019.

36. Emma Green, *The Atlantic*, 'Muslim Americans Are United by Trump—and Divided by Race', 11 March 2017, https://www.theatlantic.com/politics/archive/2017/03/muslim-americans-race/519282, last accessed 22 February 2019.

37. UK Muslims, Facebook, https://www.facebook.com/groups/UkMuslimss, last accessed 22 February 2019.

38. Muslim Changemakers, Facebook, https://www.facebook.com/groups/1671108939771013, last accessed 22 February 2019.

39. Aisha Gani, BuzzFeed, 'These Young Black British Muslims Were So Fed Up With Being Erased They Made Their Own Web Series And It's Lit', 4 October 2017, https://www.buzzfeed.com/aishagani/black-and-muslim-in-britain, last accessed 22 February 2019.

40. Black and Muslim in Britain, YouTube, 'S1 | Ep. 1: Should faith be a pivotal part of Black History Month?', 4 October 2017, https://www.youtube.com/watch?list=PlxnhIlMhs7OKYK-PoPXGE869sj9c40 Xyj&time_continue=1&v=39VfYfduGJg, last accessed 22 February 2019.

41. Najma Sharif, *PAPER*, '#BlackOutEid Celebrates Fashion and Black Muslimhood', 21 June 2018, http://www.papermag.com/blackouteid-muslim-fashion-series-2580097078.html, last accessed 22 February 2019.

42. Ikran Dahir, BuzzFeed, '45 Beautiful #BlackOutEid Selfies From Eid Al-Adha', 2 September 2017, https://www.buzzfeed.com/ikrd/45-beautiful-blackouteid-selfies-from-eid-al-adha, last accessed 22 February 2019.

43. FMC, Instagram, https://www.instagram.com/femalemuslimcreatives, last accessed 20 February 2019; Näjwä The Light, Instagram, 11 December 2017, https://www.instagram.com/p/BckB5HwnWKv/?taken-by=poelitical, last accessed 22 February 2019.

44. Hassan Gazali, Instagram, https://www.instagram.com/niftysoawesome, last accessed 22 February 2019.

45. Mohamed Abdulle, Instagram, https://www.instagram.com/mabdulle, last accessed 22 February 2019.

46. First Model Managament, Ramla Jamac, http://www.firstmodelmanagement.co.uk/talent/ramla-jamac-7900, last accessed 20 February 2019.

47. Khaled Siddiq, YouTube, '"MUSLIMS, STOP ACTING BLACK!"—Baraka Boys Podcast (Ep. 5)', 2 October 2018, https://www.youtube.com/watch?v=yMvJS1mBJ5g, last accessed 22 February 2019.

48. Ikran Dahir, BuzzFeed, 'People Are Loving This Student's Twitter Thread Highlighting Black Muslims', 14 October 2018, https://www.buzzfeed.com/ikrd/this-student-is-highlighting-black-muslims-throughout, last accessed 22 February 2019.

CONCLUSION

1. Bethan McKernan, The Guardian, 'Endgame for the Isis "caliphate" looms in small Syrian town', 20 February 2019, https://www.theguardian.com/world/2019/feb/20/endgame-for-the-isis-caliphate-looms-in-small-syrian-town, last accessed 22 February 2019.

2. BBC News, 'After the caliphate: Has IS been defeated?', 7 February 2019, https://www.bbc.co.uk/news/world-middle-east-45547595, last accessed 22 February 2019.

3. Lizzie Dearden, The Independent, 'More than 400 British Isis jihadis have already returned to UK, report warns', 24 October 2017, https://www.independent.co.uk/news/uk/home-news/isis-british-jihadis-

return-uk-iraq-syria-report-islamic-state-fighters-europe-threat-debate-terror-a8017811.html, last accessed 22 February 2019.

4. Dina Tokio, YouTube, 'The Bad, the Worse and the Ugly', 1 January 2019, https://www.youtube.com/watch?v=i3kIJd-_yiY, last accessed 22 February 2019.

5. VR Karbala, https://www.vr-karbala.com, last accessed 22 February 2019.

6. Shaikh (Dr) Haitham Al-Haddad, Islam21c, 'Fatwa on Bitcoin & Other Cryptocurrencies', 25 January 2018, https://www.islam21c.com/islamic-law/fatwa-bitcoin-cryptocurrencies, last accessed 22 February 2019.

7. Olivia Rudgard, *The Telegraph*, 'Bitcoin can be halal, mosque declares as it becomes the first in the UK to accept cryptocurrency donations', 22 May 2018, https://www.telegraph.co.uk/news/2018/05/22/bitcoin-can-halal-mosque-declares-becomes-first-uk-accept-cryptocurrency, last accessed 22 February 2019.

8. British Muslims for Secular Democracy, https://www.bmsd.org.uk, last accessed 22 February 2019.

ULYSSES S. GRANT

AND THE STRATEGY OF VICTORY

THE HISTORY OF THE CIVIL WAR